Talking Over the Years

It is now widely recognised that older adults can benefit from psychodynamic therapy and that psychodynamic concepts can help to illuminate the thorny issues of ageing and the complications of later life.

Talking Over the Years begins by examining how ideas of old age are represented by the key psychodynamic theorists of the twentieth century, including Freud, Jung, Klein and Winnicott. Contributors go on to draw on their own experiences in a range of settings to demonstrate the value of psychodynamic concepts in clinical practice, covering subjects including:

- Brief and long-term work with individuals, couples and groups.
- The expressive therapies – art, music, dance and movement.
- Ethical considerations.
- Training, supervision and support.
- Sexuality.

Illustrated by a wealth of clinical material, *Talking Over the Years* increases psychodynamic awareness, helping practitioners become more sensitive to their patients' needs to the benefit of both the patient and the professional.

Sandra Evans is a psychiatrist working with older adults at the Homerton Hospital and St Bartholomew's Hospital in London; she is also a group analyst.

Jane Garner is a consultant psychiatrist leading an old age psychiatry service at Chase Farm Hospital in London.

Talking Over the Years

A handbook of dynamic psychotherapy with older adults

Edited by Sandra Evans and Jane Garner

Brunner-Routledge
Taylor & Francis Group

HOVE AND NEW YORK

First published 2004
by Brunner-Routledge
27 Church Road, Hove, East Sussex BN3 2FA

Simultaneously published in the USA and Canada
by Brunner-Routledge
270 Madison Avenue, New York NY 10016

Brunner-Routledge is an imprint of T&F Informa plc

Typeset in Times by RefineCatch Limited, Bungay, Suffolk
Printed and bound in Great Britain by
TJ International, Padstow, Cornwall
Paperback cover design by Caroline Archer

This publication has been produced with paper manufactured to
strict environmental standards and with pulp derived from
sustainable forests.

British Library Cataloguing in Publication Data
A catalogue record for this book is available from the British Library

Library of Congress Cataloging-in-Publication Data
Evans, Sandra.
    Talking over the years : a handbook of dynamic
psychotherapy with older adults / Sandra Evans and Jane Garner.
        p. cm.
    Includes bibliographical references and index.
    ISBN 1-58391-143-X (hbk. : alk. paper) – ISBN 1-58391-144-8
(pbk. : alk. paper)
    1. Psychotherapy for the aged.   2. Psychodynamic
psychotherapy.   3. Psychoanalysis.   I. Garner, Jane, FRCPsych.
II. Title.

    RC480.54. E95 2004
    618.97′689–dc22   2003025187

ISBN 1-58391-143-X (hbk)
ISBN 1-58391-144-8 (pbk)

Contents

Contributors

Mark Ardern has been a consultant psychiatrist working with older adults in St. Charles Hospital in west London since 1984. He is a founder member and currently Chair of the Older Adults Section of the Association for Psychoanalytic Psychotherapy in the NHS (APP). Mark is currently on the executive committee of the Faculty of Old Age Psychiatry at the Royal College of Psychiatrists and provides liaison with the Psychotherapy Faculty on matters which affect older patients.

Lorenzo Bacelle is a psychiatrist trained in Italy and London. He is a Jungian Analyst trained at the Society of Analytical Psychology in London. Until recently, Lorenzo led an NHS psychotherapy service at Northwick Park Hospital in London, and now leads a sector psychiatric service in South Essex Partnership NHS Trust.

Siân Critchley-Robbins is a clinical psychologist working with older people in the Oxleas Mental Health Trust. She is currently on the national committee of PSIGE, Psychology Specialists Working with Older People, which is a faculty of the British Psychological Society, Division of Clinical Psychology. She is also a member of the Older Adults section of the APP.

Rachel Darnley-Smith trained as a music therapist at the Guildhall School of Music and Drama and has worked for many years in the National Health Service with Older Adults. She is currently working in private practice and is Senior Lecturer in Music Therapy at Roehampton University, London. She is co-author (with Helen Patey) of the new introductory text *Music Therapy*, Sage Publications, London.

Rachael Davenhill is a psychoanalyst and consultant clinical psychologist in psychotherapy at the Tavistock Clinic in London. She is director of the 2-year CPD course 'Psychodynamic Approaches to Old Age', and co-convenor of the joint Tavistock and APP annual conferences with Mark Ardern.

Sandra Evans is a psychiatrist working with older adults at the Homerton Hospital and St. Bartholomew's Hospital in London. She is a senior lecturer in old age psychiatry at Queen Mary University of London and is an IGA trained Group Analyst, a member of the Group Analytic Network in east London, and a member of the Older Adults Section of the APP.

Jane Garner is a consultant psychiatrist leading an old age psychiatry service at Chase Farm Hospital in north London. Jane is a founder member and secretary of the Older Adults Section of the Association for Psycho-analytic Psychotherapy in the NHS. She has been secretary of the Faculty of Old Age Psychiatry at the Royal College of Psychiatrists. With Mark Ardern and Ruth Porter, she has been part of the burgeoning interest in psychodynamic psychotherapy for older people nationally.

Noel Hess trained and qualified as a clinical psychologist in Queensland, Australia. He is a psychoanalytic psychotherapist trained with the British Association of Psychotherapists, a specialist clinical psychologist in psychoanalytic psychotherapy in University College Hospital in London, and is a psychoanalytic psychotherapist in private practice. He is currently Chair of the Association for Psychoanalytic Psychotherapy in the NHS (APP).

Rosamund Oliver is an accredited psychotherapist with a private practice in north London. She studied with the Karuna Institute in Devon where she is now a staff member. She gives training seminars on death and dying in hospices and care organisations in Ireland, France, Germany and the UK. She worked with older people as a psychotherapist in an east London hospital for three years, specialising in bereavement work. She is a member of the Professional Conduct Committee of the UKCP.

Joan Reggiori is a BAP qualified analytical psychologist, having first trained in psychiatric social work. She is a training therapist, training supervisor and lecturer with the BAP where she has formerly been Chair of Training Committee. She is a supervisor on the IGA MSc course. Her MA is in analytic psychotherapy, focusing on analysis in the post midlife period, the theme in a number of her published works. She is analytic supervisor in the NHS in the department of psychological medicine at St. Bartholomew's Hospital in London, and works in private practice.

Kimberley Smith is a head IV art therapist at Fulbourn Hospital, Cambridge. She is the Regional Delegate's Coordinator for the British Association of Art Therapists. She is the creator of the Special Interest Group for Art Therapists working with Older People (ATOLL). She is currently under-taking research into art therapy with older patients for a Masters Degree and lectures on her work in Britain and America.

Erdinch Suleiman describes himself as a 'community activist'. He has been working in east London for over 25 years, the past 5 at least as the co-ordinator of Hackney Bereavement Service, a registered charity providing bereavement counselling to local residents in their own homes, mainly people over the age of 55 years. Erdinch is a qualified counsellor, group worker and accredited mediator specialising in grief work in the community.

Marion Violets-Gibson SRDMT has worked with dance and movement as a major therapeutic tool for the past twenty years. Her clinical practice has been set within the NHS as part of the mental health for older people service at the Homerton Hospital. She has also been responsible for initiating and running the 'LINKS' training programme for staff in Camden and Islington, and in Hackney in London. Marion has presented her work and run workshops in the UK, France and the USA.

Roger Wesby is a consultant psychiatrist working with the elderly at the Julian Hospital in Norwich, part of Norfolk and Waveney Mental Health Partnership NHS Trust. He is a Jungian Psychotherapist trained with the British Association of Psychotherapists (BAP). Roger is a member of the Older Adults Section of the APP.

Foreword

Older adults can benefit from psychodynamic therapy. This idea no longer provokes astonishment and disbelief. What is still unusual, however, is what this book provides: detailed descriptions of psychoanalytic theory together with the use of psychodynamic concepts in clinical practice.

The two editors, with vision and hard work, have brought together theory and practice. Ideas from Freud, Jung, Klein, Kohut, Erikson, Bion, Foulkes and Yalom are discussed; the psychotherapy described includes brief and long-term work with individuals, couples and groups; and there are chapters on the expressive therapies – art, music, dance and movement – as well as the older-established treatments. A chapter on intercultural work was withdrawn, to the great disappointment of the editors, when it was too late to commission another paper. (There are two descriptions of intercultural work in Chapter 18 on bereavement). The authors all work in the UK and in the NHS or other public and private settings. They are all actively involved in the clinical care of older adults, mainly those with psychiatric problems although these ideas also apply to individuals without major mental health difficulties. I know of no other book that covers such diversity.

It is timely to publish this material: dialogue between the proponents of different theoretical schools is increasing; experience of the psychodynamic approach in clinical settings is more than enough for the work to be brought together and published; and expressive and other therapists are finding common ground. The two editors, Jane Garner and Sandra Evans, are experienced old age psychiatrists who use psychodynamic ideas in their work with individuals and groups, and with their teams. Through their skill and determination they have succeeded in bringing together theoretical and clinical strands to produce an interesting, unusual and readable book.

'Old age is a sensitive time' an 80 year old commented. 'Age is no place for softies,' from another older person (Garner, personal communication). Softies or not, however, older individuals may be unduly sensitive, perceiving offers of help as patronising and condescending (which sometimes they are). Through psychodynamic awareness professionals can become more sensitive to their own as well as to their patients' needs – the patient and the professional benefit. The material in this book shows some of the ways in which sensitivity to unconscious factors can inform the practice of old age psychiatry and of psychotherapy with older adults. It is a good time for this book to be written; equally, it is a good time for it to be read.

RUTH PORTER
22 March 2003

Introduction

When we started on this project, a unified volume on the theory and practice of psychodynamic psychotherapy in old age, it was as much for ourselves as for the imagined readership. While we hoped that colleagues from all the professional disciplines working with older people would find it of interest and of some use in their professional lives, we also thought that a book like this should exist because we would like to read and consult it.

We hoped to pull together some of the old knowledge, with the new. We chose authors to describe and comment on established writing from the icons of the psychoanalytic world, icons who either had something to say on ageing, or whose ideas could be extrapolated to the experience of growing old. These were juxtaposed with newer writings and concepts in the practical arena of clinical old age psychiatry. The result is a book that appears in two parts, theory and practice. The first part is aimed at theoretical knowledge, mostly provided by our analytic predecessors, but updated in a specific sense to apply to older patients.

Assumptions common to all psychodynamic work include the idea that symptoms and personality difficulties have meaning which is hidden or unconscious; individuals have a complex inner world of which they may be unaware but that interacts with their conscious life, and may be experienced in the therapeutic relationship. The relationship with the therapist may be diagnostic as well as therapeutic. Life is a developmental process and each stage remains with the individual throughout life and interacts with the person's current state. If these assumptions are accepted there is no reason why they will not apply to older as well as to younger people, nor is there any indication that older patients do less well than younger ones when these ideas and techniques are employed.

Part I of this book includes case illustrations which demonstrate not only the application of a particular theory, but also what we ourselves might experience as practitioners within an NHS setting or in the private sector. Included are issues for the patients relating to accessibility, issues of ethics and confidentiality, and ideas about training, supervision and support for this kind of work. We particularly wish to endorse the validity of working in this way with older people, while being mindful of a climate within therapeutics that demands evidence, and which often favours the medical or pharmacological over the psychological or social.

NHS old age psychiatry services see patients with major difficulties, both those who enter the senium with longstanding problems and also those who have managed well until the adversities and losses of old age have upset a previous equilibrium. Services are active in utilising biological treatments and have understood the need to incorporate social aspects of life into a management plan, but psychological needs are easy to ignore in a service facing many demands.

Part II of the book is an applied section, drawing on a number of practitioners, some of them new to writing but established in their particular field of therapy with older adults. We hope that colleagues will be encouraged or even inspired to try a psychodynamic approach with their patients. It is our experience that just taking the time to think psychodynamically about an individual, particularly the person who is 'getting under your skin' can be both fruitful and enriching.

A psychodynamic perspective to work emphasises the uniqueness of each patient and addresses the feelings, fears and fantasies of the staff working with this patient group. It is an approach which may be an alternative to current treatment as a specific therapy, but mostly it is an additional view of patients' lives, difficulties and relationships which may inform general psychiatric work with older people.

Our choice of authors is by no means an exclusion of other writers in the field. We are most grateful to those who did contribute and thank them for their generous and excellent work. It may be that this is the earliest such a book could be written; a time when we could draw on experience of working dynamically with older people. Although there is not as yet a section of old age psychotherapy at the Royal College of Psychiatrists, there is a special interest group at the BPS, the British Psychological Society, and an older adults section of the APP, the Association of Psychoanalytic Psychotherapists in the NHS.

The discipline of Old Age Psychiatry is still in its infancy. We look forward to its coming of age.

SANDRA EVANS AND JANE GARNER

Part I

Theoretical frameworks

Chapter 1

Old and new: Freud and others

Rachael Davenhill

> Two themes run through these pages: the story of my life and the history of psychoanalysis. They are intimately interwoven. This Autobiographical Study shows how psychoanalysis came to be the whole content of my life and rightly assumes that no personal experiences of mine are of any interest in comparison to my relations with that science.
>
> (Freud's 1935 'Postscript' to his 'An Autobiographical Study', 1924)

Psychoanalysis has always held fast to its radical origins, and no more so is this true than in the area of old age. Although in his early paper, 'On Psychotherapy' (1904), Freud was pessimistic as to the relevance of the psychoanalytic method with older people, his life and thinking, and that of post-Freudian analysts such as Segal, King, Hildebrand, Martindale and Waddell, have given us a framework for addressing those factors which can impede or support development across the lifespan, including further development right up until the end of life. Understanding factors that can support normal development can also give insight into those things which can interfere with growing up and into one's own personality – something Waddell (1998) refers to as '. . . the extraordinarily difficult process of growing up on the inside as well as on the outside'.

The first half of this chapter will give an introduction to Freud's life along with an overview of his key psychoanalytic concepts which, taken together, will give a framework to focus on aspects of ageing and their impact on the individual older person and those around them. The second half of the chapter will describe a particular way in which such concepts can be made accessible as a component of pre and post qualification trainings for clinicians wanting to deepen their understanding of the unconscious factors involved in the experience of old age, through a form of experience-based learning called the psychodynamic observational method.

FREUD – THE EARLY AND MIDDLE YEARS

Whilst it is not necessary to be familiar with Freud 'the person' to appreciate his theoretical contributions, nonetheless some familiarity with aspects of his life and death add a richness to the reading of his writings. Sigmund Freud was born in 1856 in Freiberg, Moravia, to poor Jewish parents. His father, Jacob, was 40 and had been married twice previously with two sons from his first marriage. His third wife, Amalia, was half his age, 20 years younger than himself. When Freud was 17 months old, his mother gave birth to a second baby boy, Julius, who died after only 7 months in 1858. Immediately after this, the family moved first to Leipzig, and then in 1860 to Vienna. The years from 1860 to 1866 were filled with pregnancies and births. Freud had four sisters and a young brother. As an adult he looked back with nostalgia for his early days as an infant and little boy in the countryside of Freiberg rather than the crowded city of Vienna which he always professed to hate. In his exemplary biography of Freud, however, Peter Gay (1988) points out that for

> someone who hated Vienna as fiercely as Freud told everyone he did, he proved uncommonly resistant to leaving it. He had excellent English, good foreign connections, repeated invitations to settle abroad, but he stayed until he could stay no longer. 'The feeling of triumph at liberation is mingled too strongly with mourning,' he wrote, a very old man, just after his arrival in London in early 1939, 'for one had still very much loved the prison from which one has been released.'

In 1873, Freud began his study of medicine at the University of Vienna, which he completed in 1881 after which he took up a junior post in the General Hospital in Vienna. He wrote in his 'Autobiographical Study' that his choice of medicine was not so much that he wanted to become a doctor, either in his early or later years, but 'Rather, I was moved by a sort of greed for knowledge.' A year later, aged 26, he met Martha Bernays, but it was to be four years before he married her. They had six children, three daughters and three sons, in the ensuing nine years. It was during his university years that he visited England for the first time, in order to see his two older half brothers in Manchester. This visit, he wrote to Martha Bernays, had a 'decisive influence' on him. In another letter to his friend Eduard Silberstein he commented that he liked England better than Austria despite the 'fog and rain, drunkenness and conservatism'! He also became interested in English writers such as Huxley and Darwin.

Throughout this time, Freud was moving towards his identity as a psychoanalyst rather than an anatomist or neuropsychologist. He threw himself into writing his 'Project for a Scientific Psychology' and found himself on the verge not of a psychology for neurologists, but of a psychology for psychologists. The physiological and biological substrata of the mind never lost their importance for Freud but for several decades they faded into the background as he explored the domains of the unconscious and its manifestations in thought and act – slips, jokes, symptoms, defences, and, most intriguing of all, dreams.

(Gay, 1988)

In 1885 Freud was granted a bursary which enabled him to spend some months in Paris studying hysteria and hypnotism under Charcot. This was a formative experience in Freud's move from the physical sciences towards a driving, lifelong investigation of the mind. On his return, he worked in the laboratory of Carl Claus, searching, inconclusively, for the gonads of eels – a search which was to sharpen his powers of patience and observation. Following this he moved to Brucke's laboratory, where he was much happier, and it was there he made friends with Josef Breuer, whose role in Freud's development as a psychoanalyst was critical.

Breuer was an older colleague of Freud who had made use of hypnotic suggestion in the treatment of a young woman regarded as suffering from hysteria. Hysteria at this point was thought to stem from physical trauma which had been forgotten by the patient. The idea of hypnosis and suggestion was to enable the patient to remember the traumatic event along with its accompanying emotions. Freud rapidly became dissatisfied with hypnosis as a treatment method. His eventual rejection of the use of hypnosis was decisive for the development of his new ideas as to how the mind worked – ideas which came to be referred to as psychoanalysis.

In 1896 when Freud was 40, his father died, by now an old man of 81. In his introduction to the second edition of the 'Interpretation of Dreams', Freud commented that the paper had in part been a response to the impact of his father's death, which had affected him greatly. From this point on, from an external viewpoint, what is striking is the settled nature of Freud's domestic life – living and working from the same house in Vienna until his move 47 years later to England. During these years, however, Freud was to struggle with, ripen and bring to fruition a comprehensive theory of mind which was able to take account of unconscious as well as conscious factors involved in the human ability to either develop and thrive or, conversely, undermine and destroy the capacity to love and the capacity to work which Freud saw as two of the great endeavours in life.

The notion of the *unconscious* was revolutionary in its time in terms of the blow such a concept gave to the narcissistic belief that men and women could take conscious control of their destiny. Freud developed the concepts of *transference* and *countertransference* as clinical phenomena naturally stemming from this central concept of the unconscious. Here Freud thought that it was not just the patient who transferred feelings from earlier primary relationships (usually with parental figures) onto current relationships (transference), but that the analyst/clinician also could bring their own unresolved feelings towards figures in their own past and transfer them onto their patient (countertransference).

Another cornerstone of the new psychoanalytic treatment depended on what Freud referred to as *free association*. Here, the only thing patients were required to do was to feel free to say whatever came into their mind in as unedited a way as possible. Freud was taken aback by the powerful emotional response encountered in both his patients and in himself in the course of treatment, and it was his struggle to make sense of the strength of his own, as well as his own patients' feelings, that led him to develop a number of key concepts which are as useful and relevant clinically today as they were when he first began to put forward his ideas in the late 1800s. He quickly noticed that despite being given the freedom to speak freely about whatever was on their mind, through the method of free association, patients found this difficult. In fact the contents of the mind are often censored, not available to be spoken about at first hand, but may be accessible through, for example, dreams, or 'slips of the tongue'. Early on Freud developed the concepts of resistance and repression, using the latter term interchangeably with *defence mechanisms*.

Defence mechanisms act as a kind of perimeter fence coming into force in order to protect the mind from overwhelming anxieties and conflicts which can arise from within or outside the self – often a mixture of the two. They operate from very early on in life in order to protect the infant against anxieties regarding survival itself, and include splitting, denial, identification, projection, introjection and idealisation. In later years, Anna Freud, Freud's daughter, published a book called *The Ego and the Mechanisms of Defence* (1936), classifying and further developing the defence mechanisms her father had described so many years before.

FREUD – THE LATER YEARS

From 1911 onwards, Freud wrote a number of meta-psychological papers which contained his continued explorations in developing his theory of psychoanalysis. At the age of 61, he published a paper called 'Mourning and Melancholia' (1917) which is crucial for the understanding of the psychodynamics and treatment of severe depression in people who are older. The paper is important in giving an explicit account of the role of identification in the formation of the individual's internal world. Freud thought that a world of internal object relationships came about through projection and identification which, in the case of melancholia (depressive illness) remained more alive to the individual in a quite deadly way and interfered with the possibility of the person being able to acknowledge and make use of relationships available to them in their current reality.

Clinical Illustration

Mrs Y, a 63 year old woman, went to see the practice nurse at her GP's surgery. She said she was living a 'shadow-life' when she tried to describe how she felt in the initial meeting. The nurse, through listening carefully and enquiring as to what her patient meant by this, was able to establish that Mrs Y felt that she had turned into a shadow of her former self since the death of her husband when she was 50 and had not been able to fully mourn her husband or move on from his death in terms of getting on with the rest of her life. A template of the marital relationship began to emerge as Mrs Y talked – her husband was perfect, he had done everything for her, they had gone everywhere together. All competencies seemed to be lodged in her husband. When he died, instead of being able to re-acquire aspects of herself that had been lodged with him through the process of projection, Mrs Y held onto her way of relating to him as the solution, and replicated this in her relationships with her daughter, neighbours, and potentially in her contact with the nurse. She presented extremely passively – the nurse would know the answer to all of this, her daughter did all her shopping, she had a rota of neighbours calling in each day to check she was all right, etc.

The nurse, however, was able to resist the pressure to 'do' something at the patient's request, and held onto her curiosity. This enabled her to explore the patient's difficulties further over a couple more meetings. It became clear that although chronologically in her 60s, the patient had never negotiated the ordinary transitions of infancy and childhood. She still had an extremely enmeshed relationship with her own mother (who visited the patient every other day, though she herself was now in her 80s), and was only able to leave home by marrying a man who cared for her in the same way as her father had. Rather than acquiesce to the patient's request that she, the nurse, was the solution – if she could just pop in on her every now and then, she would probably be fine – the nurse instead was able to point out how that would be replicating the exact problem Mrs Y was presenting with – everyone else getting on with things so that she did not need to. She offered to refer Mrs Y on for brief psychodynamic therapy, which Mrs Y eventually accepted, though not before an angry outburst at the nurse for her neglect and lack of caring attitude in wanting to pass her on. This explosion was a catalyst for fruitful exploration into the patient's absolute rage, rooted in infancy, at having to separate which was taken up first in brief individual treatment and then through her joining a longer term psychoanalytic psychotherapy group.

This example of Mrs Y is a variation of the kind of depression with which GPs, old age psychiatrists, CPNs, psychologists and other mental health workers may find themselves dealing on a daily basis.

Extremely valuable work can be done in those first contact meetings when the clinician is trying to assess the situation and struggling to make sense of some of the unconscious as well as conscious pressures the patient is bringing into the consultation. In the example above of Mrs Y, the nurse was able to use her skills to assess 'where next' for her patient, and refer her on for a formal assessment for psychotherapy. The transitions across the later years of life involve mourning, both in connection with that which has been had and lost, as well as for those things which may never have been experienced. The capacity to cope with transition, loss and change in later life is rooted in ways of facing loss forged much earlier on in life. Whilst living in the shadow of death is a well known colloquialism, its corollary, for older people presenting with depressions related to an unconscious fear of death, is the inability to fully live the life that is still available.

Although Freud himself was inevitably preoccupied with death and dying in relationship to his objects and his own illness and ageing, it is clear that he never stopped struggling with both the anxieties and the exhilarations of taking one new step after another in developing and deepening his own clinical understanding of his patients and in continuing to convey the development of his theory to others through discussion and writing. In stark contrast to his now oft-quoted sentence (written at the age of 48!) that 'Near or above the age of fifty the elasticity of the mental processes . . . is as a rule lacking . . .' (1904), Freud's own life and continued mental capacities remained a testament to the possibilities and potentialities residing in the latter half of life. In 1923, just before publishing his paper 'An Autobiographical Study', Sigmund Freud discovered he had cancer of the jaw and thought he was going to die. In fact he was operated upon and lived for another 16 years until his death in London in 1939. During this time he continued both his clinical work with patients, and further writings.

Freud revised his whole theory of mind with his paper 'The Ego and the Id' in 1923. Here he developed what is now referred to as the structural model of the mind based on psychological forms of internal as well as external object-relatedness. He proposed a tripartite mental apparatus, consisting of the ego, the id and the superego.

In brief, the id is the font of instinctual drives, and its contents are entirely unconscious. The superego links to what would popularly be called conscience, and is made up of images of internalised parental figures, which undergo constant modification through the process of projection and introjection. The superego may be experienced at times as a terribly cruel and judgemental presence in the individual's internal world. Alternatively, the superego may be experienced as a benign force, enabling the individual to develop a capacity for making good and realistic judgements in a helpful way. The ego is the mediator between the demands of the id and the superego, and the demands of the internal and external world. Freud's structural model of the mind laid the foundation from which post-Freudian analysts were able to develop an understanding of object relationships and the world of internal objects residing within the personality, and to explore further the complex psychological mechanisms of identification, projection and introjection.

In Freud's terms the ego, id and superego develop within the context of human relationships (referred to in analytic writing as 'object-relationships') and develop very early on from the infant's perceptions of their relationship with their parents, partly real, partly based on unconscious phantasy. This blend of conscious and unconscious perception can vary and change within the individual depending on the prevailing internal mental state in interaction with the external environment. This is what provides a basic template for the mapping of future relationships. The way in which the child builds up a view of the world from its perceptions both in reality and in imagination of their relationships with key people in that world is of central interest to psycho-analysts. It is also relevant to any curious clinician in contact with, say, an older person presenting with a chronic depression in understanding the com-plexity of factors, past as well as present, which may be contributing to the entrenched nature of the difficulty.

In his book *Immaterial Facts* (1988), Robert Caper looks further at Freud's move from a mechanistic to a psychological model of the mind in his explor-ation of the concept of *psychic reality*. According to Caper, the notion of psychic reality does not predetermine what is internal and what is external. However it does give us the freedom in our own minds and in our thinking with our patients to consider not just the external event in itself, but also the individual's subjective experience of such an event. Two aspects are involved here – the cognitive associations and the emotional associations of the event, which come together and form the *unconscious phantasy*, the ether that permeates the internal world of every individual. Once the notion of unconscious phantasy is allowed into the picture, a much richer and deeper colour and texturing of understanding can come to the fore for both patient and clinician. Psychic reality allows in and recognises the emotional signifi-cance of human experience and its qualities, and underlines the importance of looking at the emotional significance of the event rather than the 'facts of the event' alone. Later on in life, memory will be influenced both by the actual event and by the way in which it may be distorted by the internal meaning bestowed upon it by the individual. Caper says that 'by shifting from the raw, literal event toward the melding of external and internal instincts, then Freud became a psychoanalyst'.

In thinking about the processes which combine to produce 'who we are', the psychological processes of *projection* and *introjection* are helpful to understand. The basic template for these ideas is the raw human need to feed and expel, to take in and to push out, or get rid of. In thinking of a tiny baby, there is usually an instinctive move to turn towards the breast and feed when hunger is felt, and to expel faeces when discomfort is felt. But these physical processes are imbued with psychological resonance both for the baby and his or her carer. The way in which the baby learns to navigate, and is helped to navigate, his or her way through complex emotional states such as love, hate and frustration can powerfully influence the course that future psychic development can take at later points in life.

In taking forward Freud's thinking, two further psychoanalytic concepts are relevant for the understanding of mental states in people who are older and those who work with them. These are the concepts of *projective identification* and *containment* which were developed by the psychoanalysts Melanie Klein and Wilfred Bion respectively, and will be explored in greater detail in Chapters 8 and 17. In her recent paper on observing confusional mental states in people with dementia, Waddell (2000), referring specifically to Klein and Bion, linked the understanding of the very early states of mind of the infant to 'the opaque mental states of old age'. She highlighted the way in which the caregiver's capacity to unconsciously register, reflect and think, can give meaning to the infant or older person's world, and this meaning is conveyed through the caregiver's capacity to care responsively. Waddell emphasised the importance of both projective identification and containment as concepts crucial to our understanding of this area as follows:

> By the mechanism of projective identification the baby/child/elderly person who cannot understand, think or talk about his or her frag-mentary or fragmenting experience, may nonetheless be able to engender in the care-giver some version of that basic experience. If . . . the care-giver can offer a mentally receptive state of mind, conscious or unconscious, the communication can be received, modified if it is one of pain and rage, appreciated if one of love and pleasure and recom-municated, whether in more manageable, or in reciprocal mode. The caregiver's mind functions as a container for, and a sorter of, the pro-jected emotional fragments which, as a consequence, become 'the con-tained'. Care of the very elderly, those so often lacking the capacity to speak, yet so intensely riven by extreme emotional states, requires a pain-ful reversal of the original pattern of container–contained (the young now struggling to offer states of reverie to the old).

Freud's mother died at the age of 91. In the same year, Freud was awarded the Goethe Prize for merit. He regarded this as the climax of his life as a citizen. In his 1935 'Postscript' to the original 'Autobiographical Studies' he wrote, now in his 80s:

> I myself find that a significant change has come about. Threads which in the course of my development have become entangled have now begun to separate; interests which in the course of my development had become intertangled have now begun to separate; interests which I had acquired in the later part of my life have receded, while the older and original ones become prominent once more . . . My interest, after making a lifelong

detour through the natural sciences, medicine and psychotherapy, returned to the cultural problems which had fascinated me long before, when I was a youth scarcely old enough for thinking . . .

In June, 1938, with the escalation of anti-Semitism and the spread of Nazism, Freud left Austria for ever, escaping to England with his wife, sister-in-law and daughter Anna. He lived in London, and continued to work on his final papers 'Moses and Monotheism' and 'Outline of Psychoanalysis' which came to a halt in September when he had another operation in a final attempt to reach the tumour in his jaw. This was to be the last operation before his death on 23 September 1939 following the outbreak of the Second World War. Freud had commented that he knew the journey from Vienna to England was in part to enable him 'to die in freedom'. He died knowing that his immediate family were safe, not knowing that all four of his older sisters perished in the concentration camps of Theresienstadt and Auschwitz.

THE RELEVANCE OF PSYCHOANALYSIS FOR MEANINGFUL CONTINUED PROFESSIONAL DEVELOPMENT

The psychic reversal, where often much younger clinicians may be working with people much older than themselves, is not a straightforward matter. Despite the many papers that now exist on psychoanalysis and psycho-dynamic psychotherapy with older people (for example Abraham, 1919; Segal, 1958; King, 1980; Hildebrand, 1986; Martindale, 1989), as well as recent research (Fonagy & Roth, 1996) and explicit recommendations in the recently published National Service Framework for Older People (DoH, 2001) that brief psychodynamic psychotherapy by an experienced prac-titioner is an effective treatment of choice for depression in later life, it is still the case that people over the age of 60 are not referred for psychotherapeutic help in the same way as younger adults. Whilst it is likely that this will change over time, as life expectancy increases along with public expectations regard-ing the provision of social and health care and what we know can be effective, it is worth bearing in mind the unconscious factors which may inhibit both the referral of older people for psychological help as well as the capacity to take on for treatment a person much older than oneself.

In working with people who are older, unconscious anxieties in connection to our own aggressive and sadistic as well as more loving impulses to parents and maybe grandparents can easily be aroused. Hinshelwood and Skogstad (2000) point out that we may be drawn to this area of work in part because of an unconscious motivation to repair damage which we feel has been done in our internal phantasy life to primary carers, often our mother or father, who will have assumed an internal as well as an external significance for us. The difficulty here is that whilst the guilt about our own destructive impulses and wish to repair and make good may sustain us through very difficult work tasks, if, in the work setting, repair cannot take place perfectly, then the more omnipotent expectation we or the organisation may have of us, namely to cure, becomes a burden that it is impossible to fulfil. This can leave us in the grip of a hopeless paralysis in terms of thoughtful functioning – or alternatively in a state of hatred towards the person we are caring for who, in reality, may well be extremely helpless and induce such feelings of helplessness in us. Inevitably for some old people, mental and physical faculties have deteriorated to a major degree, and cure is not an option. How then can anxieties about deterioration and helplessness be better contained? Repeatedly we are reminded of the wish for joined up and seamless thinking in national policy documents. Whilst a hopeful thought, seamless thinking or preventing mindlessness is unrealistic so long as the unconscious factors which lead to fragmentation and breakdown of thinking in this area are not fully acknowledged and given a formal place to be understood.

Martindale (unpublished Tavistock Conference paper, 2000) highlights the importance of the containment of workers' anxieties through an understanding of the transference/countertransference relationship as one component in the ongoing provision of what he terms thoughtful care (as opposed to cure), in working with people who are older. Without such containment we know that the physical and mental abuse of older people takes place (Garner & Evans, 2000), as it does with babies whose parents do not have sufficient internal or external resources to support them in continuing to bear what is often felt to be unbearable.

In this complex and disturbing area, understanding the unconscious factors involved in the physical and psychological abuse of people who are older will involve a more open acknowledgement of the degree of hatred that dependence in the older person can stir up. For the younger carer, there may be a profound disappointment with the person they are caring for who, with the very fact of their ageing, may face the young person at an unconscious level with unresolved primitive infantile anxieties about the abandoning parent. Facing dependence from people upon whom we have relied can be very difficult. In the provision of clinical care services, such feelings of hatred need a place to be discussed and thought about rather than condemned and split off. The importance of developing a capacity to tolerate feelings of hate as well as love towards the other person was highlighted by Winnicott many years ago in his paper 'Hate in the Countertransference' (1949) and is discussed further in Chapter 8. More recently, the dangers of disowning unwanted aspects of the personality have been highlighted by Steiner (1993) in his work on psychic retreats, and Davenhill (1998) in a paper on unconscious factors involved in the provision of long-term care for people in later life.

How is such containment to be provided? One way is through having the experience of personal therapy or analysis ourselves, as a way of understanding more about our own unconscious which will include the countertransference response we have all the time to the people and situations surrounding us. A second way is through consistent, ongoing clinical (rather than line management) supervision with an experienced practitioner. Whilst this is integral to ongoing practice as a psychotherapist, it is not necessarily automatically built in to the core professions, particularly at more senior level. With the emphasis in the NHS clinical governance framework on continuing professional development and lifelong learning as a means of underpinning and sustaining good professional practice, there is now a real acknowledgement regarding the importance of supervision, which needs to be actively pursued and argued for on a uni- and multidisciplinary basis. An example of the latter has been described by Stern and Lovestone (2000) in their paper describing a weekly case discussion seminar run on an acute admission old age psychiatry in-patient unit.

A third way is through the psychodynamic method of observation in old age settings, which allows the observer to come closer to the experience of the older person and their carers (Davenhill, 2003). This will be described in more detail in the final section of this chapter as an example of a contemporary psychoanalytic training tool for experience-based learning happening at the Tavistock Clinic, which can take place at both pre and post qualification level for those working with older people.

The psychodynamic method of observation

The observational method was developed at the Tavistock Clinic by a psychoanalyst called Esther Bick in the 1940s, who asked her child psychotherapy trainees to undertake an observation of a baby and his or her caretaker in the first year of life as a means of learning about the basic foundations of personality development. This approach to observation is valuable in helping the observer to 'discover the value of being and themselves becoming a receptive observer. In this exercise there is no obligation to do anything beyond observing . . . indeed, one has to refrain from action' (Dawes & Boston, 1977).

Psychodynamic observation continues to be used successfully as a core aspect in the training of child and adult psychotherapists within the NHS, and the method of observation is of equal relevance to core professions working with people who are older. The use of observation has been illustrated by Mackenzie-Smith (1992) in a paper describing multiple observations of older patients in a hospital setting. Terry (1997) described his experience of supervising a clinical psychologist on placement in the final year of training, whom he encouraged to undertake an observation on a continuing care ward.

The aim of this form of observational enquiry is to allow the observer to come close to the older person's experience and to develop an attuned capacity to see and retain detail. In becoming aware of the emotional impact the interplay between the individual and their environment may produce, it is hoped that the observer will learn from their own experience about factors, conscious and unconscious, which can support or impede development and adjustment to transitions in the later part of life.

The psychodynamic method of observation differs from other methods of qualitative observation such as dementia care mapping. The two methods, by no means mutually exclusive, are propelled by different motivations. In dementia care mapping, the observer or mapper is 'looking in' to observe the quality of care in a particular environment, and then gives constructive feedback from the outside in. In psychodynamic observation, the observer is looking at, or into, their own subjective experience of what it is possible to look at, take in and think about at both a conscious and unconscious level.

In core training, a trainee may have been fortunate enough to have had a placement supervisor who suggested that they go and spend some time looking at a particular setting without doing anything 'in role'. This allows the trainee to get a feel for the sort of work area into which they are entering. Psychodynamic observation is a formalisation and a deepening of this process and has five basic components as follows:

- The observation takes place for an hour, once a week, usually at the same time for a minimum of 10 weeks, preferably longer. It may occur in an institutional setting, or in a large extended family setting with the family's permission.
- The person undertaking the observation sits in a discreet position in whatever setting they are carrying out the observation. This will have been carefully negotiated and agreed beforehand with the users and staff of the setting.
- No notes are taken at the time.
- The observer tries to write up detailed process notes as soon as is possible afterwards, outside the observational setting. Although this is demanding and time consuming it is often the case that paradoxically much of the observation may not be consciously observable to oneself until some time has passed. A process of further digestion can then take place as things not originally at the surface of the mind come to the fore in the process of writing up.
- Further processing of the observation takes place in a weekly supervision group of between four and six participants. Each member of the group is able to present an observation in detail on a rotational basis. There is an advantage in meeting as a group in that the observer is exposed to the associative process of the group setting. The group allows a multi-faceted perspective to emerge on the observation, so by the end it is hoped that the observer will feel it is possible to have a truthful and more rounded picture of the many different aspects of the experience to which they have allowed themselves to be exposed.

Psychodynamic observation provides the individual worker with a powerful tool for understanding unconscious as well as conscious processes taking place in the world both of the older person and their carers. This understanding in itself can provide a strong containing function and is invaluable in understanding more about individual responses to working with people at the particular point in the lifespan which they are negotiating.

In thinking about one of Freud's earliest and most important discoveries referred to at the beginning of the chapter – that of *free association* – it is possible to see the way in which psychodynamic observation provides a basic template from which the observer is exposed to the process of free association in an unthreatening and supported setting by being encouraged to see whatever comes into the mind during the course of the observation. It is neither personal therapy nor clinical case supervision, but emphasises the person within the professional who is undertaking the observation as well as the personhood of all those inhabiting the observed setting.

Psychodynamic observation is not purely a training method. It is also an important research tool in allowing a particular way of coming close both to the more normal aspects of ageing, as well as to the disturbance both of the older person and of staff which the deterioration of mental and physical capacities can arouse. One of the core aims of psychodynamic observation is to enable clinicians, when undertaking the observation and when back in their own work setting, both to be in a powerful emotional context and to retain the capacity to think about what they see happening inside themselves as a reflection of what is happening around them.

CONCLUSION

Obholzer (in Hinshelwood & Skogstad, 2000) describes the difficulties for frontline workers who in their everyday work are up against the raw emotional states in the people with whom they are working. He describes such workers as going about their tasks at times 'irradiated with distress'. This is a powerful phrase, and one that we need to note when thinking about the implementation of the recent National Service Framework for Older People. To gloss over the degree of difficulty which may confront workers at an unconscious level, workers in their daily contact with older patients facing the extremes of mental and physical deterioration, is dangerous and can lead to an osteoporosis of thought – a crumbling and fragmentation of thinking in the individual worker and the institutional or community atmosphere within which they operate. Nowhere can this be seen more clearly than, at the time of writing, the false division embedded in current government policy agreeing to pay fees for nursing care and not for 'personal care'. This serves to dehumanise the real meaning of nursing and the truth of its function in containing the holistic health needs of the older person both physically and emotionally. Far from being past history, Freud's core concepts, along with contemporary psychoanalytic ideas, continue to develop and can provide living, working tools both dynamic and relevant to the core task of thinking about and working with people who are older, as the following chapters in this book will illustrate.

REFERENCES

Abraham, K. (1919). The applicability of psychoanalytic treatment to patients at an advanced age. In: *Selected Papers of Karl Abraham*. London: Hogarth Press, 1927, pp. 312–317.

Caper, R. (1988). *Immaterial Facts: Freud's discovery of psychic reality and Klein's development of his work*. Northvale, NJ: Jason Aronson.

Davenhill, R. (1998). No truce with the furies: Issues of containment in the provision of long-term residential care for older adults. *Journal of Social Work Practice*, 12(2), 149–157.

Dawes, D., & Boston, M. (1977). The Tavistock training and philosophy. In: M. Harris Williams (ed.) *Collected Papers of Martha Harris and Esther Bick*. Scotland: Clunie Press.

Department of Health (DoH) (2001). *National Service Framework for Older People*. London: DoH.

Fonagy, P., & Roth, A. (1996). *What Works for Whom? A Critical Review of Psychotherapy Research*. Hove: Guilford Press.

Freud, A. (1936). *The Ego and the Mechanisms of Defence*. London: Hogarth Press.

Freud, S. (1904). On psychotherapy. Standard Edition 7. London: Hogarth Press.

—— (1917). Mourning and melancholia. Standard Edition 11. London: Hogarth Press.

—— (1923). The ego and the id. Standard Edition 11. London: Hogarth Press.

—— (1924). An autobiographical study. Standard Edition 20. London: Hogarth Press.

—— (1924). Inhibitions, symptoms and anxiety. Standard Edition 20. London: Hogarth Press.

Garner, J., & Evans, S. (2000). *Institutional Abuse of Older Adults*. Council Report CR84. London: Royal College of Psychiatrists.

Gay, P. (1988). *Freud: A life for our time*. London: J.M. Dent Ltd.

Hess, N. (1987). King Lear and some anxieties of old age. *British Journal of Medical Psychology*, 60, 209–215.

Hildebrand, P. (1986). Dynamic psychotherapy with the elderly. In: Colarusso, C. & Nemiroff, R. (eds) *The Race Against Time*. New York: New York Press.

Hinshelwood, R.D., & Skogstad, W. (2000). *Observing Organisations: Anxiety, defence and culture in health care*. London: Routledge.

King, P. (1980). The life-cycle as indicated by the nature of the transference in the psychoanalysis of the middle aged and the elderly. *International Journal of Psychoanalysis*, 61, 153–160.

Mackenzie-Smith, S. (1992). A psychoanalytical observational study of the elderly. *Free Associations*, 3.3.27, 355–390.

Martindale, B. (1989). Becoming dependent again: The fears of some elderly persons and their young therapists. *Psychoanalytic Psychotherapy*, 4(1), 67–75.

Segal, H. (1958). Fear of death: Notes on the analysis of an old man. In: *The Work of Hanna Segal: A Kleinian approach to clinical practice*. London: Free Association Books.

Steiner, J. (1993). *Psychic Retreats: Pathological organizations in psychotic, neurotic and borderline patients*. London: Routledge.

Stern, J.M., & Lovestone, S. (2000). Therapy with the elderly: Introducing psychodynamic psychotherapy to the multi-disciplinary team. *International Journal of Geriatric Psychiatry*, 500–505.

Terry, P. (1997). *Counselling the Elderly and Their Carers*. London: Macmillan Press.

Waddell, M. (1998). *Inside Lives: Psychoanalysis and the growth of the personality*. London: Duckworth.

Waddell, M. (2000). Only connect: Developmental issues from early to late life. *Psychoanalytic Psychotherapy*, 14, 239–252.

Winnicott, D.W. (1949). Hate in the countertransference. *International Journal of Psychoanalysis*, 3, 69–74.

Chapter 2

Loneliness in old age: Klein and others

Noel Hess

> Alack! The night comes on, and the bleak winds
> Do sorely ruffle; for many miles about
> There's scarce a bush
> (Shakespeare; *King Lear* II, iv)

Loneliness is a fact of life, something we do not usually view as pathological and possibly therefore rarely discuss. This is, perhaps, not because we easily accept it as a fact of life, as something we all have to contend with to varying degrees at different times of our life, but rather because it often evokes painful feelings of shame and inferiority to make an admission of feeling lonely. It is also a particularly heightened and debilitating feature of old age. This chapter will discuss some ways of understanding the experience of loneliness in old age, mainly with reference to the work of Melanie Klein, but also other psychoanalytic writers, to see what light these ideas shed on something our elderly patients often, overtly or covertly, bring to us for help.

THEORETICAL CONSIDERATIONS

Melanie Klein is best known for her pioneering work on primitive infantile anxieties which, though arising in infancy, pervade our unconscious mental life and structure our inner world and thus also structure our experience of external reality. Although considered radical and challenging at the time they were formulated, these ideas have now gained a degree of acceptance across all schools of psychoanalytic thought. Specifically, she proposed two main levels of anxiety. The first, persecutory anxiety, arises in a paranoid schizoid mode of functioning, and is an anxiety formed by the projection of aggressive impulses and the splitting, both of self and objects, into extremes of good and bad. The splitting and projection are means of protecting the good inside from contamination by the bad, so as to maintain some semblance of balance and order in an inherently fragile and unstable internal world. Alternating with persecutory experience is idealised experience, in which a sense of perfection is felt as attainable.

Gradually, as the result of the dominance of good experience over bad – of feeling loved and cared for and exposed to manageable frustrations – the extremes of good and bad are modified into something less extreme and eventually come together; the loved (idealised) and hated (persecutory) versions of mother (represented concretely in the infant's mind, according to Klein, as good and bad breasts) come together in the infant's mind to form a representation of mother who is experienced as good and needed but also human and vulnerable. This movement heralds the second level of anxiety, depressive anxiety, which has as its focus concern about the wellbeing of the good and needed internal object. Whereas persecutory anxiety is focused on the survival of the self in the face of hostile and attacking objects, depressive anxiety is concerned with the survival of the good internal object when faced with greedy or aggressive attacks from the self. Damage to or loss of this object would mean a loss of all that is good and nourishing and a return to a paranoid state of mind.

According to this model, these two levels of anxiety, persecutory and depressive, dominate our internal world and colour our experience of external reality, not only in infancy but throughout life. Depressive anxiety, and its relation to clinical depression, has been thus described:

> [Klein's] most important contribution . . . both theoretically and clinically, was the idea that a good internal mother is felt to be lost, leaving the infant's internal world devoid of goodness and in a dangerously unstable state, as bad objects predominate. It is this internal loss, triggered, or represented, by an external loss, which the depressed patient is actually troubled by and needs help to address, because the ramifications of such a loss on the balance of their internal world are felt to be catastrophic.
>
> (Hess, 1999)

Klein applied these ideas to the experience of loneliness in the last paper she wrote before her death. Before describing the paper, some biographical background is worth filling in. The paper was written for an International Congress in Copenhagen in 1959 and presented there, so is likely to have been written in the year or so preceding, when Klein was 77 years old. The editors of her papers note that 'though nowhere it is specified, there is a premonition of approaching death' in this paper. She in fact died in August 1960, a year after the paper was delivered, and it was published posthumously in 1963. Klein's biographer (Grosskurth, 1986) describes her struggles with loneliness in old age, so there is reason to believe it was written from the heart, and from a basis of personal experience.

In this paper Klein's interest is in the *inner* sense of loneliness, of feeling lonely even when among friends or receiving love. The source of this feeling she relates to a number of underlying factors: paranoid insecurity, in which persecutory anxiety is dominant and one feels isolated in a loveless and hostile domain; fear of the failure of integration of the good and bad parts of oneself and one's objects, occurring in such a way that the bad will overwhelm the good and one feels left alone with only the bad or contaminated parts of the self; and the fear of death, which signifies the loss of the good internal object necessary for survival and growth.

Perhaps the most interesting source of this inner sense of loneliness is the pervasiveness of idealisation. Klein defines this loneliness as 'the result of a ubiquitous yearning for an unattainable perfect internal state', which is a feature of the earliest relation to the mother and is a search for 'a state of being completely understood, of understanding without words'. This idealised state is yearned for and the loss or absence of it felt very painfully; the wish for it, however, is never given up.

The factors she sees as mitigating loneliness are principally a capacity for enjoyment and generosity, in which envy is not so marked and so corrosive that there can be a wish to return goodness with gratitude. A rare and specific mention is made of the experience of loneliness in old age, and how it can be counteracted by an identification with the satisfactions of youth and a gratitude for past pleasures and successes, although an idealisation of the past is always a feature of old age to some degree. Most importantly perhaps, Klein emphasises that although these various factors can mitigate loneliness, they cannot eliminate it, and may in fact be used as a defence against loneliness so it does not have to be experienced. It seems that Klein is warning us against an idealised view in which loneliness does not exist; it is there to be felt by all of us.

In addition to the possibility of the paper arising out of Klein's own experience of old age and the loneliness which is an inevitable part of it, it is interesting to speculate about the relation it might have had to Winnicott's paper on the capacity to be alone (1958). It is likely that she knew of this paper, as it was published in the previous year. Winnicott's focus is somewhat different, though related, in that he understands the capacity to be alone, to enjoy solitude, as an achievement of emotional maturity, and to derive from the infant's experience of being alone in the presence of an object (i.e. mother). The paradox he offers is that it is the awareness of mother's existence and reliability that makes it possible for the infant to be alone, because good enough mothering instils a belief in a benign environment. Klein would perhaps view this as a somewhat idealised picture, in that it is never fully achievable. Although she does not make reference to Winnicott's paper (surprisingly, given that it covers such similar ground) it is tempting to wonder if hers was written as a counterbalance to his contribution.

It could be argued that Klein and Winnicott are discussing apparently similar but subtly different states of mind: Klein's focus is on the pain of inner loneliness as a universal experience; Winnicott's is on the mature capacity to bear solitude and even use it creatively. Holmes (1993), discussing loneliness in adolescence, argues for a distinction between loneliness and solitude, such that loneliness implies awareness of a lack, and a yearning to fill it, whereas solitude can be self-sufficient and free of tension. Whether or not one agrees with this distinction, or sees these states as part of a continuum, both Klein and Winnicott are interested, from their different angles, in the experience of being alone with oneself, and what renders this experience more or less painful and more or less bearable.

Cohen (1982) relates these concepts to the role of narcissism in ageing, both in terms of how the narcissistic personality experiences the process of ageing and also how ageing may further stimulate the use of narcissistic defences. According to psychoanalytic thinking, narcissism is a way of retreating from object-relating and the fundamental anxieties it evokes – dependence, envy, separation and loss – into a state of apparent self-reliance, usually with a superior, omnipotent and self-aggrandising quality. The narcissistic personality appears to believe that he possesses within himself all the necessary sources of goodness, wisdom, understanding, etc., and that what his objects can offer him is of little value. Cohen states that narcissism 'is bound up with the inability to mourn, recognition of dependence, separation and death [all of which are] features basic to a successful adaptation to ageing'. He also relates narcissism and ageing to the experience of loneliness which he defines as 'an inability to communicate internally with parts of oneself or one's objects'. This loneliness, he argues, with reference to a narcissistic patient who presented for help in his mid-fifties, is accentuated because narcissism attacks possible connectedness, both internally and externally, creating a vicious circle which propels the patient into further isolation and sense of futility. Cohen details this vicious circle of narcissism and loneliness as seen in his patient:

> the awareness of his dependency, and with it the awareness of separation, increases his narcissistic defences; but his pathological narcissistic defences increase his loneliness making him unable to achieve a sense of belonging. It is this which makes it difficult for him to approach mourning and thus facilitate adaptation to the problem of ageing.

Also concerned with the relation between narcissism and old age, Hess (1987) has described how narcissistic defences are a common means of dealing with the anxieties of old age, especially the terror of being left alone without an organising and containing part of the self. This is often feared to be lost in the catastrophes of old age such as strokes and dementia, and is why elderly patients often forcibly conscript their objects into the role of an auxiliary organising ego. Equally often, this occurs without acknowledgement or awareness of the degree of dependence involved. It is well known that narcissism hates dependence. It is therefore perhaps not surprising that this defence or that this defensive structure becomes heightened in old age, given the reality of increasing physical and emotional vulnerability. Envy of youth, of their vitality and their sense of having a future, further escalates loneliness, as it renders it impossible to want to share one's knowledge and experience with the young in a generous way (Joseph, 1986).

While the focus here is, necessarily, on narcissism as a pathological force within the personality – attacking dependency and relatedness, increasing isolation, etc. – Zachary (1995) makes the helpful point that narcissism is also a source of confidence, dignity and self-preservation, and that we need to distinguish between 'healthy' narcissism in ageing and pathological narcissism. One way of making this distinction is to take note of the effect a patient's narcissism has on their objects – 'healthy' narcissism will usually be tolerated; and may even evoke admiration; pathological narcissism will usually alienate those in contact with it.

What understanding, then, do these various writers give us of the meaning of loneliness in old age? That the seeds of this universal experience are sown in infancy and in the earliest object relations; that loneliness might be thought of as a failure of the capacity to be alone in a benign and secure way, or possibly as an experience of being alone with only the bad parts of oneself; that envy and narcissism accentuate loneliness by attacking connectedness and dependence; and that loneliness can never be banished, in part because of our attachment to idealised states of mind and idealised object relations which are never really given up.

Clinical Illustration
With these thoughts in mind, a case will be described which illustrates some of these features. At the time of seeing this patient, the clinician was an experienced clinical psychologist but a relatively inexperienced psychotherapist in his late thirties.

Mrs Jones was referred for psychotherapy in an NHS psychotherapy service. She was 65 years old, divorced and childless, and had retired about 10 years ago from her job in the helping professions. The referring psychiatrist described her as anxious and depressed and having experienced episodes of depersonalisation. She had had a number of periods of psychoanalytic help before in her life, often in the private sector.

After he had sent her an appointment for an initial interview, she rang to confirm that the time offered was suitable for her, and they had a brief, business-like but rather stilted conversation. He felt that the patient was disturbed by something, but was unsure what, so he was not surprised when she rang back a few minutes later. She then registered her concern about her referral to him – she had not heard of him, was he experienced enough to see her, how old was he, and what was his training? He felt very much put on the spot and said that perhaps they could discuss these issues when they met. What he picked up from this brief telephone contact was the patient's prickly, interrogative and rather superior manner, such that he was put in the position of having to justify himself as good enough or experienced enough to see her. Not fully aware of all the implications at the time he felt sure that he felt somewhat attacked and defensive. He was certainly aware that Mrs Jones experienced the referral, to a younger man and to an NHS service, as a cause of shame and narcissistic injury.

They met a few weeks later, and she began the interview straight away by telling him that she felt really quite insulted at being referred to such a young man, that he was 'obviously' too young and too inexperienced to really under-stand or help her, that his name was German and associated with Nazis and how could she, a Jewish refugee, possibly come to him for help? This went on for some time, during which he felt rather taken aback at being subjected to such an attacking and contemptuous scrutiny by his patient, and during which he felt that anything he said would be likely to be either defensive or cruelly retaliatory.

Eventually he was able to gather his thoughts together sufficiently to say something like, 'It must feel very difficult to come here and ask for help'. This triggered further withering comments on his obvious incompetence and insensitivity, but she was then able to tell him that, though she had suffered with anxiety and depression throughout her life, she was presenting for help now in part because she was suffering with a degenerative condition which caused a great deal of pain in her neck, and which was likely to worsen as she got older. This allowed him to see something of the mental pain behind the grandiose façade, and to be able to empathise with her despair and misery. He said some-thing about the painful comparisons she was making in her mind between herself and himself, and how difficult it was to face her envy of younger people given that she felt herself to be old and falling apart; but that she wanted him to know how lonely and miserable she felt. This seemed to enable her to become somewhat more thoughtful, and she said that although she was quite sure he could not help her, she would like to come back again in order to clarify this comment of his.

She began the second interview by reiterating her criticisms and complaints of him, that much of what he had to say in the previous meeting was obvious proof of his inadequacy, defensiveness and insensitivity, but that she was caught off-guard by something he said about her loneliness. She was reminded of this during the past week, when she had been to see a production of a Strindberg play, in which one of the characters said, 'I have no-one'. She found this very moving and, indeed, cried telling him about it. However, it was striking to observe how quickly she seemed to recover from this rare demonstration of vulnerability and quickly returned to a litany of his shortcomings which seemed more familiar and reassuring ground. He could recall feeling that a window of opportunity for making contact with her suffering had passed, as he watched her defences regroup and reposition her in a more secure and superior state of mind in relation to him.

Despite this, he found it altogether easier to feel sympathetic in this second meeting. He said that he thought she was wanting to show him how a lonely and miserable woman was trapped inside someone who could be quite contemptuous and dismissive, and that she wanted him to know what it felt like to be weighed in the balance and found wanting, because this was something she felt on the receiving end of herself. Further, she needed to know that he could stand this, in order to know if he could help her. Again, she was thoughtful and quiet for a few minutes, and then said that she really was not sure about having help from him, she would have to think about it and would let him know. A week or two later, he received a letter from her to say that 'it would be impossible because of the age gap' for her to see him and she had asked her doctor for a referral to see someone privately. He recalled feeling disappointed and relieved – disappointed at his failure to engage this interesting but challenging patient, and relieved that he would not have to face further such stormy encounters.

DISCUSSION

This is perhaps an atypical clinical example, but not entirely uncommon, and one which does illustrate some of the ideas put forward earlier, albeit in a rather dramatic and heightened way. From her first contact with him on the telephone, Mrs Jones conveyed an intense preoccupation with what was wrong with her object. This is complex, and is a communication which operates on many levels. At its simplest, it derives from the painful reality of an elderly person asking for help from a younger therapist. As Martindale (1989) has described, this difficult dynamic can result in an idealised transference in which the therapist is experienced as the ideal son or daughter caregiver, with the envious feelings often split off and projected elsewhere. For Mrs Jones, the envy was very much in the foreground.

Second, her preoccupation with his shortcomings was a projection into him of a part of the patient which feels inadequate, vulnerable and under attack from what Bion (1962) has described as an ego-destructive superego, so that what is then played out between them is a version of an internal object relation. In a sense, Mrs Jones rather helpfully, if unnervingly, brought her internal difficulties to his attention immediately, just as she accurately perceived his inexperience as a likely source of his vulnerability. Klein has described how a persecutory superego increases feelings of loneliness, because its harsh and unforgiving demands increase paranoid and depressive anxieties, and both of these anxieties were present in the patient in a complex and mixed way.

Third, it is an expression of the patient's underlying feelings of shame and failure at needing help, and in particular of the failure to locate an idealised object, who would be just the right age, sufficiently experienced, well trained, etc. to be able to offer perfect understanding. Paradoxically, the patient's denigration of her therapist was a communication of her fantasy of an idealised therapist who exists somewhere and who could cure her of getting old and falling apart. Had this idealised fantasy been addressed, perhaps by reference to her disappointment in him compared to what she had hoped or imagined he might be, it may have been more possible to engage the patient in treatment.

Cohen's notion of the vicious cycle of narcissism is particularly well illustrated by this case. Such is the force of her fear and hatred of dependence that any possible connectedness must not be risked, resulting in the burden of loneliness and isolation from a potentially helpful object becoming even more entrenched. It could be argued that she was also seeking to discover to what degree her attacks on his clinical competence and experience would invoke his narcissism and his use of narcissistic defences (e.g. contempt and denigration) to deal with this perceived threat to his sense of his professional self.

It is important to emphasise that what this patient was asking for help with was not only or simply her loneliness, but also feeling persecuted by ageing, such that the physical degeneration is experienced as an internal attack, coming from a Nazi-like part of her mind identified with cruel superiority and oppression, and utilising a narrowing of perception, including perception of the object, down to one aspect, i.e. the object's age (Brenman, 1985). The help she sought was to be freed from this sadomasochistic (or Strindbergian) internal relationship. One of the crucial and painful consequences of this internal situation, however, is the isolation of a vulnerable part of the patient who feels trapped, but also separated from a good or helpful object. Her communication via the character from the play who complains of 'having no-one' and being lonely is a communication from this part of the patient. This was the point of deepest emotional contact between them. Unfortunately, it was not possible to build on this contact so that the loneliness of this part of the patient's mind could be mitigated by understanding, however imperfect.

For a patient such as Mrs Jones, as for many of us, the admission of feelings of loneliness is a shameful one, because it threatens an idealised and narcissistic self-image constructed around the notion that it is weak and despicable to need others, and to feel lonely without them. It is usually not possible to help a patient towards an admission of loneliness without interpreting the feelings of shame such an admission evokes. To 'admit' is to let in – to allow something painful and alien into our minds which we may have needed to keep shut out, because the emotional cost of such an admission may feel too high.

The experience of growing old tests many things which all of us find painful and difficult. It tests our capacity to be vulnerable and dependent, which may be either a tolerable reality or hated and unbearable; it tests our capacity to deal with loss – of loved objects, of functions and abilities – and loss of opportunities, hopes and ambitions; it tests our willingness to face the fact of death, which, as Jacques (1965) has discussed, becomes a reality rather than a theoretical notion from the time of mid-life onwards. Most fundamentally and underpinning all of these aspects, growing old tests the security of our internal world, the balance of love and hate, envy and gratitude, good and bad, inside us. The degree to which we are painfully afflicted with feelings of loneliness in old age will be mostly determined by how separated we feel internally from a loved object who can accept our vulnerability and ultimately help us to bear the reality of our loneliness. As described previously, the pain of being alone is fundamentally related to the pain of being alone with oneself, and what we feel to be inside us, be it predominantly persecutory, critical and aggressive, or loving, supportive and forgiving.

REFERENCES

Bion, W.R. (1962). *Learning from Experience*. London: Karnac.

Brenman, E. (1985). Cruelty and narrow-mindedness. *International Journal of Psychoanalysis*, 66, 273–282.

Cohen, N. (1982). On loneliness and the ageing process. *International Journal of Psychoanalysis*, 63, 149–155.

Grosskurth, P. (1986). *Melanie Klein*. London: Maresfield.

Hess, N. (1987). King Lear and some anxieties of old age. *British Journal of Medical Psychology*, 60, 209–215.

Hess, N. (1999). Psychoanalytic psychotherapy for chronic depression. In: Ruszczynski, S. & Johnson, S. (eds) *Psychoanalytic Psychotherapy in the Kleinian Tradition* (pp. 117–134). London: Karnac.

Holmes, J. (1993). Adolescent loneliness, solitude and psychotherapy. In: *Between Art and Science: Essays in psychotherapy and psychiatry* (pp. 42–57). London: Routledge.

Jacques, E. (1965). Death and the mid-life crisis. *International Journal of Psychoanalysis*, 46, 502–514.

Joseph, B. (1986). Envy in everyday life. *Psychoanalytic Psychotherapy*, 2, 13–22.

Klein, M. (1963). On the sense of loneliness. In: *Envy and Gratitude and Other Works*. London: Hogarth Press, 1975.

Martindale, B. (1989). Becoming dependant again: The fears of some elderly persons and their younger therapist. *Psychoanalytic Psychotherapy*, 4, 67–75.

Winnicott, D.W. (1958). The capacity to be alone. In: *Maturational Processes and the Facilitating Environment*. London: Hogarth Press, 1965.

Zachary, A. (1995). Narcissism in ageing. In: Cooper, J. & Maxwell, N. (eds) *Narcissistic Wounds: Clinical perspectives* (pp. 94–100). London: Whurr.

Chapter 3

On becoming an old man: Jung and others

Lorenzo Bacelle

> Not being able to grow old is just as absurd as not being able to outgrow child's-size shoes.
>
> (Jung, 1934)

Carl Gustav Jung (1875–1961) grew up in a village environment in Switzer-land. He was a solitary and introverted boy, unforgiving of the unwillingness or inability of his father (a vicar) to respond to his attempts to challenge religious beliefs and disquieted by what he saw as his mother's two person-alities, which he called No. 1 and No. 2. He later recognised a similar duality in himself as well as in many of his patients (Jung, 1963).

He graduated in medicine and then, between 1900 and 1914, trained and worked as a psychiatrist under Eugen Bleuler at the Burghölzli Mental Hos-pital in Zürich, his main interest being the observation of psychotic states of mind and their investigation through the word-association test. He became internationally known after the publication of 'The Psychology of Dementia Praecox' in 1906. Freud approached him then and a close association between the two men followed (McGuire, 1979), with Jung becoming the first president of the International Psychoanalytic Association in 1910. Such association broke down in 1914, following Jung's publication of 'Symbols of Transform-ation', in which he proposed an extension of Freud's notion of the unconscious to include a collective component. This was rejected by Freud as a product of mysticism incompatible with psychoanalysis. In the same year Jung left the Burghölzli Hospital, thus also ending his association with Bleuler.

Jung's disappointment with and rejection by an older mentor (Jung was 39 and Freud 58), who he believed deprived him of a dialogue in response to his challenging ideas, was extremely painful and reminiscent of the conflict with his father (Jung, 1963). As a result Jung went through a period of psycho-logical disturbance which continued throughout World War I, until 1918. Traces of the same affect can be seen in his remarks on Freud present in many of his writings for at least the next twenty years. Jung continued his work outside psychoanalysis and founded a new discipline, which he called

Analytical Psychology. This he meant to be an extension, not an alternative, to psychoanalysis whose value as well as limitations he continued to recognise. His intention was to generate hypotheses rather than theories, which (in covert reference to Freud) 'should not claim to be the finally attained and only valid truth' (Jung, 1931a).

In later decades, as psychoanalysis evolved, ideas remarkably similar to Jung's did find acceptance within psychoanalytic circles. Perhaps there were personality issues between Freud and Jung or perhaps Jung, together with several other post-Freudians, came too early for his time, at a stage in which the psychoanalytic movement could not risk losing its cohesiveness (Haynal, 1988).

Analytical Psychology has also evolved. Much of Jung's work has been revised, especially in London by the 'Developmental School', which has re-established connections with its psychoanalytic roots (Samuels, 1985). In practical terms, the work of a contemporary Jungian therapist in the NHS does not differ substantially from the work of a psychoanalytic therapist – both approaches are represented in the British Confederation of Psychotherapists and the United Kingdom Confederation of Psychotherapists.

This chapter aims to elucidate some Jungian ideas, with special reference to male psychology and to old age. The ideas are illustrated with clinical material and elaborated with observations drawn from psychoanalysis, anthropology, literature and from Jung's own history.

COLLECTIVE UNCONSCIOUS/ARCHETYPES – PERSONAL UNCONSCIOUS/COMPLEXES

According to Jung, the collective unconscious and its contents, the archetypes, refer to a structure of the human psyche common to all, that is innate and thus transmitted from generation to generation – presumably through the fertilised egg. Jung spoke of a two million-year-old being, present in a newborn baby (Samuels, 1985).

The personal unconscious and its contents, the complexes, refer to a structure that develops for each individual as a result of an interplay between the collective unconscious, with which the individual is born, and the environment in which he or she grows up (see Chapter 7). For Jung, the concept of archetype is rooted in biology. He wrote:

> This term is not meant to denote an inherited idea, but rather an inherited mode of psychic functioning, corresponding to the inborn way in which the chick emerges from the egg, the bird builds its nest, a certain kind of wasp stings the motor ganglion of the caterpillar, and eels find their way to the Bermudas. In other words, it is a 'pattern of behaviour'.
>
> (Jung, 1948a)

Contemporary analytical psychologist Anthony Stevens, influenced by ethology and by developmental psychology (particularly Bowlby's attachment theory), has researched the genetic nature of archetypes, which he views as unconscious predispositions to certain patterns of behaviour formed through natural selection.

> The repeated selection of fortuitous mutations occurring through hundreds of thousands of generations and over millions of years, has resulted in the present genome of the human species. And the genome expresses itself as surely in the structure of the psyche and in human patterns of behaviour as it does in the anatomy of the human physique.
>
> (Stevens, 2000)

The unfolding of archetypal predispositions, imprinted in the genome, follows a built-in biological clock that continues throughout a person's life, in interaction with an environment that either fulfils or fails to meet them. For example, in keeping with Bowlby's theory (Stevens, 1990), we could say that a baby is born already predisposed to relate to 'a mother' in an intimate bond. This 'mother' we may call archetypal in that she includes a variety of aspects (loving, nurturing, abandoning or destroying) experienced, in the process of being mothered, by the human species during its evolution. Jung thought we could have a glimpse of her from representations in myths, fairy tales, religions, anthropology, art, literature, dreams, fantasies, neurotic and psychotic symptoms. It is, however, the personal mother who, incarnating, so to speak, her archetypal counterpart, will provide the baby with real experience. The interplay between the baby's archetypal predisposition to relate to a certain type of mother and the real mother will determine the quality of the mother/baby bond and, with it, the foundations for the developing personality. Similar processes occur in determining the quality of the bond between the baby and his father, with an interplay between archetypal expectation and actual experience.

A further step in archetypal development is for the son to leave the world of women and to enter the world of men, in order to achieve full masculinity. This is enacted in tribal societies through 'rites of passage', in which the boy, in an exclusively male setting, is initiated to experiences that are to remain a shared secret amongst men. He is usually expected to endure an ordeal in which he tolerates courageously some deliberately inflicted pain, such as cuts to his body or circumcision (La Fontaine, 1985). In some cases his submission to men includes oral or anal sexual practices, enabling him to incorporate the men's semen. This is sometimes viewed as a source of nourishment and strength superior to mother's milk (Herdt, 1984). Similar cases in our contemporary society would be regarded as child abuse or criminal assault, although remnants of the same dynamics can be found in the modern world in areas such as religious, educational and military systems and in sport.

Psychopathology (in the form of complexes) is the result of a failure of the personal environment to meet one or more archetypal needs (Stevens, 2000). By the term 'complex' Jung meant 'a collection of images and ideas, clustered round a core derived from one or more archetypes, and characterised by a common emotional tone' (Samuels et al., 1986). For example, the exposure to an incompetent father (tyrannical or absent) for a child who is innately genetically predisposed towards paranoid feelings about fathers, is likely to evoke a state of mind characterised by a conflict with authority figures, either idealised or denigrated. Such state of mind, or complex, sets in the developing personality (which is controlled by the ego), with a tendency to an active, separate and autonomous existence. 'In this way a new morbid personality is gradually created, the inclinations, judgements and resolutions of which move only in the direction of the will to be ill. This second personality devours what is left of the normal ego' (Jung, 1906). According to Jung, we do not have complexes, but rather complexes have us. They are said to be 'fragmentary personalities' or 'splinter psyches', operating as 'independent beings' (Jung, 1948b).

The main value of Jung's theory about the complex is in addressing a vertical split of the personality – a split whose nature was subsequently examined in greater detail by psychoanalysts such as Klein (1946), Bion (1967), Rosenfeld (1992) and, perhaps more radically, by Sinason (1993).

ADULT DEVELOPMENT

Jung has been the forerunner in describing a model of personality development that, with the unfolding of our archetypal programme, is imprinted, as Stevens suggests, in our genome, and goes beyond the onset of maturity to occupy the whole of life (Samuels, 1985).

In his paper 'The stages of life' (1931b), echoed by Erikson twenty years later (see Chapter 6), Jung drew an analogy from the daily course of the sun, to describe four stages, following a 180-degrees arc: childhood, maturity, middle age and old age. Each stage was said to be separated from the next by a period of crisis or transition and to have its own goals and meanings. He spoke about a 'morning psychology' in the first half of the life cycle, reminiscent of the ascending sun and characterised by a movement of expansion and adaptation to the environment, for example by establishing a place in the social hierarchy, accomplishing courtship and marriage, child rearing, fighting, participating in religious rituals and ceremonials (Stevens, 1990). But, Jung said, 'At the strike of noon the descent begins . . . The sun falls into contradiction with itself. It is as though it should draw in its rays instead of emitting them . . . After having lavished its light upon the world, the sun withdraws its rays in order to illuminate itself' (Jung, 1931b).

This contraction of light Jung thought was a characteristic of the second half of life. He associated it with the process of individuation, by which he meant an introspective and self-reflective experience, searching for and coming to terms with who one is, both individually and collectively.

> The afternoon of human life must also have a significance of its own and cannot be merely a pitiful appendage to life's morning . . . Unfortunately [there is] not enough meaning and purpose for those who see in the approach of old age a mere diminution of life and can feel their earlier ideals only as something faded and worn out . . . for many people all too much unlived life remains over – sometimes potentialities which they could never have lived with the best of wills, so that they approach the threshold of old age with unsatisfied demands . . . an old man who cannot bid farewell to life appears as feeble and sickly as a young man.
>
> (Jung, 1931b)

Jung did not specify particular age groups for the developmental stages he described, as he was interested in a fluid and symbolic rather than a concrete model. His idea of a psychopathological continuity throughout such stages is confirmed by the impression clinicians often have of late life depression as an extension of a fear to live life as a younger person. For a psychodynamic exploration of this issue the reader may refer to the clinical illustrations in this chapter and in Chapter 17.

Although Jung thought the process of individuation happened in the second half of life, probably few contemporary analytical psychologists would agree with his idea, arguing that in healthy development individuation happens throughout the life cycle, beginning in infancy (Fordham, 1969). For them individuation is the goal of a Jungian analysis with a patient of any age. However, maybe Jung did have a point.

Commenting on the lameness of the simile with the sun, he wrote: 'Fortunately we are not rising and setting suns . . . But there is something sunlike within us, and to speak of the morning and spring, of the evening and autumn of life is not merely sentimental jargon' (Jung, 1931b). He wrote further: 'A young man who does not fight and conquer has missed the best of his youth, and an old man who does not know how to listen to the secrets of the brooks, as they tumble down from the peaks of the valleys, makes no sense; he is a spiritual mummy who is nothing but a rigid relic of the past' (Jung, 1934).

At the approach of old age, our archetypal programme, searching for an identity as 'senex', confronts us with opposite polarities described in many collective myths as the 'old wise man' and the 'old fool'. The process of individuation in old age includes an acceptance of such polarities as potentialities existing in us. The final developmental step is death, the great leveller as well as the unique experience each individual goes through. What does the old wise man in us think about death, and what the old fool? Inability to come to terms with these archetypal issues prevents our identity from undergoing the necessary transformation from young to old. Our collective wish as therapists to reduce the fear of death in our patients could reflect our own anxieties.

Wharton (1996) describes the analysis of a 76-year-old woman for whom unresolved conflicts in her early development created 'an urgent, final pressure toward individuation'. Wharton wonders:

> Might age and the approach of death give an extra impetus to the self to complete – or to accomplish – certain psychological tasks before, as it were, time runs out? Or is it that the approach of death recapitulates particular anxieties from earlier stages of development, and creates difficulties to the extent that these earlier anxieties were incompletely resolved? It became reasonably clear that this patient's fears of separation and of dependency were intimately linked with her attitude to death. But what does death mean to an older woman who, because of a very incomplete start in life, has, in a sense, never completely lived?

Jung thought that his method – emphasising the need to discover where a person's situation was leading him or her, in addition to the supposed causation of symptoms – was particularly suitable for older people. More than two-thirds of his patients were said to be in the second half of life (Jung, 1931c). He went through a period of severe physical illness in his late sixties, but he overcame it and afterwards published the most influential of his works. He saw patients well into his seventies and continued to write up to the last weeks of his life, which ended at the age of 85. However, he spent long periods on his own, especially after his wife died, painting, sculpting and paying attention to his 'inner voice', in search for his own individuation. As well as being described as a 'wise man' by his friends, he also exhibited traits reminiscent of an 'old fool', for example in his occasional outbursts of rage towards his old friend/housekeeper, very similar to a child's temper tantrums, to which he seemed to feel entitled. After his wife's death, he persuaded the friend to move in and look after him, warning her that he was prone to getting into terrible rages, of which however she should not take notice, because they meant nothing. One day she was in the kitchen preparing a meal of mince meat and he saw her putting two tomatoes in with the meat. Then a sudden eruption occurred: he shouted that she should not have put the tomatoes in, and stormed out, sulking for hours. She was obviously hurt and told him that she was prepared to leave if he treated her like that. He reminded her that he had warned her about his meaningless rages, which were not to be taken personally. Interestingly, he went on saying that all she had to do was to avoid those things that made him angry (Hubback, 1996)!

ON OLD AGE

'On Old Age' is the title of the oldest – but still very topical – treatise on this subject written by Cicero, when he was 61, in 45 BC. It is in the shape of a dialogue between two young men and 84-year-old Cato, famous for his wisdom. The young men put forward a series of negative views about old age which Cato refutes one by one, arguing that the quality of old age depends on the quality of previous experience in younger age. 'Blame rests with character, not with age' he says, and emphasises the need to train both mind and body to glide gradually and imperceptibly into old age. Men who grow into healthy old age are said by Cicero to be 'like skilful actors who have played well their parts in the drama of life to the end, and not like untrained players who have broken down in the last act'. They continue to experience sensual pleasures, although in a limited form – 'Just as [an actor] gives greater delight to the spectators in the front row at the theatre, and yet gives some delight even to those in the last row, so youth, looking on pleasures at closer range, perhaps enjoys them more, while old age, on the other hand, finds delight enough in a more distant view.'

But what pleases a young man may not please an old man at all: 'Let others, then, have their weapons, their horses and their spears, their fencing-foils, and games of ball, their swimming contests and foot-races, and out of many sports leave us old fellows our dice and knuckle-bones. Or take away the dice-box, too, if you will, since old age can be happy without it.'

Boyhood, early youth, maturity and old age – each has its own pursuits which are left behind in the next stage of life. 'Old age is the final scene, as it were, in life's drama, from which we ought to escape when it grows wearisome and certainly, when we have had our fill.'

Clinical Illustration
Mr M was 73 when, unlike Cicero's skilful actor, he did break down in the last act, developing depression with suicidal ideas and nervous tics in his face. He improved with pharmacological treatment, but became aware of an urgent need to explore himself psychologically before it was too late.

He presented as a slim, tall man, with a pleasing smile, anxious eyes and intermittent facial tics. His hair was tinted a dark colour and there was an overwhelming smell of aftershave, which the therapist, a younger man, felt entered into his lungs and invaded him inside. The therapist's own associations to the aftershave were images of a sickening smell of flowers at funerals and of rotting flowers in stagnating water in cemeteries; for a moment he thought he might faint.

Mr M, still a practising musician, was married, with a daughter, a son and two grandchildren. He made little mention of his family and concentrated at length, instead, on a homosexual double life he had lived for the previous fifty years, made possible by frequent periods he spent away from home because of his work. His depression started when, a few months before, his 85-year-old male partner, ill and disabled, ended the relationship and moved to a nursing home in a different part of the country, to be near his niece. The relationship had been strained for a long time, due to Mr M's anger and jealousy. He dealt with the abandonment in secret, unable to explain his pain and depressive symptoms to his family.

Mr M's problem was complex, comprising a grief reaction to the loss of his friend as well as a continuing but now unmet need for a sexual relationship with an older man, conflicting with his own age, family and superego. He did not describe specific sexual acts with his friend, but he indicated that, at least in his mind, their relationship had been sexual to the end.

He grew up in an Irish Catholic family, consumed by anger. He was angry for being displaced at 13 months by his younger sister; angry also at his mother's jealous attacks on his father and at his father's inability to stand up to her and protect his son from her rage. He developed in isolation, with no close friends and resenting the authority of men in his social group, perceived as either fearsome or inadequate. He obtained no qualifications, but he read a lot and, thanks to a natural musical talent, he developed a career as a pianist and a composer. In the process, he became alienated from his family and 'their' religion. From the age of twenty he had several relationships with older men, which continued after his marriage, ten years later. He never contemplated a relationship with a man younger or the same age as he was.

Mr M's image of himself was of being much younger. He did not feel a whole person; he felt there was a missing part that could only be found in an older man, who loved him and was loved by him totally. Outside a never-ending, perfect and holding embrace with an older man he felt he had nothing. He said this was not like the need for a 'crutch' (his choice of word) that an adult person might have, with life still possible in its absence. His need was more basic and primitive, a life-or-death issue like the feeding of a baby through the nipple or of a foetus through the umbilical cord, without which a baby or foetus would die. He felt he had not yet been properly weaned and said 'To wean myself now takes all the guts out of me'. When he was with his partner, he would put him on a pedestal, worshipping him as if he were God and feeling lost if what seemed to be God deserted him through appearing imperfect. Then his illusion of bliss would be shattered and would be replaced by uncontrollable rage and jealous recriminations.

After exploring feeding themes associated with the penis, the nipple and the umbilical cord, themes from ancient myths emerged, in association with dream material. Mr M was fascinated by Narcissus, the youth who – a seer prophesied – would live to a ripe old age, provided that he never knew himself. According to Graves (1955), Narcissus fled from the love of a nymph, Echo, and fell in love with a beautiful image in a pool, which he identified as his own reflection. Unable to kiss and embrace the image, which he possessed and yet did not possess, he was destroyed by grief. In the end he killed himself and became transformed into the flower named after him, a surviving representation of his eternal youth. This illusory quality of youth is hinted at by the etymological root of the flower's name, 'narc', in common with the word 'narcotic'. Mr M felt that the image he wanted to merge with, in his own imaginary pool, was the one of an elusive older man only attainable, in its pure form, through death.

In exploring this myth, some libido was mobilised that made him feel as if he was part of an ancient fabric of humanity, rather than an isolated monster, doomed only to associate in secret with others like himself. Another myth that interested and amused him was one described in Plato's Symposium, *a book in which a group of men at a dinner party in 4th century* BC *Greece discuss the nature of love, particularly love between a boy and a man. According to the myth each human being was originally a rounded whole made up either of two males or two females or one male and one female, representing the male, the female and the hermaphrodite sex. But they angered Zeus who split them in two so that each of us is now a mere half perpetually in search of his or her other half, with homosexuals (male and female), deriving from the first two and heterosexuals from the hermaphrodite. Plato says:*

> *This is what everybody wants, and everybody would regard it*
> *as the precise expression of the desire which he had long felt*
> *but had been unable to formulate, that he should melt into his beloved,*
> *and that henceforth they should be one being instead of two.*
> *The reason is that this was our primitive condition when we were wholes,*
> *and love is simply the name for the desire and pursuit of the whole.*

Mr M recognised in the myth his own need to seek wholeness by finding and joining again with an older man, but he felt that a potential and suitable new partner with whom to start a relationship would now be too old – indeed, that all potential partners were already dead. This forced him to realise that he too had become old.

The archetypal need of a boy to be helped by an older man (normally the father or other authority figure) in order to differentiate himself from women and to become a man, used to be enacted in initiation rites in tribal societies. Mr M grew up in an environment that failed to provide him with such a figure. As a result he remained enveloped and identified with his mother, who at times put him on a pedestal and told him he was, unlike his father, perfect, and at other times exposed him and his father to her rage.

His mother stopped breastfeeding him, after becoming pregnant with his sister, when he was four months old. He imagined that with the milk, a kind of irreplaceable intimacy was lost to his sister, one in which one body feeds from another body, thus constituting a whole. He was born early last century, in a family setting in which food was scarce. Did he receive through the umbilical cord and the breast all the nutrients he needed? Did the weaning imply also a real state of nutritional deprivation?

His idealisation of and rage with his partner repeated old patterns between him, his mother, his father and his sister. The 'God-like' and the 'failing' aspects of a father are part of the same archetype, which young sons (as Jung's own history confirms) have experienced since the beginning of time in the process of becoming men.

The therapeutic alliance was good from the start but the transference was mixed. Behind the apparent richness of the verbal communication with the therapist, there was a large area of silence, with messages coming from body language, such as facial tics and scent of aftershave. Part of him was deeply disappointed that the therapist was not an older man, and for this reason believed the therapy was hopelessly futile. Breaks were accepted as a matter of course and transference interpretations, attributing significance to the person of the therapist, were dismissed out-of-hand.

Some inroads were made when the silence behind his words, the tics and the smell of aftershave were interpreted as expressions of the language of a very private self whose views were at odds with what he recognised as his own views. This private self thought he could only be understood by getting inside the therapist through the smell of aftershave, occupying a space there in which he and the therapist existed in symbiotic union. The facial tics signalled, to the patient/therapist pair, any 'bad smells' experienced in the consulting room, for example the announcement of a break, or his perceived abandonment as an individual during intellectualising conversations about old myths. However, by contrast, the smell of aftershave and the tics were also meant to disguise the same 'bad smells' and to distract the therapist's attention from them.

There was the 'smell' of a life largely spent in what he saw as the fantasy world of a fool, unable truly to become old while relating to people not as they really were, but to the internal objects he projected onto them. He only partly knew his friend as the person he really was, so that his departure was experienced as an unreal event. The same was true with his parents, whose death left him cold. And then there were the mutilated relationships with his wife and children, whom he perceived as if they were behind a glass wall. His wife was irritated by his tics and his grandchildren laughed about them, thus reinforcing a view he had of himself as a fool. His suicidal ideas were connected with anger about the past and the present as well as despair that the future could ever be any different. Death was viewed as a return to inorganic matter, ashes to ashes and dust to dust, in an uninterrupted embrace with mother earth.

As the therapy progressed, and words were found to describe what up to then had been silent, Mr M began to feel older and to accept it. His compulsive search for an older man gradually diminished, while he established new connections with his son, giving him advice about his career and taking pride in his achievements. He became warmer towards his grandchildren, smiling in his head because he was a grandfather. And for the first time ever, he started a non-sexual friendship with a man younger than himself, another musician, whom he endeavoured to help develop a project in the field of music.

Mr M's positive changes, in his internal as well as external world, were registered in the countertransference as a decreased intolerance to the smell of aftershave. The therapist read about old age and male psychology from several different sources and discussed Mr M's case in a peer supervision group. Alongside his patient's increased confidence as an old man, he developed an increased confidence as a therapist. No doubt other factors independent of Mr M contributed, but – significantly – he felt more 'senior' and more effective as a supervisor with his own trainees.

CONCLUSION

Drawing on both analytical psychology and psychoanalysis, it could be said that a 'complex' operated, like a separate and independent being, in Mr M's personality, feeding from it, dominating it and impoverishing it. It included a symbiotic relationship with an object that combined male and female components, like the nipple, the penis and the breast.

The complex was expressed in Mr M's external world most characteristically in the form of a narcissistic relationship with an older man, who might feed him and make him whole. This undermined Mr M's capacity to experience people as real – e.g. his friend, his wife and children, and also his therapist.

Mr M's internal world could be understood as the result of a failure of his personal environment (dominant mother, ineffective father, absence of other reliable authority figures) to meet his archetypally determined need for adequate parenting.

The need to be fed and made whole by an older man could be viewed as a mixed regression to earlier individual and cultural stages of development. The former could be inferred from the feeding dynamics between an infant and his still undiscriminated mother, perceived as containing the father within her; the latter from archetypal representations of a goddess-like nourishing/starving mother and a god-like protecting/abandoning father, often merged together in different composites, deriving from both matriarchal and patriarchal societies.

His use of scent (aftershave) and his facial grimaces (tics), when he was hiding behind his words, could point to behaviours from a distant animal substrate, aiming to attract, to repel or to avoid. The therapist's countertransference images of cut dead flowers corresponded to an equivalent view of the therapy, held by Mr M's complex, as occasionally entertaining but hopelessly lonely and sterile. By contrast, Mr M's remaining personality viewed therapy as a plant, from whose symbolic roots he hoped to feed.

For Mr M, was the construct 'an old man' a pathological fetish representing a phallic pre-Oedipal mother and a defence against the fear of castration at the sight of the female genital (Freud, 1927)? Or (condensing Jung, Klein and Kohut) was it an idealised, omnipotent, perfect self object to merge with, like the great mother with her babies and penises inside her (Fordham, 1991)? Alternatively, was it simply a descriptive representation of Mr M's preferred sexual object, in the desire and pursuit of the whole, as narrated in Plato's myth? Perhaps it was all of this. But more significantly, it appeared to be a symbol for Mr M's undeveloped self, struggling with a maturational task, the 'puer–senex' (boy–old man) archetype. Thomas Mann represented the reverse form of the same theme in *Death in Venice*, with an older repressed academic seeking wholeness in his encounter with an adolescent boy, as a prelude to embracing his coming death.

After working through a painful experience of himself as an 'old fool', who had wasted much of his life, Mr M felt older and wiser, turning his search for an older man from outside to inside himself.

The ideas and clinical material described will not be unfamiliar to those who use a psychoanalytic perspective, apart from a different terminology and a different historical context for the development of Jung's thinking. Jung was well known for rejecting the validity of the term 'Jungian', claiming that only one Jung existed, i.e. himself. He had a profound distaste for 'followers' of any sort, possibly rooted in his early difficulties with his father, but no doubt the expression of a free spirit. He could not adhere to Freud's ideas any more than he expected anyone else to adhere to his own. This relativistic stance is possibly what captures the fantasy of therapists who decide to train with a 'Jungian' institution. It is an interest in 'discovering' one's own style, not to be confused with eclecticism, after a study of the literature in which Jung is represented only as a small part – neither pagan nor monotheistic, but sympathetic to both.

Why does a psychotherapist of any persuasion choose one rather than another 'school'? The 'vision' behind such choice, a mixture of fantasies and complexes as well as of rational evaluation, would be an interesting area for future exploration.

REFERENCES

Bion, W.R. (1967). Differentiation of the psychotic from the non-psychotic personalities. In: *Second Thoughts: Selected papers on psycho-analysis*. London: William Heinemann Medical Books Ltd.

Cicero (45 BC). *De Senectute*. [Trans. Falconer, W.A., 1923. *On Old Age*. Harvard University Press.]

Fordham, M. (1969). *Children as Individuals*. London: Hodder & Stoughton.
—— (1991). The supposed limits of interpretations. *Journal of Analytical Psychology*, 36(2), 165–175.
Freud, S. (1927). Fetishism. Standard Edition 21. London: Hogarth.
Graves, R. (1955). *The Greek Myths*, Vol. 1. London: Penguin Books.
Haynal, A. (1988). *The Technique at Issue*. London: Karnac Books.
Herdt, G.H. (ed) (1984). *Ritualised Homosexuality in Melanesia*. Berkeley, Los Angeles, London: University of California Press.
Hubback, J. (1996). The archetypal senex: an exploration of old age. *Journal of Analytical Psychology*, 41(1), 3–18.
Jung, C.G. (1906). Association, dream, and hysterical symptom. *C. W. 2.*
—— (1931a). Problems of modern psychotherapy. *C. W. 16.*
—— (1931b). The stages of life. *C. W. 8.*
—— (1931c). The aims of psychotherapy. *C. W. 16.*
—— (1934). The soul and death. *C. W. 8.*
—— (1948a). Foreword to Harding: Woman's mysteries. *C. W. 18.*
—— (1948b). A review of the complex theory. *C. W. 8.*
—— (1963). *Memories, Dreams, Reflections*. London: Collins, Routledge & Kegan Paul.
Klein, M. (1946). Notes on some schizoid mechanisms. In: Riviere, J. (ed) *Developments in Psychoanalysis*. London: Hogarth, 1952.
La Fontaine, J.S. (1985). *Initiation: Ritual drama and secret knowledge across the world*. London: Penguin Books.
McGuire, W. (ed) (1979). *The Freud/Jung Letters*. [Trans. Manheim, R. & Hull, R.F.C., abridged by McGlashan, A. London: Pan/Picador.]
Plato (4th century BC). *The Symposium*. [Trans. Hamilton, W., 1951. London: Penguin Books.]
Rosenfeld, D. (1992). *The Psychotic Aspects of the Personality*. London: Karnac Books.
Samuels, A. (1985). *Jung and the Post-Jungians*. London, Boston, Melbourne and Henley: Routledge & Kegan Paul.
Samuels, A., Shorter, B., & Plaut, F. (1986). *A Critical Dictionary of Jungian Analysis*. London and New York: Routledge & Kegan Paul.
Sinason, M. (1993). Who is the mad voice inside? *Psychoanalytic Psychotherapy*, 7, 207–221.
Stevens, A. (1990). *On Jung*. London and New York: Routledge.
—— (2000). *Evolutionary Psychiatry*. London and Philadelphia: Routledge, Taylor & Francis Group.
Van Gennep, A. (1960). *The Rites of Passage*. London and Henley: Routledge and Kegan Paul.
Wharton, B. (1996). In the last analysis: Archetypal themes in the analysis of an elderly patient with early disintegrative trauma. *Journal of Analytical Psychology*, 41(1), 19–36.

Chapter 4

Attachment in old age: Bowlby and others

Sandra Evans

> Attachment is the hub of human existence; around which all relationships revolve, from infancy into adult life . . . and on into old age.
>
> (Bowlby, 1980)

INTRODUCTION

In the late 1950s, John Bowlby revolutionised the way in which small children were treated as hospital inpatients and the amount of visiting access that their parents were allowed. He developed a theory of the importance of healthy attachments in early life to later mental health. As a psychoanalyst himself, his collaborations with ethologists and psychologists were perceived to be deeply suspect.

Attachment theory has, however, exemplified the continuing convergence of psychoanalytic thought and neuropsychiatric research (Gabbard, 2000). Bowlby's work continues to be highly relevant in the clinical setting in every area of psychiatry and in every age group. This chapter sets out to demonstrate the importance of attachment theory to the area of mental health care for older people.

A synopsis of Bowlby's work

The depression that ensues in children separated from their parents and handled by strangers in hospital was most movingly demonstrated on film, while documenting the admission and treatment of a 2-year-old girl (Robertson, 1952). Initially, she was distressed and protested at being removed from her family, but eventually accepted the bustling care offered by the nurses with grim and helpless resignation. She became emotionally withdrawn and uninterested in her surroundings, and in her food. She was apparently suffering from the hallmarks of depression commonly seen in adults of all ages.

From repeated infant observations Bowlby (1958) recognised that newborn babies are happy when held by a confident, emotionally warm adult. At between 4 and 6 months, older infants begin to discriminate between people. Later at 8 months or so children will become anxious when held by a stranger and will protest when their mother leaves the room. Konrad Lorenz (1935), an ethologist working with various species of animals, arrived at a theory of an innate drive of animals to attach to a care-giving object by a process called imprinting. Harlow's baby monkeys (1958) showed a preference for a soft artificial 'mother' over a hard uncomfortable 'mother' which was nonetheless equipped with food. Bowlby postulated that a similar innate drive exists in humans which enhances the individual's chance of survival, but also has important implications for their emotional development and wellbeing later in life. The dimension of security versus insecurity in attachment may be equivalent to Klein's (1948) notion of the introjection of the good object or breast. Similarly of relevance is Winnicott's 'good enough mother' (1965). The possession of secure attachment is considered to be an aspect of an individual's personality and may have a bearing on their capacity for good mental health and ability to withstand change. *Secure attachment* is thought to be derived from adequate presence of mother or the prime caregiver; adequate referring to quality of interaction as well as the amount of time spent in their company.

By contrast, an *insecure attachment* may derive from a situation where the quality of the maternal relationship was impaired, either by maternal illness or emotional distance, or physical absence at an important developmental stage; resulting in separation anxiety. The individual with anxious attachment patterns may appear unduly dependent in relationships and become anxious and insecure without obvious cause (*anxious attachment*).

Ambivalence in an attachment context refers to the type of relationship which is highlighted by alternating emotional patterns of relating, sometimes excessively loving and demanding on the part of the mother and at other times distant or rejecting. Similar patterns of relating may then develop in the child. Finally, *avoidant attachment* patterns develop in individuals who have suffered the pain of separation or the anxiety and have chosen the defensive position of not-relating and not getting too closely involved with others for fear of further hurt.

Bowlby, and later on with his colleague Mary Ainsworth (1954), started to look at styles of parenting and equated these to attachment styles in infants. Bowlby was clear that infants initially showed a preference for carers who attended most promptly and most accurately to their needs (Bowlby, 1969a). This was most often the biological mother who had become attuned to her baby's needs in a similar way to that described by Winnicott.

Later, as the child developed confidence in his attachment object, he could use her as a launch pad from which to explore his world, checking in at regular intervals to ascertain her proximity and her continuing interest. Conversely those children who were less sure of their attachment objects (mother) would explore less and cling more (Ainsworth et al., 1978). Bowlby (1960) suggested that this anxiety was expressed at the threat of loss of the mother. He conjectured that this was a result of the dynamic between mother and infant in terms of mothering interest and attunement and the constitution of the child, which comes to some degree from the child's genetic inheritance. Children who had been separated from parental figures for significant lengths of time would also become anxious at the threat of a loss more quickly and more profoundly than infants with a secure base.

ATTACHMENT

Equally, Bowlby was very clear about the effect of early separation from mother. He argued that separation during a defining point in an infant's life, particularly when a child is removed to an unfamiliar place populated by strangers, can be traumatic, and will have an effect on the developing psyche (Bowlby, 1969b, p. 31). Freud maintained that trauma is dependent on the individual's constitution and the phase of life; particularly if it occurs when the ego is immature (1940, pp. 184–185). This may explain the variation in experiences of those now elderly people who were evacuated from large towns in wartime Britain. Some had good experiences of the separation, others were miserable. Other factors would have to have included the age of the child at separation and the warmth of the family at the other end, as well as the quality of the original relationship with the parents. Using Bowlby's model, it is easy to understand how some experienced this move to safety as a banishment, or another threat to the balance of their existence.

Loss of object rather than mere separation results in profound sadness that cannot be regained in the manner described above. Bowlby (1977a) reminded us of Freud's paper 'Mourning and Melancholia' in that psychological work needs to be done in order to regain a sense of the self without the object to which one has 'cathected' or attached. Bowlby's observations are pertinent to life generally. As the infant develops so her attachment styles both shape her relationships and are shaped by them. However, the early experiences, particularly the 'secure base' from which to discover and explore, may offer the individual a resource on which to fall back in times of crisis. With respect to old age, which could be argued as a situation of one crisis or challenge after another, the relationships with people around, both personal and professional, may be the only anchor in a shifting world.

ANXIETY

Anxiety is a very common psychological disturbance in the elderly (Lindesay et al., 1989). It can occur as a primary condition with no obvious precipitating factors, or it may arise as part of a depression or secondary to an anxiety provoking situation which conveys a particular meaning to the individual concerned (Evans & Katona, 1990).

Anxiety is an emotion which carries with it an innate survival mechanism that is part of the 'fight/flight' response to potentially dangerous situations. Arguably an increased level of anxiety is appropriate to old age, as the number of challenging situations increase while the physical and sometimes mental resources with which to deal with them, actually diminish. Most of these anxieties may be understood and dealt with efficiently and effectively with relaxation and anxiety management techniques (Woods & Roth, 1996).

More severe and disabling, however, are the anxieties associated with the threat of a loss that is deeply feared. Patients who have lost their main attachment figure, often a spouse or partner, may anticipate and dread further losses. They appear to need constant reassurance of the presence of an alternative attachment figure and may cling at the point of parting. Relatives may remark that the individual has sustained a personality change, never having apparently been this way before. One may find in the personal history an early separation trauma such as a hospitalisation to a sanatorium for tuberculosis, or a premature disposal to boarding school. Alternatively, one may retrieve a history of anxious attachment as a child; the new loss having rekindled earlier anxieties.

Clinical Illustration
Mavis lost her husband of 45 years over a year ago. Her grieving for him had apparently been appropriate. She moved home to be closer to her son, but had to forgo the old family GP to whom she had remarkably free access. Last month she was mugged in the street and robbed but was left unhurt. Since then she has been unable to remain at home with any sense of peace. She prefers to go out to the shops or if she remains at home, she constantly makes demands for company.

Her family is concerned for her, but also cannot meet her need for their constant presence. She makes repeated telephone calls for reassurance. Her sleep and appetite are unaffected. Pre-morbidly, she describes herself as always having been a bit of a worrier. She was the youngest of her family; very close to her mother, from whom she only separated when she married. It is interesting to note that it is the mugging and not the death of her husband (who may have been compensated for by the GP) which has precipitated her need to seek out an authority or caring figure in order to allay her fears.

Successful treatment for Mavis, after a few other interventions were tried, was the reassuring presence of a community psychiatric nurse who would visit her twice weekly initially, and whose telephone number she had; thus recreating the attachment to the authority figure that she had had with her old doctor.

In this example, the usual front-line treatments for Mavis's anxiety were ineffective. The knowledge of her attachment style in early life was useful, as was the recognition by the treating team that she was not about to alter deep-rooted aspects of her behaviour. Eventually she was adequately contained by a reassuring alternative attachment figure. This aspect of an insecure or anxious attachment and the apparent absence of a period of appropriate separation from the object or mother-figure, seems to indicate some failure in the developmental process of the maturing infant. The re-emergence of separation anxiety appears to have occurred for the first time in later adult life. More particularly when Mavis was facing challenging times without her life partner, or her constant attachment figure.

Such disruption of normal socially acceptable behaviour is uncommon. However, examples of similar and more severely regressed behaviour do appear regularly in the caseloads of old age psychiatrists. It cannot always be explained by appearance of dementia and clearly requires a more psychodynamic formulation (Padoani & De Leo, 2000).

Secure attachment as defined by Bowlby and Ainsworth bears resemblance to the phenomenon described by Winnicott (1965) as 'the capacity to be alone'. In his seminal paper Winnicott describes the importance of play in the presence of mother, in order for the infant to develop a sense of wellbeing. He goes on to suggest that the child eventually takes 'into himself' that interested mother and maintains a 'mental image' (Damasio, 1994) of her wherever he goes. He is liable to be separate from her for increasingly long periods of time, and can explore his world in a relaxed manner. Anxiety only resurfaces at an unexpected situation or separation. Winnicott stresses the importance of child's play 'in the presence of' mother. She does not have to be busy interacting, but her attention is nonetheless implied. This attention does seem to be important in the development of the security of the child and his sense of containment, which Amini et al. (1996) suggest becomes part of an individual's unconscious memory, and forms a template for the affectional relationships later on in life; on to old age.

Although only a minority of older people develop dementia; a significant proportion do have some cognitive deficits and this can have an effect on anxiety levels, as the individual may be aware that their memory is failing. More pertinent to psychiatry of old age is when this minor cognitive deficit appears to affect the mechanism described above. In order to be competent both personally and socially an individual needs to be able to collect and retain (even for a few seconds) a number of complex thoughts and memories. Damasio (1994) insists that a number of brain parts are essential for this kind of processing, particularly the pre-frontal cortices and parts of the hypothalamus and cyngulate gyrus. Without this function the brain may be unable to retain the mental images that give the individual his or her sense of connectedness to others, and the sense of secure attachment and containment.

The author postulates that even someone who has previously shown secure attachment behaviour may, by virtue of their cognitive impairment, find this disrupted by neuro-degeneration. They may lose their sense of security, even when their short- and long-term memories for simple things appear relatively intact. This has been a feature of patients with early clinical signs of dementia, who are capable of independence in other ways. Those who live alone are most susceptible to the phenomenon of repeatedly calling out doctors, attending casualty departments or telephoning family, neighbours and even the police. Cognitive deficit appears to be the basis of this rather than affective disorder alone.

DEPRESSION

The role of loss and change in the aetiology of depression is well documented (Brown & Harris, 1978). This work was further extended to look particularly closely at the role of loss and change in older people, and at the mitigation of any ensuing depression by relationships of differing qualities (Lowenthal, 1965; Murphy, 1982; Evans & Katona, 1993). To summarise, it is held that the experience of an early parental loss or separation confers vulnerability to the development of a depressive illness in later adult life. The role of the presence of a close confiding relationship in the prevention of a depressive episode at a stressful time is somewhat less clear; but it does seem that the ability to make successful relationships is a good prognostic factor (Murphy, 1982). There is some evidence to suggest that those who commit suicide have problems with interpersonal relationships (Harwood et al., 2000).

In the event of a clinical depression, people often withdraw from others and their social milieu. They may show a detachment from the world, which may increase the risk of suicide, particularly if they believe that no one will suffer as a result. Freud (1925) decided that this detachment from the world was part of normal ageing, and he might have been correct had he been referring to the more physical and material aspects of life. He was however thought to have been depressed at the time of writing (Wolheim, 1971) and the author suggests that he had fallen into a common ageist trap, confusing the detachment associated with depression in later life with preparation for death. The 'detachment proper to ageing' that Freud wrote of 'the Death Instinct' was seemingly premature; for him at least (Evans, 1998). There exists a particular danger in late life depression that it may be considered as 'normal'. The depressed individual is at the end of their life and may have survived trauma that is inconceivable to a younger person. The individual may not seek treatment, or may not be adequately treated, and their detachment from others not subject to intervention. Their risk of suicide is also greater (Shah & De, 1998).

THE BENEFITS OF MAKING NEW ATTACHMENTS

As one gets older the opportunities for making new relationships can diminish, as does perhaps the energy for the associated niceties. Increasing the number of supportive social contacts in a clinical setting has been shown to reduce the relapse rate of depression in older people (Ong et al., 1987), and the addition of interpersonal therapy to drug treatment of depression in older people has demonstrated an improvement in outcome (Reynolds et al., 1999). It would appear that ongoing attachments may confer real meaning to continued existence (Thompson, 1993). Bowlby himself (1980) thought that meaningful attachments to others were the 'hub of human existence' and that their importance did not change, irrespective of the age of the individual.

LOSS

A common feature as we age is the experience of losing someone who is of particular importance to us. This precipitates a bereavement reaction (Parkes, 1965) but does not invariably precipitate depression. The issues pertinent to the elderly with regard to bereavement are partly due to the volume of loss likely to occur over a relatively short period of time, and in part to the significant malignant effects on the physical health of the bereaved (Parkes, 1972). The role of ambivalent and insecure attachments in the development of pathological grief is well known (Parkes & Weiss, 1983) and needs little further comment, other than to stress that although the factors are similar in old age to younger adult grief, the consequences may be much greater. The de-cathexis that is required to let go of a lost object, and free up the emotional space to form new attachments, is harder when there is no expectation of future relationships. It is relatively uncommon for older adults, particularly elderly women, to marry again after the loss of a lifetime partner (Daniel, 1997).

The importance of bereavement work in this area cannot be understated (see Chapter 18). It is of proven efficacy (Raphael, 1977) and yet has fallen somewhat in the hierarchy of importance in the treatment of psychological distress and in the prevention of more severe mental illness. (At the time of writing, the author is aware of funding crises to bereavement counselling services across the UK.)

ATTACHMENT VERSUS DEPENDENCY

This discussion of the psychodynamics of late life depression has considered the influence of the social and therapeutic environment on the course and experience of the depression. Equally one needs to consider the influence of the depression and the depressed individual on their relationships and on the therapeutic environment. A depressive illness can put strain on a partnership relationship, even one that has endured for many years. The elderly spouse or partner may be physically frail and less able to cope with increased domestic tasks left undone by the depressed partner, or with repeated visits to hospital. However, none of this is as difficult to endure as the absence of the friend and the disintegration of the usual reciprocity of support and dependence.

Elderly people do not, as a rule, seek the advice of marriage guidance counsellors. When there is a problem that is no longer tolerable, demands are made on the Health Service structures. Quite appropriately so, but one wonders how many other couples never find help, perhaps because they lack the spur of severe mental illness in one partner.

The presence of insecure attachments in the partnership seems anecdotally to be a common problem. There is little published evidence of this in older patients, although the work exists on younger populations and on the 'caregiver' partners of people with dementia. In clinical practice, the author has observed a repeating pattern of people suffering from chronic depression who have residual symptoms despite vigorous treatment and who have become increasingly dependent on a spouse. The spouse in turn is often highly capable and nurturing, or if not, has adopted the role of carer in response to the demands made on them. The illness in the index patient necessitates the continuing presence of the spouse; on occasions the threat of crisis makes it impossible for them to leave the home even to do shopping. This situation benefits the dependency needs of the individual by ensuring the emotional imprisonment of the other. Unconsciously the patient creates the phantasy of never having to suffer the anxiety or pain of separation again. An ambivalent attachment, where the unacknowledged hate combines in equal parts with the protested love, can be exceedingly problematic during the course of the relationship, as well as after the death of a partner.

> *Clinical Illustration*
> *Jack and Daisy have been together for 40 years. Jack's mother was ill for most of his early life, requiring hospitalisation and ensuring that she was not as available to him emotionally as would have been required. He loved her, but resented her for being ill.*
>
> *When Daisy develops a depressive illness, Jack begins to have episodes of extreme panic. He insists that Daisy is hospitalised as he is frightened she will kill herself, but becomes enraged at the hospital staff when she improves during the admission; feeling that the doctors are turning her against him. He is unable to acknowledge his anger at Daisy for getting ill and leaving him, lest he send her away permanently.*

The author postulated a potentiating effect of these examples of exaggerated dependency on the depression itself. Within a group analytic framework,

Evans et al. (1997) described an eclectic psychotherapeutic approach using group analysis (Foulkes, 1964), interpersonal therapy and systemic approaches to a couples group of depressed patients and their spouses. The therapeutic group demonstrated a useful diagnostic function, but also succeeded in shifting some of the carer/patient dynamic in these couples and enabled them to function more as marital partners (see Chapter 7).

John Birtchnell (1993) has built on attachment theory to look at the relationship styles of adult couples. He uses dimensions of closeness and distance, 'upperness and lowerness' (indicating dependency and care-giving). The octagons he derives from questionnaires on qualities of relating appear to be a useful research tool in the understanding of attachment styles and their stability.

FEAR OF DEPENDENCY

Dependency needs in elderly patients can cause anxiety in the care staff in hospitals and residential homes, particularly when the staff are witnessing demands from their own parents or grandparents (Martindale, 1989). If these are experienced in a persecuted or guilty way by staff they may avoid recipro-cating any emotional involvement with the patients, or worse still, this may be the basis in normal individuals to abuse or neglect the needs of the older person (Garner & Evans, 2000). Paradoxically, in an insecurely attached person this may increase the object-seeking behaviour, thus worsening in the staff the sense of being overwhelmed by need (Adshead, 1998). Under-standing the dynamics of dependency and attachment behaviour, particularly in institutional care, is an essential part of prevention of abusive behaviour.

The elderly patients themselves may avoid engagement (avoidant attach-ment), unwilling to submit themselves to a dreaded dependency similar to an unconsciously remember earlier failed attachment, when the pain of the deprivation was unavoidable (Martindale, 1989).

DEMENTIA

Miesen (1992) described the phenomenon of people with severe dementia disremembering their own parent's death as a kind of attachment behaviour. The author has cited earlier in this chapter the mental capacity to carry within ourselves numbers of internal representations of others, alive and dead. This requires certain intact functions of the brain, but does not pre-clude the possibility of maintaining a mental image of an attachment object, without the cognitive capacity to recognise whether or not the people are alive, and how old one actually is. One does not require an intact cortex to demonstrate aggression or indeed affection.

In the assumption that individuals require access to attachment objects in order to maintain emotional security, Miesen postulated that the demented person recreates his lost objects by reinventing his parents who come alive for him again. Miesen observed the searching behaviour of elderly people with dementia (object seeking), who are not uncommonly seen on continuing-care wards in a distressed and agitated state. They may be anxious that their 'parents' were to collect them, or that they 'have to get home or mummy will be worried'. Their parents have been dead for many years and yet they demonstrate continued attachment. Interestingly, these individuals tend not to attach to real-life staff or other residents; although they will often accept 'interim' care from the professional as though they might be a teacher or similar trustworthy carer. It is important not to infantilise the person by perpetuating the mistaken identity, but gentle reassurance and distraction is often helpful.

The capacity to relate and to respond to others seems to have a diffuse existence within the brain. Overt attachment behaviour to real people is a recognisable feature on dementia wards. People can and do make new attachments even when they have lost the power of articulate speech, and can be seen holding hands with staff or demonstrating or demanding physical signs of affection.

SUMMARY

Attachment theory has a unique place in old age psychiatry, a speciality which demands a range of skills from the practising clinician. Because of its scientific basis in ethology and behavioural psychology and its close working analogies to psychoanalytic theory, particularly object relations theory, it can offer genuinely useful links to the study of our patients' feelings and behaviours. It provides another useful model with which to negotiate clinical problems that are not easily solvable with the more prosaic tools of psychiatric practice – physical treatments.

Attachment theory is a developmental model which lends itself well to the understanding of ageing. It is based on observational studies as well as on listening to what the patient thinks and feels. The early observational model fits in well with studies or neurodevelopment; equally, this observational capacity is showing promise in the understanding of dementia, and of the behaviours and feelings experienced by those undergoing the process. It has proved to be useful in the ways in which we treat children in hospital; this has had a parallel effect in the more humane way in which we now treat our elderly with dementia (Kitwood, 1987). There is further scope for improvement in the prevention of abusive behaviour towards the elderly.

There is now work in progress to elucidate the psycho-biology of psychiatry. Attachment theory already provides helpful links with learning theory for which we are currently identifying biological substrates. There is a long history of biological correlates which coincide with changes in mood relating to attachment and loss; one example being changes in cortisol levels and immuno-suppression in the recently bereaved.

CONCLUSION

When we are unable to understand what we are witnessing in our patients it is often useful to look back at what went before. Twenty years ago in psychiatry, it was uncommon practice to take a full life history of anyone over the age of 65. Their life stories usually started when they got married or got a job. There is also an extraordinary lack of research on the continuities or otherwise between early and late periods of life. The lifespan approach to the study of ageing, although offered by Jung and Erikson, has not yet been fully embraced by psychiatry. It is only now that the speciality of old age psychiatry is on a firm biological footing, with functional neuro-imaging and confident pharmacology, we can begin again to explore some of the psychoanalytic, dynamic and social factors that contribute towards illness in old age (Ardern, Garner & Porter, 1998). Perhaps the linking of childhood factors to events in old age used to be considered less than respectful to older adults, but we see now that it essential (Waddell, 2000).

Attachment theory offers a sold scientific link between psychoanalytic thought and the neurobiology of the behaviours we observe in clinical practice. The possibilities for research are many; perhaps we will see prospective cohort studies taken well into old age.

REFERENCES

Adshead, G. (1998). Psychiatric staff as attachment figures: Understanding management problems in the light of attachment theory. *British Journal of Psychiatry*, 172, 64–69.

Ainsworth, M.S., Belhar, M.C., Waters, E. et al. (1978). *Patterns of Attachment: A psychobiological study of the strange situation.* Hillsdale, NJ: Lawrence Erlbaum Associate Inc.

Ainsworth, M.D., & Bowlby, J. (1954). Research strategy in the study of mother–child separation. *Courr. Cent. Int. Enf.*, 4, 105.

Amini, F., Lewis, T., Lannon, R., Louie, A., Baumbacher, G., McGuinness, T., & Schiff, E.Z. (1996) Affect, attachment, memory: Contribution towards psychobiological intergration. *Psychiatry*, 59(3), 213–239.

Ardern, M., Garner, J., & Porter, R. (1998). Curious bedfellows: Psychoanalytic understanding and old age psychiatry. *Psychoanalytic Pyschotherapy*, 12(1), 47–56.

Birtchnell, J. (1993). *How Humans Relate: A new interpersonal theory.* Hove, UK: Psychology Press.

Bowlby, J. (1958). The nature of the child's tie to his mother. *International Journal of Psychoanalysis*, 39, 350–373.

—— (1960). Separation anxiety. *International Journal of Psychoanalysis*, 41, 89–113.

—— (1969a). Instinctive behaviour. In: *Attachment and Loss Volume 1*. Harmondsworth, UK: Penguin.

—— (1969b). The ontogeny of human attachment. In: *Attachment and Loss Volume 1*. Harmondsworth, UK: Penguin.

—— (1977a). The making and breaking of affectional bonds: I Aetiology and psychopathology in the light of attachment theory. *British Journal of Psychiatry*, 130, 201–210.

—— (1977b). The making and breaking of affectional bonds: II Some principles of psychotherapy. *British Journal of Psychiatry*, 130, 421–431.

—— (1980). Loss, sadness and depression. In: *Attachment and Loss Volume III*. London: Penguin.

Brown, G., & Harris, T. (1978). *The Social Origins of Depression*. London: Tavistock.

Damasio, A. (1994). *Descarte's Error: Emotion, reason and the human brain*. London: Papermac, Macmillan.

Daniel, B. (1997). Working with older women. In: Lawrence, M. & Maguire, M. (eds) *Psychotherapy with Women: Feminist perspectives*. Basingstoke, UK: Macmillan.

Evans, S. (1998). Beyond the Mirror: A group analytic exploration of late life and depression. *Ageing and Mental Health*, 2(2), 94–99.

Evans, S. & Katona, C. (1990). Treatment of anxiety disorders in the elderly. In: Wheatley, D. (ed) *The Anxiolytic Jungle: Where next?* Chichester, UK: John Wiley & Sons.

—— (1993). The epidemiology of depressive symptoms in primary care attenders. *Dementia*, 4, 327–333.

Evans, S., Winnet, A., Birtchnell, J., & Goodwin, M. (1997). *Group couple psychotherapy for the depressed elderly: Qualitative and quantitative data from a thirty-week group*. Abstracts. World Psychiatric Association Conference, Israel.

Foulkes, S. (1964). *Therapeutic Group Analysis*. London: Allen & Unwin.

Freud, S. (1905). On psychotherapy. Standard Edition 7. London: Hogarth.

—— (1914). Remembering, repeating and working through (further recommendations on the technique of psycho-analysis II). Standard Edition 12. J. Strachey (trans. & ed), pp. 145–156. London: Hogarth.

—— (1917). Mourning and melancholia. Standard Edition 14. Trans. J. Riviere. London: Hogarth.

—— (1925). The death instinct. Standard Edition. Trans. J. Strachey. London: Hogarth.

—— (1940). An outline of psychoanalysis. Standard Edition 23. London: Hogarth.

Gabbard, G.O. (2000). A neurobiologically informed perspective on psychotherapy. *British Journal of Psychiatry*, 177, 117–122.

Garner, J., & Evans, S. (2000). The abuse of elderly people in institutions. CR84. London: Royal College of Psychiatrists.

Harwood, D., Hawton, K., Hope, T., & Jacoby, R. (2000). Suicide in older people: Modes of death, demographic factors, and medical contact before death. *International Journal of Geriatric Psychiatry*, 15(8), 736–743.

Harlow, H.F. (1958). The nature of love. *American Psychology*, 13, 673–685.

Kitwood, T. (1987). Dementia and its pathology: In brain, mind or society? *Free Associations*, 8, 81–93.

Klein, M. (1948). *Contributions to Psychoanalysis 1921–1945*. London: Hogarth.

Lindesay, J., Briggs, K., & Murphy, E. (1989). Guy's/Age Concern Survey: Prevalence of cognitive impairment, depression and anxiety in an urban elderly community. *British Journal of Psychiatry*, 155, 317–329.

Lorenz, K.Z. (1935). *Instinctive Behavior*. C. Schiller (ed). New York: International Universities Press, 1953.

Lowenthal, M.F. (1965). Antecedents of isolation and mental illness in old age. *Archives of General Psychiatry*, 12, 245–254.

Martindale, B.V. (1989). Becoming dependent again: The fears of some elderly patients and their younger therapists. *Psychoanalytic Psychotherapy*, 4(1), 67–75.

Miesen, B. (1992). Attachment theory and dementia. In: G. Jones & B. Miesen (eds) *Care Giving in Dementia: Research and applications*. London: Routledge.

Murphy, E. (1982). Social origins of depression in old age. *British Journal of Psychiatry*, 141, 135–142.

Ong, Y.L., Martineau, F., Lloyd, G., & Robbins, I. (1987). A support group for the depressed elderly. *International Journal of Geriatric Psychiatry*, 2, 119–123.

Padoani, W., & De Leo, D. (2000). Severe and persistent regressive behaviour in three elderly subjects without cognitive decline. *International Journal of Geriatric Psychiatry*, 15(1), 70–74.

Parkes, C.M. (1965). Bereavement and mental illness. *British Journal of Medical Psychology*, 38, 1–26.

—— (1972). *Bereavement: Studies of grief in adult life*. London: Tavistock Publications.

—— & Weiss, R.S. (1983). *Recovery from Bereavement*. New York: Basic Books.

Raphael, B. (1977). Preventive intervention with the recently bereaved. *Archives of General Psychiatry*, 34, 1450–1454.

Reynolds, C.F., Frank, E., Perel, J.M. et al. (1999). Nortriptiline and IPTs maintenance therapies for recurrent major depression: A randomised controlled trial in patients older than 59 years. *Journal of the American Medical Association*, 281(1), 83–84.

Robertson, J. (1952). Film: *A two-year-old goes to hospital*. London: Tavistock Child Development Research Unit.

Shah, A., & De, T. (1998). Suicide and the elderly. *International Journal of Psychiatric Clinical Practice*, 2, 3–17.

Thompson, P. (1993). I don't feel old: The significance of the search for meaning in later life. *International Journal of Geriatric Psychiatry*, 8, 685–692.

Waddell, M. (2000). Only connect: Developmental issues from early to late life. *Psychoanalytic Psychotherapy*, 14(3), 239–252.

Winnicot, D.W. (1965). *The Maturational Process and the Facilitating Environment*. London: Hogarth.

Winnicott, D.W. (1965). *The Capacity to Be Alone*. London: Tavistock.

Wolheim, R. (1971). *Freud*. London: Fontana.

Woods, R., & Roth, A. (1996). Effectiveness of psychological interventions with older people. In: A. Roth & P. Fonagy (eds) *What Works for Whom? A critical review of psychotherapy research*. London: Guilford.

Chapter 5

The old self: Kohut, Winnicott and others

Sandra Evans

Lear: 'Who is it can tell me who I am?'

(Shakespeare; *King Lear* II, iv)

Heinz Kohut initiated a strand of psychoanalytic theory devised principally for the treatment of narcissistic disorders. He was a Viennese physician who escaped Nazi Austria around the same time as did Freud who was near the end of his life; Kohut was 25. At that time he had recently qualified as a physician, and from Vienna moved to Chicago where he studied neurology, once more as Freud had done. Despite being a brilliant clinician (Wolf, 1996), he left neurology to train as a psychoanalyst at the Chicago Institute of Psychoanalysis.

After qualifying and while still quite young, he began to teach Freudian psychoanalysis at the Institute. Kohut was thought of as a gifted teacher and one whose understanding of Freudian theory was outstanding. He had the advantage of being able to read Freud in the original, and perhaps as a result had a purist attitude towards a number of the ideas which had been misunderstood and misused since Freud's death. As a student of classical Freudian Analysis, Kohut understood the evolutionary nature of Freud's ideas and identified strengths and flaws in the master's thinking. Of particular note was Freud's tenacity to the Oedipal Situation, and Kohut's own difficulty with making, as he saw, it reflex oedipal interpretations. Kohut insisted that it simply did not work with some patients and although he was aware that this may consist of resistance in part, he also felt that there was something else that his patients were saying.

One of Kohut's greatest legacies was to exhort us to listen to our patients and let them speak for themselves. Analysts should not attempt to fit patients into a theoretical framework that is not appropriate. Kohut was fond of quoting Freud on empathy and he himself wrote extensively on the subject.

A path leads from identification by way of imitation to empathy, . . . to the comprehension of the mechanism by means of which we are able to take up any attitude at all towards another mental life.

(Freud, 1921: 110)

Meaning that without empathy we cannot hope to access another's internal world closely enough to understand or form an opinion about them (Wolf, 1996).

Kohut was called a sociologist, by way of criticism. His accusers insisted that a psychoanalyst should not be concerned with the environment. Kohut's riposte was that he was interested in the effect of the environment on the individual's internal world. His patients' experience of trauma was coloured by a multitude of factors, of which the external environment is only one. One cannot study mental life in isolation; and from this standpoint Kohut shared some ideas with the object relations theorists (Bacal & Newman, 1993) who were developing their ideas in the United Kingdom about the same time as Kohut, in the 1950s and 1960s.

Another of the more 'independent' analysts, Winnicott (1964), for example, wrote of the 'good enough mother'; an environmental ideal which facilitates the healthy development of the child, and on into adulthood. Winnicott also suggested that 'there is no such thing as a baby' indicating that an infant cannot develop a healthy sense of self without a mother. This was the framework within which Kohut began to develop his Psychology of the Self. He did not fully explore these ideas until the early 1970s when he was diagnosed with lymphocytic leukaemia. This may have been the catalyst to help him complete the work.

Kohut was to develop further Freud's ideas on narcissism. Kohut had a different view of narcissism; that instead of being a defensive stance, it had a developmental line of its own. Negative aspects of narcissism arose from a particular deprivation at a significant stage in an individual's development. Positive narcissism also exists and requires a lifetime of feeding. This lifelong aspect of Kohutian narcissism is a helpful frame within which to understand depression in response to difficulties in the lives of older people (Evans, 1998).

Kohut did not enjoy an easy relationship with his contemporary psychoanalytic colleagues. He was perceived as something of a revolutionary and an audacious one at that. He presumed to improve upon classical Freudian theory. Freud had left a considerable body of work and his mourning followers had perhaps begun to adopt a rigid post-Freudian ego psychology of which further evolution, so soon after Freud's death, might have seemed in some way to defile the original.

KOHUTIAN SELF-PSYCHOLOGY

The centrepiece of Kohut's work is his move away from drive theory classical psychoanalysis, for which Freud is thought to have been influenced by Darwinism, to the more dynamic approach of the 'selfobjects'. Whereas Freud's dynamism was vertical, between the levels of consciousness, Kohut's dynamism was more lateral, between the individual's mind and the experience of the important others in his or her life (Kohut, 1977). The running of the words self and object together highlights Kohut's approach; which was that the selfobject is a part of the self that holds the experience of the other person (object). Selfobjects are experienced as part of our self and are the materials from which our internal world is made. The expected control we have over them is akin to the adult's normal sense of agency over his or her limbs (Kohut & Wolf, 1978). In infancy the selfobjects are likely to be mother and father. Their healthy responses to the child ensures his or her normal development. Kohut went further than the Object Relations Theorists in that he asserted that one continues to make use of different selfobjects throughout one's life, and that these selfobject experiences are essential to ongoing mature development through adulthood, right up to the end of life.

Kohut described three selfobject functions. The first two are the basic mirroring and idealising roles of normal parenting. Mirroring is the positive regard in which the infant is held – the pride and admiration for being and for the mastery of new skills; using the potty, reading, writing and so forth. Without this positive mirroring the individual cannot develop a positive sense of self and will be depleted and vulnerable as a consequence; easily demolished by the slightest criticism.

The idealising function of selfobjects is to provide the perfect template with which to merge, in order to provide calm omnipotence. This becomes the idealised parent imago. The healthy self derived from the interactions with a series of adequate selfobjects, consists of one pole containing an individual's striving for success, a second pole that harbours a moral stance, and an arc of skills between the two corresponding to the tension between ambitions and ideals (Kohut & Wolf, 1978).

The third selfobject function as 'alter ego' was a later addition, which highlighted a child's longing for belonging and constancy and the need to feel secure (Kohut, 1984). This has strong resonances with attachment theory, which was dealt with in greater detail in Chapter 4.

Common to all three selfobject functions were the pre-requisite attuned parental figures. It is important to bear in mind that parents must also be fallible. Perfect parents would not supply sufficient frustration in order to develop autonomy, and the sense of separateness considered essential to individuality (Trop, 1994).

PRIMARY DISTURBANCES OF THE SELF

Faulty mirroring or idealising selfobjects results in a damaged self; either diffusely so or seriously damaged in one or other constituents. In adult life the interactions with other potential selfobjects will be faulty, and will reactivate the specific need that was unattended at the earliest point. The *sine qua non* of this phenomenon occurs in the consulting room. The person will be considered to suffer a damaged self in Kohutian terms, the more severe of which is the primary disturbance of the self. The afflictions may be of a psychotic order, which Kohut stated was not treatable analytically, or they may develop into borderline or narcissistic states, the narcissistic behaviour disorders or a narcissistic personality disorder. It was particularly the people with narcissistic behaviour disorders who interested Kohut, and whom he felt were not assisted greatly by using a classical theoretical framework, which highlighted the Oedipus complex. He illustrated this most clearly with the example of a patient Mr Z, who completed a Freudian analysis with Kohut only to return a few years later distressed by his mother's descent into frank mental illness. He underwent a second analysis with Kohut, this time with the benefit of the more 'empathic', listening approach. On this occasion his ending was more satisfactory, and seemed to concur more genuinely with the formulation (Kohut, 1979).

Kohut developed his thinking on an individual's perpetual need for selfobjects in his later work when he had relinquished his dependence on ego psychology. He conceptualised the mature adult position as one that has relinquished its ties to its original selfobjects; those that provided the first nurturing (Kohut, 1984). However, the mature adult continues to require reflection in a lifelong pattern of empathic contact with mature selfobjects. This is also distinct from the 'autonomous' position of Erikson and others (Siegel, 1996) (see Chapter 6).

CONTEMPORANEOUS WORK FROM THE ENGLISH SCHOOL

Many of Kohut's ideas shared common ground with other theoreticians and clinicians of his time and those that have published more recently. Donald Winnicott, as a paediatrician before becoming a psychoanalyst, was able to draw upon his wealth of clinical work in observing infants with their mothers, in addition to his work with children in the consulting room. He used a combination of observing mother and child interactions, and media such as drawing, to investigate the internal world of the child. The former type of work has been successfully replicated by Daniel Stern (1985) in his work with infants, and by the late Tom Kitwood in his work with dementia sufferers. Kitwood (1990) exhorted us to use empathy in order to understand better the world of the individual who is becoming demented (see Chapter 15). Winnicott (1960) also wrote of the 'mirroring function' of the maternal gaze and its importance in the development of a healthy individual. Absence of the good enough reflective capacity or, more importantly, the excessive intrusion of maternal needs and desires, leads to an absence of sense of self and the development of the 'false self' respectively. Winnicott suggested that in this case there is no true ego-development (1956). The consequences for the adult may be far reaching. In the case of the borderline individual, just as Kohut suggested, there is vulnerability to criticism or insults of any kind including the losses of ageing.

SECONDARY DISTURBANCES OF THE SELF

The course of the lives of 'false self' individuals often looks different. False self individuals may be high achievers and are common in the Health Service and in the helping professions generally. Winnicott's 'false self' corresponds to Kohut's idea of secondary disturbance of the self. This occurs in patients whose parental objects were considered to be over involved and intrusive, or suffocating; thus resulting in the falsification or mutilation of the self by the patient. These people tend nonetheless to become high achievers, but are thought to be particularly sensitive, prone to depression, guilt and shame (Hearst, 1988). They may not suffer psychiatric problems until late life. These individuals may obtain their sense of self, or a strong selfobject experience, from helping patients or relieving other sufferers. Their problems begin when they retire, or when there is no one left to help. They may suffer a crisis of self-confidence or even an identity crisis. Their reason for existence is threatened as, without the distraction of another's needs, or the tenuous sensation of being whole by being needed, they may lose their equilibrium altogether and become clinically depressed, experiencing at last the previously avoided depression belonging to infancy, the caring role having staved this off for years.

POST KOHUTIAN SELF-PSYCHOLOGY

Since Kohut the field of self-psychology has progressed further but continues to be relevant to modern psychiatric practice. It remains relevant in the understanding and treatment of schizoid mechanisms and borderline states which are common in patients who develop secondary depressive illnesses and/or who engage in self-harm behaviour, something that still occurs in later life, but which does not achieve much attention. In fact some of the behaviour disorders of old age are thought to be displays of maladaptive adjustment to the narcissistic injuries caused by loss and infirmity (Padoani & De Leo,

2000). In addition, the emphasis that Kohut put on empathy continues to be relevant today. His ideas echo those of Rogers in 1961 on the importance of empathy as a therapeutic factor, and this still pertains in process and outcome research.

Lichtenberg (1983) proposed the use of the term selfobjects for those who perform specific functions for the individual, rather than an indiscriminate term for anyone or anything that benefits the individual. Stolorow (1995) clarifies further by defining selfobjects as *not* simply caregivers, but significant other people in the developing person's life.

SELF EXPERIENCE AND THE GENERATIONAL CONSCIOUSNESS

Although Bollas cannot be described as a self-psychologist, a number of his ideas appear to have roots in selfobject identifications. His work as an independent psychoanalyst is in the tradition of Winnicott himself (Bollas, 1993). In his seminal work *The Shadow of the Object*, Bollas (1987) describes the dynamic between the individual mind and the constantly shifting external environment, which plays both consciously and unconsciously. These daily diets of experiences are described as *transformational objects*. They are both randomly experienced and chosen, consciously and unconsciously; and impact on the individual's frame of reference, changing us by their impact. They are impacted upon in turn by us in some way, by what we bring to the experience. These transformational objects are not necessarily other people; they may be inanimate objects or aesthetic experiences such as art and music (Bollas, 1993). He goes on to describe the *generational consciousness* as that element of our selves which relates to our cohort and the singular experiences of a generation. These link us to other members of our generation and remove us, and potentially alienate us, from other generations. The cohort of patients that we see tend to be over the age of 60. They will remember the Second World War for example; something that has international relevance even though the perspective will be different depending on what part of the world they were in at the time. Those of us who are too young to remember the war or who were born after it cannot share in the experience in the same way. Bollas used the writings of Vera Brittain to illustrate the point. Music, fashion and social expectations can also be dated and can highlight similarities and differences between generations. Differences in these kinds of tastes can serve to set older people apart from younger generations, and induce fear and a sense of disaffection at worst. The fewer of one's 'sort' of fellow individuals that survive, the fewer generational objects exist for a person; resulting in a diminution in familiar things that reflect and reinforce the sense of self.

TRANSITIONAL OBJECTS AND SELFOBJECTS

Bollas's work may have provided us with a link between *selfobjects* and *transitional objects* – a term supplied by Winnicott (1974) for inanimate things that 'stand in' for mother. A selfobject, just as a transitional object, becomes invested with meaning. As an example of the transitional object, a child will invest a teddy or blanket with the part of herself that has been able to hold on to the idea of mother; in other words the child's maternal selfobject. Loss of this, even in the presence of mother, is often distressing to the child.

Some transformational objects may be considered loosely as adult versions of the transitional object. The difference is that there is often an abundance of such objects available in adult life. Personal belongings can also be invested with meaning and selfobject status. Items such as father's watch given on his deathbed can be invested with selfobject significance. Other personal items may not have quite the same degree of preciousness as a parental gift, but may reflect the self in important ways, and are therefore worthy of consideration. If one experiences living in an hotel room for more than a few days, one might sense an initial thrill at the newness and anonymity, but after a while, feel the lack of the company of one's 'things'. Some individuals admit to anxiety when packing to go on holiday, leaving behind familiarity and personal objects. The loss of people, such as friends and relatives is well documented as a potential cause of depression and anxiety in older people (Murphy, 1983); however, the loss of familiar surroundings, particularly walls which reflect years of experience, such as a family home is less well analysed. The home may have become a selfobject with meaning and a sense of belonging, and the giving up of it for a smaller, more manageable or supported flat may be experienced as an attack on the sense of self. Equally, moves to residential homes without adequate personal effects, familiar crockery, photographs and so forth, which take on a selfobject function and transitional object significance, will add to the anxiety of the loss of independence. People with cognitive impairment are still sent to hospitals and nursing homes without these familiar items. The sense of personal loss can then be exacerbated and may increase the sense of disorientation.

Clinical Illustration
Sylvia has developed a rapid decline in her cognitive function. Her family who are used to organising things for her, find her a beautiful residential home where she can be looked after. The staff are kind and attentive, and Sylvia's room is spacious and nicely furnished by the home. To the horror of her family, within days of arrival Sylvia is smearing faeces and is visibly distressed. She is unable to articulate her feelings in a more constructive way. The replacement of some of the furnishings in the room with her own armchair and some of her paintings results in an improvement in her behaviour and her mental state generally.

KOHUT'S RELEVANCE TO AGEING
AND GROUPWORK

Kohut's interest in narcissistic disturbances are of relevance to those working with older people generally, and those with psychological disturbances in particular. Weiner and White (1984) describe the self-psychology group approach to working with older adults, and give clear illustrations of how the group provides positive mirroring selfobjects in the form of other members of the group. Hearst (1988) suggests that a group is often the most appropriate therapeutic environment for people with an impaired sense of self. Evans (1998) went on to propose groups as positively beneficial to older people who have an impaired self, either from early life, or who through sustained illness and death had depleted numbers of mirroring selfobjects. For the more narcissistic and borderline patients, the group setting may have to be almost indestructible in order to resist omnipotent, demanding and controlling behaviour. The mature group with a 'healthy narcissistic group self' (Battegay, 1976) needs to be available, which can provide a reservoir of healthy narcissism for needy and 'greedy' group members (Pines, 1980). The following illustrations are adapted from the author's own practice.

Clinical Illustration

A depressed and physically deteriorated man in his seventies is persuaded to attend a group in a day hospital. He has been discharged recently from inpatient care having made only a partial recovery following treatment with ECT. He remains dejected and seemingly helpless, unable to resume his life, and is growing increasingly dependent. In the group he sits slouched and with his head bent so that he can only see his feet. He engages very little, although he does respond when people ask him questions. Other group members are patently interested in him, perhaps sensing that there is more to him than this sad old man that he himself seems to present.

The topic of conversation turns inevitably to the war, and Wilfred who had spent most of his early years in an orphanage, is asked about his time during the Second World War. He tells them of the action that he has seen and the terrible losses of young men that he himself witnessed. It transpires that he was decorated for bravery, and as he tells the tale and responds to the admiration of the group, he becomes more talkative. It becomes clear that he is eloquent and well read. He begins to command some real respect in the group and responds by engaging more with the process. His non-verbal communications are worthy of note. His posture alters in that he begins to sit up and looks at people.

Comment

The group members acted as mirroring selfobjects to Wilfred, reflecting and reinforcing some of his own positive narcissism, and improving his self-esteem. This occurred because the group was able to estimate him more accurately by talking to him and knowing him, rather than making assumptions. Judging from his non-verbal communications, there are associated changes to his mental state brought about by this intervention. The importance of empathic working with this group of individuals cannot be emphasised enough. The increasing dependency associated with ageing is accepted while the wish for independence is acknowledged. The empathic approach fosters the patient's self-esteem by accepting their version of the experience of ageing (Kohut, 1984; Weiner & White, 1984).

Clinical Illustration
Charlotte is an attractive woman in her late seventies. She had little affection from her mother whom she recalls as a critical individual. Her father was killed in the war. Her memories of him are as a magnificent soldier and a warm and loving if remote man. Throughout her life she has followed older men, hoping to regain some of that warmth, but always choosing unluckily. The men are idealised in retrospect (and may have been idealised at the time) but none fulfilled the promise of being Mr Right who would look after her and protect her. She is deeply anxious, unable to rid herself of personal belongings that are surplus to requirements. The consequence of her hoarding is an uncomfortable and unpleasant house and two exasperated daughters, with whom she has an ambivalent relationship. As she has aged she has become increasingly anxious and increasingly dependent on benzodiazepines. Antidepressant therapy improves her anxiety a little, but she develops an almost instant transference to the female doctor whom she perceives as cold and rejecting. She asks constantly for feedback on how she is experienced as a patient, and often misreads the doctor's feelings towards her. She is referred for group therapy.

Comment

Charlotte is a 'mirror hungry' individual. In Kohutian terms her early development lacked the positive admiring mirroring, and her idealising selfobject relationship with her father was cut short before it could be integrated in a mature way. Her overwhelming need for mirroring and particularly idealising selfobjects has continued on through her unsatisfactory adult relationships into her old age. Her hoarding and drug dependence appear to have roots in her need to hang on to 'selfobjects' of an inanimate kind over which she has some conscious control. However, when presented with a strongly idealised and feared figure; in this case her doctor, she develops a neurotic transference which needs to be dealt with empathically and kindly. The empathic contact is essential as the vehicle through which she might get help (White, 1984). Charlotte would be an easy casualty in a busy health service which might see her partial remission through antidepressant treatment as 'good enough'. However this does little to address the primary needs, and more particularly the compensating but problematic behavioural disturbances that act merely to alienate others rather than engage them. Her proper development, inhibited by an absent father and a depressed, possibly embittered mother, has rendered her unable to love herself (Grotjahn, 1981).

Clinical Illustration
Malcolm, an older gay man, attends individual therapy. He complains of feeling different and inferior in his life by virtue of his sexuality. Despite positive feelings for him in the countertransference, he continues to feel criticised and unsupported by the therapist. He is exquisitely sensitive to any view contrary to his own, which he perceives as an assault.

By contrast he reminisces about a previous analyst from whom he felt total understanding. When describing his 'coming out' he remembers the excitement of having his gay self to go to, which is imagined by the therapist as another rather beautiful man with whom Malcolm can merge and feel whole. The therapist is aware of a failure of empathy on his part when he does not adequately reflect Malcolm's need to merge with another, nor wholeheartedly sympathise with the resultant loneliness.

Too late, the therapist appreciates that he had accepted the sexuality 'problem' at face value. He had thought of it as a part of Malcolm, rather than as an expression of his primary disturbance of narcissism; the profound lack in his childhood of mirroring or idealising selfobjects (Garland, 1982). Malcolm's father had been harsh and his mother ineffectual (he rarely mentioned her). It would seem that his experience with his former analyst, although not accepting of his homosexuality (an aspect of himself), had been accepting of something deeper and more profoundly required in the therapy.

Comment

The therapist came to realise that his empathic failure prevented Malcolm from fulfilling the longed-for idealising transference in which he could possibly have revisited the mirroring and idealising experiences essential to the development of a healthy sense of self. In the past Malcolm sustained a profound lack of these experiences and consequently developed a narcissistic disturbance. It is proposed that although not all homosexuality arises in a developmental line out of narcissistic disturbance, in Malcolm's case this was his solution to the problem. Unfortunately he lost relationships of either orientation, and as he got older, relationships in which this could have been improved were becoming less likely. His 'gay self' may have been the key to the resolution, as the imagined other man who would be Malcolm's twin. This twinship idealising transference could not sustain, since it only existed in fantasy.

CONCLUSION

The post Freudian object-relating psychology provides a bridge to the understanding of social groups as well as individuals, and also the changing relationships between people, and between people and society as we age. Kohutian self-psychology and Winnicott's theories on the development of the personality add a coherence to the notion of the self. They also provide an understanding of how developmental problems in early life may contribute to vulnerabilities in an individual's personal resources when meeting the exigencies of old age. The narcissistic vulnerabilities in particular may go some way to understanding the risk of suicide in later life (Rosenfeld, 1971; Singer, 1977; Evans, 1998).

Development of the self is also a lifelong characteristic; it is no longer sufficient to think of it as input at the beginning of life, which ends at adolescence. The self cannot be acted upon by a lifetime of experience and remain unchanged and rigid. Bollas uses a microscopic lens to examine the minutiae of everyday experiences, and these ideas help us to value experiences in their myriad forms, throughout life, helping us to ensure we do not neglect the experiences of the old, the very old, and the demented old. People need reinforcing and mirroring as a part of normal life – for the whole of life.

REFERENCES

Bacal, H., & Newman, K. (1993). *Theories of Object Relations: Bridges to self psychology*. New York: Columbia University Press.

Battegay, H. (1976). The concept of the narcissistic group self. *Group Analysis*, IX/3, 217–220.

Bollas, C. (1987). *The Shadow of the Object: Psychoanalysis of the unthought known*. London: Free Association Books.

Bollas, C. (1993). *Being a Character: Psychoanalysis and self experience*. New York: Hill & Wang. [Reprinted by Routledge, London in 1997.]

Evans, S. (1998). Beyond the mirror: A group analytic view of late life and depression. *Ageing and Mental Health*, 2(2), 94–99.

Freud, S. (1921). *Standard Edition*. London: Hogarth.

Garland, C. (1982). Taking the non-problem seriously. *Group Analysis*, 15(2), 4–14.

Grotjahn, M. (1981). The therapeutic group process in the light of developmental ego psychology. *Group*, 5, 11–16.

Hearst, L.E. (1988). The restoration of the impaired self in group psychoanalytic treatment. In: N. Slavinsky-Holy (ed) *Borderline and Narcissistic Patients in Therapy*. New York: IUP Inc.

Kitwood, T. (1990). The dialectics of dementia: With particular reference to Alzheimer's disease. *Ageing and Society*, 10, 177–196.

Kohut, H. (1977). The need for a psychology of the self. In: *The Restoration of the Self*. New York: International Universities Press.

Kohut, H. (1979). The two analyses of Mr Z. In: P. Ornstein (ed) *The Search for the Self*, Vol. 4, pp. 395–446. New York: International Universities Press, 1990.

Kohut, H. (1984). *How Does Analysis Cure?* Chicago & London: University of Chicago Press.

Kohut, H. & Wolf, E. (1978). The disorders of the self and their treatment: An outline. *International Journal of Psychoanalysis*, 59, 413–425.

Lichtenberg, J. (1983). *Psychoanalysis and Infant Research*. Hillsdale, NJ: Analytic Press.

Murphy, E. (1982). The social origins of depression in old age. *British Journal of Psychiatry*, 141, 135–142.

Murphy, E. (1983). The prognosis of depression in old age. *British Journal of Psychiatry*, 142, 111–119.

Padoani, W., & De Leo, D. (2000). Severe and persistent regressive behaviour in three elderly subjects without cognitive decline. *International Journal of Geriatric Psychiatry*, 15(1), 70–74.

Pines, M. (1980). What to expect in the psychotherapy of the borderline patient. *Group Analysis*, XIII/3, 168–176.

Rogers, C. (1961). *On Becoming a Person*. London: Constable.

Rosenfeld, H. (1971). A clinical approach to the psychoanalytic theory of the life and death instincts: an investigation into the aggressive aspects of narcissism. *International Journal of Psychoanalysis*, 52, 169–177.

Siegel, A.M. (1996). *Heinz Kohut and the Psychology of the Self*. London & New York: Routledge.

Singer, M. (1977). The experience of emptiness in narcissistic and borderline states: II The struggle for a sense of self and the potential for suicide. *International Review of Psychoanalysis*, 4, 471–479.

Stern, D.N. (1985). *The Interpersonal World of the Infant: A view from psychoanalysis and developmental psychology*. London: Basic Books, Harper-Collins.

Stolorow, R. (1995). An intersubjective view of self-psychology. *Psychoanalytic Dialogues*, 5(3), 393–399.

Trop, J.L. (1994). Recent developments in self-psychology. *Current Opinion in Psychiatry*, 7, 225–228.

Weiner, B.M., & White, T.M. (1984). The third chance: Self psychology as an effective group approach for older adults. In: Discussion of 'Narcissistic transferences: Implications for the treatment of couples' by G. Schwartzman. *Dynamic Psychotherapy*, 2, 15–17.

White, M.T. (1984). Discussion of 'Narcissistic transferences: Implications for the treatment of couples' by G. Schwartzman. *Dynamic Psychotherapy*, 2, 15–17.

Winnicott, D.W. (1953). Transitional objects and transitional phenomena. *International Journal of Psychoanalysis*, 34, 42.

Winnicott, D.W. (1956). On transference. *International Journal of Psychoanalysis*, 37, 386–388.

Winnicott, D.W. (1960). The theory of the parent–infant relationship. In: Winnicott, D.W. *The Maturational Processes and the Facilitating Environment*. London: Hogarth Press.

Winnicott, D.W. (1964). *The Child, the Family and the Outside World*. Harmondsworth, UK: Penguin.

Winnicott, D.W. (1974). Fear of breakdown. *International Review of Psychoanalysis*, Pts 1 & 2.

Wolf, E.S. (1996). The Viennese Chicagoan. In: A.M. Siegel (ed) *Heinz Kohut and the Psychology of the Self*. London: Routledge.

Chapter 6

Growing into old age: Erikson and others

Jane Garner

For age is opportunity no less
Than youth itself, though in another dress
And as the evening twilight fades away
The sky is filled with stars, invisible by day.
(Longfellow)

Psychoanalytic theory is a theory of development. Freud, emphasising early experience, originally conceived of this development as passing through predetermined stages, each stage linked to an 'erotogenic zone', with instincts and behaviour also equated with physiological development. There are limitations to the paradigm of Freud's instinct theory (oral, anal, genital phases) and difficulties in equating stages with parts of the body. The idea of passing through different predetermined psychological 'stages' tends to negate the influence of the external environment; there will be many different potential developmental pathways, only some of which are likely to unfold in particular environmental circumstances. Psychological stages or phases are neither traversed and left nor stopped at particular points but remain active throughout life to different degrees and may be stimulated at different times (see Bateman & Holmes, 1995). Problems arising from external reality continue throughout life. Later environmental experience also influences functioning.

THE LIFE CYCLE

The Neo-Freudians restated Freud's theory in sociological terms with a greater focus on the external world and developed an interpersonal (cf. intrapersonal) model with less emphasis on the 'individual', and more on how persons interact on and with one another. Out of this tradition Erik Erikson supplemented and developed Freud's ideas which ended in early adulthood. Erikson was a professor of human development at Harvard University. He saw development continuing beyond libidinal development throughout the life cycle with different, specific tasks to be negotiated in each of the eight phases he described. Although he called his model 'epigenetic', which until then had been a term used exclusively for a biological theory, he moved away from an emphasis on the body. He departed from a framework derived from bodily needs, to the subject's attitude to and interaction with the world. He was mindful of the criticisms which could be made of a psychological theory of development that proceeds in and through stages. Erikson's developmental schema (see Erikson, 1959, 1966; Rapaport, 1959) emphasises cultural as well as intrapsychic factors; the life cycle is charted through social science and psychoanalysis; 'each successive stage and crisis has a special relation to one of the basic elements of society, and this for the simple reason that the human lifecycle and man's institutions have evolved together' (Erikson, 1966). The infantile ego has its origins in organised social life, and social organisation has its bearing on the individual ego.

Erikson charts the history of psychoanalytic research. First 'man's enslavement by the id' was studied; then man's enslavement by 'ego (and superego) strivings'; Erikson suggests that psychoanalytic study would not be complete unless finally it investigates 'man's enslavement by historical conditions'. It is because these processes are apparently autonomous that man is seen as slave to them.

Table 6.1 lists the 'eight ages of man'. The title of each age distinguishes a stage of psychosocial development and indicates the nuclear conflict to be negotiated at that time, a phase-specific developmental task. Human growth is seen as a series of alternative basic attitudes, each at the same time being a way of experiencing, a way of behaving and an unconscious inner state. The solution to each of these developmental crises is carried forward to the next and subsequent ones, and each is also dependent upon the solution of earlier ones. There is an interaction between current development and previous and early experience.

Erikson points out that the positive attitudes are not 'achievements', rather the negative ones persist alongside as the dynamic counterpart throughout

Table 6.1 Eight ages of man

Stages of development	'Basic virtue'
Basic trust vs basic mistrust	Hope
Autonomy vs shame and doubt	Willpower
Initiative vs guilt	Purpose
Industry vs inferiority	Competence
Identity vs role confusion	Fidelity
Intimacy vs isolation	Love
Generativity vs stagnation	Care
Ego integrity vs despair	Wisdom

(Erikson, 1959, 1966)

life. However if the negotiation between the two contentions is reasonably successful with a ratio between the two balanced towards the positive, a 'basic virtue' may evolve relevant to the human spirit of the individual and to society from generation to generation.

The two assumptions underlying the model are first, that the personality develops in stages which are determined by the readiness of the growing individual to engage with an increasing range of social interactions. Second, that society is constructed to invite these interactions and to safeguard and encourage this ordered development, for example parental care, schools and teachers, marital arrangements, a variety of occupations, workers who care for and support older people. The sequence of phases is universal – different cultures and societies respond with varying solutions to ensure the child will be a viable future participant in society.

Although a sequence of stages, this model is also a gradual development. Erikson writes of 'crises' but he does not consider the whole of development a series of crises, rather there are 'decisive encounters' within the environment. There are particular moments in psychosocial growth, turning points, which may be crucial and portend progress and integration or regression and retardation. The epigenetic principle is one of programmed or planned growth, each part growing at its particular time until there is a functioning whole. After birth the organism continues to grow physically and socially in a prescribed sequence. Erikson, the psychoanalyst, described the growth of the personality using similar language and ideas. Epigenetic denoted a theory of autonomous ego development, that is, with independent roots from the id. Developmental stages prior to old age will be mentioned briefly.

Basic trust vs basic mistrust

This first stage is the basis for all future psychosocial functioning. A sense of basic trust is the first component of mental health to develop in life, 'the cornerstone of a healthy personality', initially trust that mother and food will be reliably available for the oral, sensory baby; subsequently that others and institutions in whom one is emotionally invested will be sufficient for one's needs. The way this stage progresses depends not on quantities of food or demonstrations of love but on the quality of the maternal relationship and care. If basic trust is not established, the adult may withdraw into schizoid or depressive states. Erikson relates this stage to the institution of religion, which over centuries has restored a sense of trust while promising to ban evil – the faithful surrender childlike to an almighty provider.

Autonomy vs shame and doubt

In the second stage a sense of autonomous will develops. The anal phase toddler, with a maturing musculature, is now standing and manipulating objects in his world. He may measure himself unfavourably in size and power against those around him. If self-control can be learned and self-esteem maintained, the individual develops a sense of personal pride rather than fearing 'loss of face'. The child needs to coordinate conflicting action patterns, not only directly in relation to retention and elimination but more widely, including socially, 'holding on' and 'letting go'. If this stage is not negotiated well, the child may overmanipulate himself, developing a precocious conscience, setting the infantile model for a compulsion neurosis. The institutional safeguard related to this stage is the principle of law and order and a sense of justice.

Initiative vs guilt

In the third stage the child develops a sense of initiative, with increased language and locomotion skills, and the imagination expands tremendously. Freud describes this as the Oedipal complex, for Erikson (1966) the time when 'infantile sexuality and incest taboo, castration complex and superego all unite . . .'. Social goals are contemplated and possibly achieved by the two genders taking the initiative in different ways. Guilt may be engendered by the particular goal set or by enjoyment of one's bodily actions with fear of punishment for eroticised fantasies. The individual may have a deep sense of guilt for deeds which in reality were not committed and would have been biologically impossible. This is the cornerstone of morality for the individual. In laying foundations for the future this stage may help the individual realistically identify with others in a spirit of equality or be oppressed by an over-restrictive moral sense. Social institutions offer the child an economic ethos, an understanding of the necessities of an economic life.

Industry vs inferiority

In the latency period the child at school and home enjoys work and the pleasure of producing things but risks feeling mediocre or inadequate. With guidance, the child does not only do things which are the product of play and fantasy, but also those which give a sense of participating in the adult world, of being useful and of being recognised for being productive. Erikson considers this socially to be a most decisive stage, the child learning to do things with others while at the same time getting an idea of division of labour and of differential opportunity. Along with increased skills a technological ethos develops.

Identity vs role confusion

Here youth begins, and physiological revolution. Ego identity is more than the sum of childhood identifications but is the integration of previous successive stages. In puberty and adolescence the search for continuity and inner sameness may be refought in previous childhood battles with a concern for how one appears to others. A problem at this stage may be 'identity diffusion'. The danger of overidentifying with 'heroes' may lead to confusion over personal identity and role. Cliques may develop which are intolerant and exclusive and be joined as a defence against this confusion. Ego identity implies that one has continuity for oneself but also sameness in meaning for others too. Erikson considers the adolescent has to confront the 'problems of ideology and aristocracy', those who succeed personify the nation's ideals, 'the best people will come to rule and rule develops the best in people'; without this notion there is cynicism or apathy.

Intimacy vs isolation

This is the first of the three stages of adulthood. The young adult having found identity is now eager for affiliation, partnership, intimacy and fusing that identity with another. The fear and avoidance of this self-abandonment may presage isolation and self-absorption. Erikson comments that true genitality can fully develop at this stage. For him, writing in his historical context four to seven decades ago, this would be expressed in heterosexual mutuality and supremely in mutual orgasm. The 'foreigner' encroaching on one's personal or national territory may be subject to fierce prejudice unless the adult develops an ethical sense.

Generativity vs stagnation

In adulthood, generativity is primarily the concern for establishing and guiding the next generation, although the concept also includes non-genital productivity and creativity. The counterpart to this creative generativity is a sense of stagnation and interpersonal impoverishment. Not everyone has children and not all who do are successful in negotiating generativity with its expansion of ego-interests and libidinal investment in what is generated. All social institutions codify the ethics of generative succession in terms of 'care' and of 'charity'.

Ego integrity vs despair and disgust

For Erikson, ego integrity lacks a clear definition, but the one who possesses integrity in old age sees his personal life, his position in world affairs and history to be as it had to be. He accepts his family of origin as it was and that one's own life is one's own responsibility, albeit that his own life cycle has accidentally coincided with a particular time in history. Without emotional integration the individual is beset by despair, that time is too short, death is too near to try out different routes in life, and one is faced with 'not being' rather than valuing the experience one has had 'to be . . . through having been'. For those without integration, the life cycle they have had at that time in history is not accepted as the ultimate 'one and only' possible life. Despair may not be obvious but clothed in disgust, misanthropy, contempt and displeasure.

Elderly patients often feel in a state of physical and psychological disintegration. The ego can feel too frail to be containing and integrated. Whereas the mother can give the child a sense of containment and an internal space so that anxieties are modified, helping the older person involves therapist and patient in recognising loss, acknowledging grief and anger for a life which did not feel integrated and trying to hold on to what were the worthwhile aspects of life, of having been lovable and having loved.

Each phase is related to all others, each strength and weakness has its precursors or its derivatives in each stage. The infant has the seeds of all crises to come, and in the elderly a mark has been left by the previous seven struggles, some of which may be stimulated again by the exigencies of old age. With increasing dependency and the practical necessity, or anticipation of a necessity, of relying once more on others, family, friends or institutions, the capacity for trust is again to the fore (Martindale, 1989, 1998). Some carry with them a benign acceptance of possible future dependency and have an inner idea that if they are in difficulties others will provide care, having sufficient good will towards them, and that the dependency, loss, hatred and sacrifice will be tolerated by both sides.

Good enough experiences of dependency early in life can now be transferred on to others. Older people without sufficient of this basic trust may be referred with anxiety or depression in the face of consciously or unconsciously feared dependency. The pseudo-independent older person who, despite major incapacitating difficulties, vociferously maintains that they can cope and dismisses all attempts to help is well known to old age psychiatry services, as is the one who could do much more for themselves but rather chides, complains and denigrates as not good enough others' attempts to help.

Whatever one's thoughts about the particulars of the stages described by Erikson, his extension of the idea of development throughout the life cycle has influenced later analysts and writers to consider old age and its potential for psychological work both for individual patients and for the service as a whole.

A further contribution he makes is of the idea that psychoanalysis is not complete unless it includes consideration or study of the historical situation in which the ego developed. There is a crucial relationship between the developing individual and his social environment. Erikson leaves us 'a beginning of a formulation of integrity based on clinical and anthropological experience' (1959). Setting the individual experience in history may be particularly important in thinking of older patients who have lived in different times from most of the staff who care for them and even different times from each other. The ages of patients seen in old age psychiatry departments span over 30 years. Individuals may have been influenced by two world wars, poverty and economic depression and may themselves have been raised by parents who grew up in Victorian times.

Clinical Illustration

Mr R at the age of 86 came to the attention of services in a panic about himself, his limited mobility and his expiring future. He was admitted to the day hospital where he was an assiduous attender of all scheduled occupational therapy groups, giving staff the impression that as well as being fearful he was avidly looking for something, some answer that he was unable to find. His greatest fear seemed to be of ending his days as his mother had, with a dementing illness in a mental hospital. Mr R showed no evidence of organic cognitive impairment but angrily berated himself and others if he was unable immediately to answer a question or if something temporarily slipped his mind. When not actively occupied he seemed in gloom and despair, not interacting with others attending the hospital but sitting apart and apparently uninvolved with anything except himself and his zimmer frame which he gave an occasional and presumably painful kick. The occupational therapist who took the current affairs group which Mr R attended was interested and intrigued by the paradox of some of his comments. He was self-deprecating while showing evident intelligence and thoughtfulness. She felt she could offer him a series of individual sessions with the theme of life review. Life review is a component of most psychological work with older people and can be adapted to the model in use – in this case psychodynamic. Reminiscence can of itself be adaptive, helping to maintain a sense of continuity of the self.

Mr R, in common with many older patients, was fearful and querulous that the person he had spent his life becoming had started to decay. He had been good at sports and proud of his body and attractive physique which were now letting him down. He had held the post of director of research for a well known engineering company and was anxious that his intelligence and skills would collapse as had his legs.

He had been married. Following a series of affairs about which he was subsequently apologetic his wife had divorced him. He did not remarry but was always sad not to have had children. In part this regret was that he would have liked to have had the opportunity to give a child some of the things he felt he had missed, his own father having died in World War I.

It was not easy for the therapist to see Mr R weekly for six months. He was frequently angry with her and with himself but at the same time he also gave the impression that he was eager to learn how to use what time remained for him, both in the day hospital and in life. Over the weeks he seemed to realise it was possible to grow up as you grow old, and that old age may be not only a time of loss but also of consolidation. Certainly it may be a time to regret mistakes and failings, but also one in which to view with pleasure and appropriate pride one's successes and achievements. The increased time alone may be spent in productive dialogue with internal objects – for Mr R with his father who died when he was six but not before he had developed an admiration for and identification with him. That his father had died a soldier's death fighting the enemy somehow encouraged Mr R to face his own death with determination 'not to let it beat me before it happens'.

He acknowledged mistakes he felt he had made in his life but with help was able to make some steps towards ameliorating a few of them. As a previously enthusiastic local historian he now became involved with a primary school project helping children understand the history of the area where they lived and went to school. He recontacted a widow with whom he had had a relationship following his divorce. The affair had ended in some acrimony and he wanted to try to put it right. He traced a friend with whom he had been close in the RAF during the war and for many years after. He had lost touch when his friend had moved to a different part of the country. He wrote a will, painful for him as it emphasised his childlessness. He decided to leave some of his estate to a nephew and a niece, and a large legacy to the RAF Benevolent Fund. He continued to have times when he felt despairing and disgusted with his ageing self but he was also able to value his experience, to apprehend his part in his own and others' lives, to acknowledge his role of being fatherless from World War I and a successful pilot in World War II, to give something to peers and to younger generations, and to achieve some degree of ego integrity.

OTHER DEVELOPMENTALISTS: EARLY AND CONTEMPORARY

The notion of change over time has been associated with the idea of inevitable decline. We are familiar with Shakespeare's ages of man in *As You Like It*. The sardonic Jaques does not make any of the seven ages sound particularly inviting, but by far the worst is the 'last scene of all', 'sans teeth, sans eyes, sans taste, sans everything'.

However, although change is certain, change is not synonymous with decline. Old Adam in the same play describes his advanced age 'as a lusty winter, frosty but kindly'. Reading Cicero (45 BC) is a reminder that ideas of positive change in old age are centuries old: 'It is not by muscle speed or physical dexterity that great things are achieved, but by reflection, force of character, and judgement; in these qualities old age is usually not only not poorer but is even richer.' Eastern philosophies have the concept of 'the way', suggesting a journey through life, a path to be taken of self-awareness to self-realisation. Jung (1931) (see Chapters 3 and 17) was the first contemporary adult developmentalist. He was interested in the psychology of the second half of life which he understood to be governed by different principles from the first half. For the young person whose life is mounting and unfolding his aims are those of nature, entrenchment in the world, propagation and care of children. He should not be too much occupied with himself. Whereas 'for the ageing person it is a duty and a necessity to give serious attention to himself'. Jung explains that this attitude is not in order for old people to be 'hypochondriacs, niggards, doctrinaires, applauders of the past or eternal adolescents' but for illumination of the self. In the second half of life one's focus is more on culture and spirituality. Jung cites so-called 'primitive tribes' where the old people are custodians of cultural heritage, mysteries and secrets, whereas in Western societies there is a confusion about age, with mothers being sisters to their daughters and fathers brothers to their sons.

The converse of and perhaps a defence against the idea of inevitable diminishment in old age is to erect an iconography of age (Garner & Ardern, 1998), to create idealised images of venerable wisdom, profound knowledge, fearless generosity and increasing creativity. Jung added the description 'wise' to the archetype senex, perhaps even for himself fearing a lessening of intellectual and creative powers. Culverwell and Martin (1999) remind us that it is just as much an illusion that older people develop wisdom through the passing of the years alone as is the view that people necessarily decline: 'like wine some mature better than others'. 'You are only young once but you can stay immature indefinitely' quipped Ogden Nash, touching on the idea of enduring character traits which may help or hinder one's passage through life. The same thoughts had occurred to the aged Cephalus who, in response to questioning about what the later years were like, replied:

> The truth is, Socrates, that these regrets, and also the complaints about . . . [relatives], are to be attributed to the same cause, which is not old age, but men's characters and tempers; for he who is of a calm and happy nature will hardly feel the pressure of age, but to him who is of an opposite disposition youth and age are equally a burden.
>
> (Plato, p.3)

So we learn that people take into the senium the character strengths and weaknesses developed over the years. These attributes and failings will not be static but fluctuate and interact with each other, whatever the age, as will different states of mind from different stages of development. Growth and development are not a linear chronological progression. They may even be discontinuous. Mental attitudes appropriate to a particular stage may be found throughout life, always with an interplay between different mental states which need to be accommodated and integrated (Waddell, 1998).

Throughout life disturbances in earlier phases can produce psychopathological change later. The ability to face loss is founded in very early capacities to bear psychic reality. Terry (1997) reminds us, 'in working with the elderly there is a tension between keeping in mind an awareness of developmental issues specific to phases of later life and understanding what has been revived from earlier times'.

Colarusso and Nemiroff (1981) present a series of seven hypotheses as a theoretical foundation for development in adulthood (Table 6.2). If development occurs in adulthood, so too can developmental arrest, fixation or regression. Nemiroff and Colarusso (1985) discuss *developmental resonance*. This is a more particular concept than empathy. It is about the therapist's ability to share and respect patients' experiences from all ages because they have either been there themselves or will be at some point in the future, all of us having a similar developmental framework. However, Nemiroff and Colarusso also point out that countertransference issues are affected by the fact that the therapist is likely to have had their training analysis/therapy at a relatively young age, and not to have dealt yet with this more adult time of their own lives. In addition, working with older patients the therapist will be the object of transference feelings from all stages in the life cycle. Not only the childhood past but also the adult past is a source of transference.

Hildebrand (1982), drawing on the work of Erikson and of King (1974, 1980), has delineated particular developmental tasks and difficulties which need to be negotiated for successful later life (see Table 6.3). For King (1980) it is clear that in the analysis of older people whatever infantile material needs to be addressed, in addition the traumas and psychopathology of puberty and adolescence must be re-experienced and worked through in the transference. Sandler (1978) reports the case of a narcissistic patient in which 'senescence revived adolescence'. For Schmid (1990) positive attempts at self-consolidation which are part of ageing may put people in conflict with society's norms. 'Having nothing to lose' in this situation he likens to

Table 6.2 Seven hypotheses for adult development

I	The nature of developmental processes is the same in the adult and the child
II	Development during the adult years is an ongoing dynamic process
III	Adult development is concerned with the continuing evolution and use of psychic structure rather than its formation
IV	The fundamental issues of childhood continue in altered form as central aspects of adult life
V	Developmental processes are influenced by the adult past, not only by childhood
VI	Bodily changes influence development in adulthood
VII	A central theme is the growing awareness of the finiteness of time and inevitability of death including one's own

Reproduced from *Adult Development: A new dimension in psychodynamic theory and practice* by Colarusso and Nemiroff (1981), with permission from Kluwer Academic/Plenum Publishers.

Table 6.3 Developmental tasks and difficulties in later life

- Fear of diminution/loss of sexual potency
- Threat of redundancy in work roles; being replaced by younger people
- The need to reconsider and possibly remake the marital relationship after children have left
- Awareness of one's own ageing, illness and possible dependence
- Awareness that what one can achieve now is limited
- The feeling of having failed as a parent (paradoxically exacerbated in the childless)
- Loss of a partner and of intimacy
- The fact of one's own death in terms of narcissistic loss and pain

(Hildebrand, 1982)

adolescent rebellion. For those of us beyond adolescence but not yet old enough to 'wear purple with a red hat that doesn't go' (from a poem 'Warning' by Jenny Joseph) we envy this confidence and insouciance which age brings to some.

That earlier developmental issues re-emerge in concentrated form in later life raises the question of definition of maturity. Bob Dylan's paradoxical lines from the song 'My Back Pages' (1964) suggest something about flexibility and a willingness to see something anew. For Freud (see Chapter 1) being mature meant being able '*Lieben und arbeiten*' (to love and to work). For Klein (see Chapter 2) it was an increased capacity to live in the depressive position – for Bion (1970) being able to go on developing. Waddell (1998) writes:

> The difference between maturity and immaturity hinges not on the fact of chronological years but on a person's capacity to bear intense emotional states; on the extent to which it is possible to think about, and reflect on psychic pain as a consequence of having found and sustained a relationship with external and internal figures who are able so to do.

REALITY

'Is it not strange that desire should so many years outlive performance?' says Poins in Shakespeare's *Henry IV*, Part II. For many people advancing years do bring multiple problems of performance. Those who have psychological strength in old age are able to manage these exigencies and even to take pleasure in younger relatives and friends being able to do things, without envying them. One of the skills in working therapeutically with older people is to be able to acknowledge the physical reality of their lives and incorporate this into the therapy along with external relationships, transference and the intrapsychic world. A reluctance to work with older people is in part due to prejudice and fear, a denial that development occurs or is possible in old age so near to the feared death or an assumption that all patients will have cognitive impairment and therefore it is not possible to work psychologically (see Chapter 15).

One does not become old suddenly. Adults of many ages are preoccupied by body changes. Although the body–mind relationship is emphasised in child development, it tends to be ignored in work with adults. Nemiroff and Colarusso (1985) suggest that the therapist needs to continually return to this because adult patients are deeply influenced by the body, its appearance, function and ageing. The patient may avoid examining this because of the narcissistic injury involved as one ages. The same unfortunately may be true for the therapist, who will have similar views and feelings about their own bodily decline.

McLean (1995) writes, not specifically about older patients, that therapists must be aware of biological issues and the realities of these for the patient. This needs to be about not only the biological research into psychiatric disorder, but also the handicaps which multiply and accumulate for older people, engendering pain and disability which are unlikely to be alleviated by the exploratory approach of psychotherapy. The goal of therapy may need to be adaptation to biological and social reality. Psychological mindedness is an important mitigating factor in dealing with adverse experiences.

CREATIVITY

Classical psychoanalytic theory attributes creativity to the sublimation of drives. Chasseguet-Smirgel (1984) expands on this, suggesting that the sublimated creative act may be used to achieve integrity. Many people are able to use later life as a time of positive development. Although for some retirement from work closes the door on creativity, for others the increased time available is put into further education, the realisation of undeveloped skills and talents, and keeping and making relationships. Some creative individuals have continued to work until advanced age. Giuseppe Verdi (1813–1901) composed the passionate opera *Otello* when he was 73 and continued to work for many subsequent years.

Perhaps ageing itself can, for those with sufficient internal resources, be a creative process in developmental adaptation. Although a number of new experiences at this time of life will be negative ones, even these may strengthen the internal world. Development may be stimulated by changes and losses. Settlage (1996) reports work with a centenarian patient whose development at this time included the acceptance of necessary dependency involving mutual trust and adaptation within role reversal with her daughter; a revision of values, perceiving their relativity; the acquisition of wisdom; and the acceptance of mortality. Other writers have focused more on development through mourning and the acceptance of loss; the outcome of earlier struggles determines how grief is managed later. Although loss can be a powerful stimulant of anger and depression, moving into something new always involves some loss. Pollack (1982) writes of 'mourning-liberation' – the ability to age well depends on the capacity to mourn for the self. Salzberger-Wittenberg (1970) writes of losses and mourning, strengthening and developing the individual:

> some losses are an inevitable part of our life experience and are indeed necessary for the attainment of mature adulthood. For the work of mourning can lead to a greater integration, strengthening of character, the development of courage, and to deeper concern for others as we come to appreciate the preciousness of others' and our own time of life.

Psychotherapy aims to help change, development and growth. In order to do this the patient needs to give up and lose maladaptive behaviour, erroneous values and beliefs, unrealistic infantile wishes and illusions. What is first experienced as a loss can become the starting point of a new development (Wolff, 1977). In the same way, things need to be given up in order to move on through the phases of life, to develop concern and integrity. Losses are not absolute, everything lost has left its trace. Some find even when friends or relatives are lost through death that conversations may continue within the memories and structures of the internal world, communication may be held with internal objects and earlier aspects of the self. Limentani (1995) states that 'we should regard old age as the fruit of our own creative actions'.

CONCLUSION

The phrase 'to grow old', although it has many negative connotations, also suggests something productive, something growing. Life review dominates old age, either as a purely personal task or with the help of the therapist. Through developing a personal narrative and understanding of the route one has taken, it is possible to see its commonality and its singularity, its pattern of intra- and interpersonal relationships. Ageing is a developmental task but one in which timing and sequencing is not always predictable. Development is an evolutionary process interacting with experience.

Erikson emphasises that into old age there are periods for potential change when there is still the possibility of influencing mental life. The details of development and possibilities for change are dependent not only on the individual but also on the social and historical context in which the individual finds himself. In a later work Erikson (1981) suggests that to be healthy in old age, one will be free of neurotic anxiety, but that is not the same as being 'absolved from existential dread' which affects all humans as they bring themselves into question.

Erikson's use of the word integrity, implying an emotional integration, brings to mind Klein's 'integrative processes' which is an acceptance of impulses to loved and valued objects that can be destructive as well as loving. *Growing* well into old age is not about striving to be young, but involves accepting oneself and one's life in all its complexities as it was and now is, accepting others with their positive and negative sides, accepting loss and disability as well as opportunities for new experiences and developing a balance of integrity over despair.

REFERENCES

Bateman, A., & Holmes, J. (1995). *Introduction to Psychoanalysis: Contemporary theory and practice*. London and New York: Routledge.

Bion, W. (1970). *Attention and Interpretation*. London: Tavistock Publications.

Chasseguet-Smirgel, J. (1984). Thoughts on the concept of reparation and the hierarchy of creative acts. *International Review of Psychoanalysis*, 11, 399–406.

Cicero, M.T. (45 BC). *De Senectute*. [Trans. Falconer, W.A. (1923). *On Old Age*. Harvard University Press.]

Colarusso, G.A., & Nemiroff, R.A. (1981). *Adult Development: A new dimension in psychodynamic theory and practice*. New York: Plenum Press.

Culverwell, A., & Martin, C. (1999). Psychotherapy with older adults. In: Croley, G. (ed) *Older People and Their Needs*. London: Whurr.

Erikson, E.H. (1959). Identity and the life cycle. *Psychological Issues Monograph, No. 1*. New York: International Universities Press.

Erikson, E.H. (1966). Eight ages of man. *International Journal of Psychiatry*, II, 281–300.

Erikson, E.H. (1981). Elements of a psychoanalytic theory of psychosocial development. In: S.I. Greenspan and G. Pollock (eds) *The Cause of Life. (Vol. 1): Infancy and early childhood*. Washington DC: US Department of Health and Human Services.

Garner, J., & Ardern, M. (1998). Reflections on old age. *Ageing and Mental Health*, 2(2), 92–93.

Hildebrand, H.P. (1982). Psychotherapy with older patients. *British Journal of Medical Psychology*, 55, 19–28.

Jung, C.G. (1931). The stages of life. *Collected Works 8*, 387–403. London: Routledge.

King, P.H.M. (1974). Notes on the psychoanalysis of older patients. *Journal of Analytical Psychology*, 19, 22–37.

King, P.H.M. (1980). The life cycle as indicated by the nature of the transference in the psychoanalysis of the middle aged and elderly. *International Journal of Psychoanalysis*, 61, 153–160.

Limentani, A. (1995). Creativity and the third age. *International Journal of Psychoanalysis*, 76, 825–833.

McLean, D. (1995). Two models, one mind: Integrating the biological and psychological. *Psychoanalytic Psychotherapy*, 9(2), 133–144.

Martindale, B. (1989). Becoming dependent again: The fears of some elderly persons and their younger therapists. *Psychoanalytic Psychotherapy*, 4(1), 67–75.

Martindale, B. (1998). On ageing, dying, death and eternal life. *Psychoanalytic Psychotherapy*, 12(3), 259–270.

Nemiroff, R.A., & Colarusso, C.A. (1985). *The Race Against Time: Psychotherapy and psychoanalysis in the second half of life*. New York and London: Plenum Press.

Plato (4th century BC). *The Republic*. [Trans. Jowett, B. (1894). Dover Thrift Edition 2000, p. 3.]

Pollack, G. (1982). On ageing and psychotherapy. *International Journal of Psychoanalysis*, 63, 275–281.

Rapaport, D. (1959). A historical survey of psychoanalytic egopsychology. Introduction to Erikson, E.H. *Identity and the Life Cycle*. New York: International Universities Press.

Salzberger-Wittenberg, I. (1970). *Psychoanalytic Insight and Relationships: A Kleinian approach*. London: Routledge & Kegan Paul.

Sandler, A.M. (1978). Psychoanalysis in later life: Problems in the psychoanalysis of an aging narcissistic patient. *Journal of Geriatric Psychoanalysis*, 11, 5–36.

Schmid, A.H. (1990). Dementia, related disorders, and old age: Psychodynamic dimensions in diagnosis and treatment. *American Journal of Psychoanalysis*, 50(3), 253–262.

Settlage, C.F. (1996). Transcending old age: Creativity, development and psychoanalysis in the life of a centenarian. *International Journal of Psychoanalysis*, 77, 549–564.

Shakespeare, W. (1971). *The Complete Works*. London: Oxford University Press. [*As You Like It*, 217–242. *Henry IV, Part 2*, 438–469.]

Terry, P. (1997). *Counselling the Elderly and Their Carers*. London: Macmillan.

Waddell, M. (1998). *Inside Lives: Psychoanalysis and the growth of the personality*. London: Duckworth, Tavistock Clinic Series.

Wolff, H.H. (1977). Loss: A central theme in psychotherapy. *British Journal of Psychology*, 50, 11–19.

Chapter 7

Group psychotherapy: Foulkes, Yalom and Bion

Sandra Evans

> The essence of man is social, not individual, unconsciously as well as consciously.
>
> (S.H. Foulkes, 1964)

HISTORICAL OVERVIEW

The Second World War, 1939–1945, was an important time for psychiatry generally and psychotherapy more particularly. Psychological trauma, 'shell shock', became recognised as a valid psychiatric condition, and soldiers were sent to military hospitals for treatment instead of being shot for cowardice. It was in Northfield, a military hospital, that 'Michael' Foulkes used a group therapy model to treat large numbers of traumatised soldiers. (His widow, Elizabeth Foulkes, has explained that when he moved to Britain, Sigmund preferred to drop his German name in favour of a more anglicised one.) Wilfred Bion and Tom Main, two of Foulkes' contemporary psychoanalysts were also using group, milieu and therapeutic community models at this time (Main, 1977).

Bion's work in a military hospital stemmed from the need to re-introduce discipline into the lives of traumatised soldiers (Harrison & Clarke, 1992). The small 'Bionic' group was a form that initially examined how the men could best perform a task. This task could be something that was outside the group, such as fighting a common enemy, or it could be formed to address issues within the group itself, for example, the issues of leadership or of taking personal responsibility.

Bion noted in detail features that are common in small groups. He termed these *Basic Assumptions*. These are part of primitive group activities. The three basic assumptions are as follows. (1) *The group looks to its leader for nourishment in all modalities.* In all new groups people will look for rules and for direction. In groups of older adults in institutional settings, this is often expressed as the desire for a 'class': a learning forum. The therapist is looked to for guidance, as in most new groups. (2) *The group allows pairings (non-heterosexual included) that instil hope from the phantasy that a Messiah will be delivered from this union.* Bion understood the tolerance which groups often show towards exclusive pairings in these terms; that groups await the coming of someone or something that will rescue them from their condition. This may indeed refer to the Human Condition, about which Beckett had much to say in *Waiting for Godot.* (3) *The group meets to either fight a common enemy, or to flee one.* This is a task element of the group, and may give the group a sense of purpose and cohesiveness. The enemy may be neurotic difficulties within group members (Bion & Rickman, 1943).

Bionic groups tend to maintain the leader as more prominent and active. Communications tend to be between patients and the leader and less concentrated on interpersonal issues between members. If the Bionic group is a therapeutic one, there is more emphasis on the intrapsychic than the interpersonal, although 'group as a whole' interventions are also possible.

In the United States a group therapy movement developed along slightly different lines, although many essential similarities exist. The original idea of group psychotherapy has been attributed to Moreno (1959), better known for his work in psychodrama.

The therapeutic factors that appear to be common to all groups are elucidated thoroughly by Yalom (1985), an American group psychotherapist who has also published vignettes of older patients in individual therapy. Most prominently, he cites the factor 'universality' – the fact that our problems are common and shared by many people. This is of significance particularly to those who are feeling isolated and uniquely impoverished. To find solace and power from like-minded or afflicted individuals is common to self-help groups and political lobbies alike. Yalom emphasised the factor he called 'altruism'. This is the ability to help others, usually by problem solving, but also by sharing something of one's own life to which other group members can relate. This can be of importance to an isolated older person who feels they have become useless.

Foulkes often fantasised about what his psychiatric outpatients would make of each other and their symptoms if they were all to meet in the waiting room. The reality of the group proved a fruitful area for the understanding of the processes that take place as a group evolves, and enabled the development of a theory of group analysis which derived a great deal from the field of social theory as well as from psychoanalysis.

GROUP THERAPY WITH OLDER PEOPLE

That working together in groups can be good for older people is no longer in dispute, and there are many accounts of the benefits of small group therapy with elderly people (Hunter, 1989; MacLennan et al., 1988; Canete et al., 2000; Evans et al., 2001). There are also some few examples of practice-based research on the subject (Ong et al., 1987; Woods & Fonagy, 1996; Radley et al., 1997). What we lack at present are adequate data on which older people can benefit best from group work, and which treatment models are most useful. It is well known that older people have high levels of depressive symptoms and anxiety (Evans & Katona, 1993) and that a great deal of this is related to losses and changes in circumstances (Murphy, 1982). Personality structures appear to be important aetiological factors, with a suggestion that those with pre-elderly personality disorder find negotiating the challenges of ageing more difficult (Reich et al., 1988; Abrams, 1995). Interpersonal problems and lack of ability to form intimate and confiding relationships (Lowenthal, 1965) have long been thought to be particular problems.

It is important to emphasise that there are negative aspects of groups about which the practitioner should be informed. Despite reports of benefits, agreement that older people can benefit from psychological therapies (Evans, 2000) and lively accounts of groups, they are not widespread in the Health Service generally. There exists for patients a resistance to working therapeutically in groups. There are those who are likely to see the sharing of a therapist or facilitator as a dilution of therapeutic effect, and as utterly pointless to those individuals who are seeking to recreate a 'special' and intimate relationship with one other. The post-modern culture of individuality sees community as a threat and as a loss of personal freedoms.

The presence of others in the group may represent another kind of threat; that of merging with other people beyond existence, resulting in the loss of the self (Bion, 1961). The additional threat for an older person joining a group of elderly people is that of the double projective identification or malignant mirroring (Zinkin, 1983). This is what happens when two or more people project onto each other split-off and unwanted aspects of themselves to such an extent that they cannot tolerate each other's company. The chapter author has proposed that this occurs with respect to ageing when older people refuse to have anything to do with venues for 'old people'. The negative images of ageing exhibited by the media and in our modern culture generally are absorbed unconsciously by all of us, including older people. They may shun offers to attend venues with other elderly persons, in order to avoid feeling contaminated and further stigmatised (Evans, 1998; Garner & Ardern, 1998).

Professionals may be anxious about working with older patients in a psychological or psychodynamic way, suggesting they feel a lack of experience to work with this client group (Murphy, 2000). Professional staff may be equally resistant to running groups, perhaps feeling that they are offering their patients second-best treatment. The fact that offering a group treatment can be cost-effective does not mean that it is necessarily inferior. Group conductors may dislike the exposure they have in facing their patients. It is more difficult to be a blank screen as a group therapist. In a small group of seven or eight patients, nuances of one's reactions may be picked up and exposed in the group and become part of the group currency; this applies as much to the therapist as other group members. One's personal resilience in the face of potential hostility is therefore required to be greater than is necessary when working individually.

The effort of forming a new group is significant and may therefore defeat professionals working in short-term placements. They may find working therapeutically with older people unattractive, and may anticipate a Monty Pythonesque catalogue of somatic complaints being discussed, rather than moving accounts of personal lives. In fact one can expect all of the above to be possible from groups of older people.

FOULKESIAN GROUP ANALYSIS

Despite these negative preconceptions, many people find group therapy useful. There are psychotherapy organisations which offer a training almost exclusively in group work, and which continue to produce academic papers on theory and practice of psychotherapeutic work in groups. Those exponents of S.H. Foulkes work from a particular therapeutic framework, which includes the group itself as an entity to be analysed in addition to the individual members. This 'figure–ground' framework draws a great deal on the work of Norbert Elias (1969) and his perspective on social theory. Essentially, the Eliasian school did not see the individual as isolated from their community or from history (1978). It viewed society as the central theme around which humans revolved and with which we are infused (Dalal, 1998). This idea has particular resonance for working with older people because of the quasi-anthropological nature of working with an age-distinct cohort who will often have different cultural and historical reference points than those of the younger therapist (see Chapter 18). The older adults themselves will need to be examined in terms of their environments, past as well as present, in order to understand the personal transformations that have gone before (Boyd, 1991).

Foulkes put forward the idea that the social group provides a 'norm' within which individuals have some latitude but which serves as a kind of 'check' on 'deviant' behaviour. For this reason he encouraged the small therapy group to be filled with as diverse a number of people and psychopathologies as possible. The differences between individuals would offer alternative ways of being and behaving, and the peer-group effect would be powerful enough to extinguish problem behaviours (Foulkes, 1964). It is clear from this that there are cognitive and behavioural mechanisms at work in small group therapy, as well as intra- and interpersonal ones.

Foulkes described the matrix (Foulkes & Anthony, 1984), a web of human experience and understanding that was constructed between individuals in a group over time, and which connects people. The matrix also highlights differences between people when new people arrive into a group, or indeed move countries and cultures. Their lack of knowledge of the group history and culture defines them as new. They may or may not be given the opportunity to learn this information. This aspect of the group functioning will define the group also. Anthropologists choose to study group culture; but will perceive aspects of culture more quickly if it differs from their own. Reflexive anthropologists will recognise the dynamic effect of themselves on the study group, and the study group on them in turn.

Foulkes wrote of the 'group unconscious' which has resonances with Jung's collective unconscious (1951) and which he treated as an entity in itself. Individual members may vocalise something that they feel is personal to them, only to find that they speak for everyone. It may also refer to primitive affects and desires that are attributable to the human condition. This is also akin to the notion of social unconscious which Hopper has attributed to Fromm (Hopper, 1996), which describes to some extent the particular anatomy and culture of a social group. As Bollas described in 1987, individuals begin to know things from before birth that are not consciously available to them. These 'unthought known' things are part of the social unconscious.

ASSESSMENT

In terms of assessment for group psychotherapy, the principles of individual psychotherapy prevail. Assessment should be made of a patient's willingness to enter into treatment, and to challenge and explore aspects of themselves and their relationships. Poverty of ego-strength, extreme narcissism and a tendency to relate to the world in a primarily paranoid manner, are all features that should be treated with caution. There would be no absolute contra-indication, except perhaps a facility for becoming psychotic. The group therapist needs to bear in mind the goals of treatment, the type of group available and the nature of the patient's problem (Barnes et al., 1999).

Nitsun, in 1989, described how a new group with its new patients could be likened to a newborn infant, with similar fragmented sense of self and similar anxieties. The early group needs a great deal of containment, reverie (Bion, 1962) and primary maternal preoccupation (Winnicott, 1960) from the therapist. As the group matures and the reliance on the group conductor minimises, as do the projections of strength and omniscience, individual group members feel less anxious and more inclined to play and explore. The mature group can contain more anxiety and can accommodate more disturbed new members without significant threat to its integrity.

When assessing a patient for group therapy, one needs to be mindful of these issues. It is also helpful to imagine how a particular patient will relate to others in the group under consideration. When making these assessments, it is useful to think about factors in the patient which may isolate or stigmatise him or her. Issues such as race, religion, sexual orientation and age can be displayed as a problem when they are not really the issue; and this can detract from the real work of the group. Patients may also hide behind these superficial qualities. Having other members of different races or age in twos or threes reduces a sense of heightened difference or isolation.

THERAPEUTIC FACTORS IN GROUP ANALYSIS FOR OLDER ADULTS

Negativity about old age is learnt in the social group. It is a logical step to consider that it might also be unlearned in a therapeutic group which acts as a mirror counteracting negativity (Pines, 1984). The small group can develop to encourage people to look at themselves from different viewpoints, from the perspectives of people sitting opposite and beside them for example. In this way they can challenge entrenched views about themselves and about old age. There is the opportunity to take back projections. Initially these may be projections of ageing, decrepitude and dependency; unwanted parts of themselves which they cheerfully put into other old people. Since the other group members are also old, they will have to examine this at some point, if they remain in therapy. Equally, but later on as time progresses and the maturity of the group develops, idealised parts of themselves such as wisdom and strength with which the probably younger therapist is imbued, can be 'taken back' and owned by the older group member, thus enhancing their personal strength and resilience. This taking back of aspects of the self theoretically strengthens the ego, which Foulkes himself called 'ego training in action', and helps to develop positive coping strategies to deal with the narcissistic injuries of ageing. The small group may offer opportunities to think in new ways and give strength and support to people in making significant changes in their lives.

Clinical Illustration
Harry, now in his mid-seventies, has fallen in love with a younger woman whom he does admit he idealises somewhat, although he freely admits that he is enjoying the deliciousness of the experience. The group colludes for a while with the fantasy element of it, but are struck by Harry's reluctance to declare his love to his partner. He readily describes his fears that he will damage the affair by such a declaration; particularly that he will feel trapped by a sense of commitment. He goes on to describe previous relationships with women where he played games and was dishonest about his feelings.

The group encourages him to look at his fear of dependency and his real anxiety that a declaration of love from him will scare off his partner; a prospect which he could not bear. He returns some time later to tell the group that he has asked his partner to marry him. She has accepted.

The therapist links his behaviour towards the group – that of arriving late in a whirlwind of new anxieties and demands, or not at all – to his behaviour towards the significant women in his life. He is capable of sustaining short bursts of intimacy with the group, but cannot commit fully and admit his dependency. Reference is then made to his previously aired regret that his mother was unable to show him love or tenderness, and that his love for her had been rejected.

The example above gives some insights into the possibility for change in group analysis. One model for the anatomy of the process of therapeutic interventions suggests the need for a triangular model of interpretation (Malan, 1979). The above demonstrates the first two sides of the triangle, in which the member has recreated in a behaviour towards his therapy group, a repeated pattern of behaviours towards significant past relationships. The third side of the triangle links the here and now behaviour to the there and then, and to the early object relations. Linking the two offers the individual an opportunity to see what he or she does to others. The third side of the triangle is often available to the therapist (or other group members), and if it is known, may be considered as worth bringing up (see Chapter 11). Linking all three is thought to provide sufficient power to make some of these unconscious repetition compulsions conscious, thus enabling an individual to begin to alter the entrenched behavioural patterns which contribute to his or her difficulties.

REPORTED BENEFITS

Groups have been shown to provide improvements in reality testing, depression and self-esteem, as well as changes in maladaptive behaviour and readiness for discharge from institutions (Tross & Blum, 1988).

Martindale (1995) cited a paper by Kelly recording the benefits of groups for acutely mentally ill inpatients. This described additional improvements in staff morale and ability to understand the people in their care. Hunter (1989) reported on groups with institutionalised elders with dementia, where she noted people regaining self-esteem and a sense of connectedness. Furthermore, she argued that older people can be more motivated to work dynamically than younger adults. Groups on a general psychiatric unit ameliorated a number of psychological problems associated with ageing in a small number of sessions (Goodman, 1998).

MODIFICATIONS FOR GROUPS OF AGED PEOPLE

It is not unreasonable to consider tailoring the type of therapeutic setting in order to accommodate people's needs. One may have to modify the physical environment or the timing and length of group to minimise discomfort, or to cope with variations in ability to concentrate. Despite the Foulkesian model of relative non-interference and trusting the group, one may need to be more active as the therapist; more prepared to intervene. This is in order to reduce anxiety and to prevent hurtful rejection of fragile individuals (Evans et al., 2001; Martindale, 1995), for example by racial or sexual prejudices and other differences, which older people can be alarmingly unafraid to discuss. More anxious and depressed individuals may be frightened by too much silence and may not return.

A heterogeneous group is important in terms of its psychopathology (Foulkes, 1964). A reasonable mix of problems provides a mean of normality and prevents stagnation into one kind of difficulty, particularly with depressed individuals. Groups of elderly and 'pre-elderly' (Esquerro, 1989) may counteract the sense of older people being 'lumped together' while maintaining a sense of common interest, e.g. retirement, illness, problems with children, etc. Consideration needs to be given to cognitive functioning, as too great a difference in this area may increase an individual's sense of isolation. Equally, motivation for change needs to be present, and identifiable at assessment. Those who just want a bit of company will frustrate a hard-working group and will be better joining a social activity which will not be so challenging or demanding (Martindale, 1995).

Working with a co-therapist may help by increasing the opportunity for monitoring countertransference, and allows a sharing of frustration and negative feelings about a group in an informal way. Therapists also experience the projective identifications of group members. It is essential to isolate these and distinguish them from countertransference; but this can also be checked out by discussion after the group with a co-facilitator or supervisor. Feelings about patients in the group may be complicated by generational difficulties in the therapist's own life.

Clinical Illustration

Nettie presents herself to her new bereavement group in a similar way to the way she faces the world. She displays a 'victim' quality, which belies her underlying aggression and anger. The therapist's mother behaves in a similar manner and has done all her life. This may have been an unconscious factor in the therapist's motivation for training as a mental health professional, but they enjoy a good relationship normally.

The therapist is aware of disliking Nettie, and of finding her too demanding. At the same time she finds herself willing to spend less and less of her free time with her own mother, who is also widowed. Her co-therapist thinks Nettie is needy, but he quite likes her and denies a similar visceral response to her demands.

Goals may need to be modified; one may have to strive for acceptance of loss and a decline in mastery rather than the standard need to 'get better'.

Independence may not be possible; many people fear dependence or have unconscious memories of an earlier persecuted dependence (Martindale, 1989). The therapist may need to withstand much envious or enraged attack before an alliance is gained.

One has to accept that denial or 'flight' (Bion, 1961) may be an important defence: a constant onslaught of pain and grief is difficult to bear without the diversion of the banal and the prosaic. 'Bus stop talk' can still add to group cohesiveness and can be supportive; but the therapist must also be alive to the possibility that it excludes some members and can be used to avoid some painful issues inappropriately. The therapist must be clear about the boundaries of the group, particularly the timing of its end. This is one of the key tasks of the conductor. Resistance to ending therapy may be unconsciously linked to death (King, 1980) and is a phenomenon experienced by therapists and staff in NHS settings as much as by the patients themselves (Evans et al., 2001).

Clinical Illustration
Morris has a wife who is gravely ill. He has been looking after her diligently for several years but his health is suffering and he is depressed and feels guilty when he finds it difficult to tolerate Frankie's sickness. He comes to a group for support but finds it difficult to talk about himself and his needs. Frankie is his 'passport' to the group, but then he feels bound to talk about her rather than his own sadness. The group is coming up to a break; a fact which no one has been able to address.

Nora, a flirtatious woman in her mid-seventies, is talking about love (something that is absent in her life). Morris becomes visibly agitated, makes his excuses and leaves. The group is left feeling terrible, aware that Morris wanted something but was unable to ask for it, and now there would be a month before they would meet again. The therapist is aware of perhaps failing to intervene early enough for Morris, but tries to retrieve the situation for the others by acknowledging the need to fly into phantasy when life gets painful. For Morris however, his need at that time was to have space to feel pain and the loss of his wife and for a while, the group's support.

ASSOCIATED DIFFICULTIES AND SIDE EFFECTS

Groups are places where all sorts of unpredictable things can happen and where people sometimes abdicate responsibility. Feelings change rapidly in small and large groups and can be magnified greatly (Agazarian, 1994). One can feel excited and exhilarated in a group; the converse is also possible. There exists an inherent negative potential of all kinds of groups including organisations (Nitsun, 1996), which has the power to destroy the group structure and which can have adverse effects on its members. For example, a group that cannot tolerate or admit to negative characteristics may identify them prominently in one individual who is then attacked. The 'scapegoat' may then be ejected or may choose to leave the group, making everyone feel better for a while. However, because they have been projected rather than 'worked through', the characteristics will creep back into consciousness again eventually.

Groups can become part of a pathological institutional ritual that is introduced into hospital services without thought. It is not uncommon to see the most junior member of a team being told to run a group. Inexperience and lack of training in the running of groups is serious and this is an area where it matters. At best these groups will be a pleasant experience for most and supportive for some. At worst, vulnerable people can be exposed to scapegoating, intolerance and a variety of projective mechanisms. This is not to suggest that everyone who runs groups must be a psychoanalyst. Sincerity and a genuine affinity for working with older people is more important, but staff need to be supported by proper supervision and the opportunity to think in a self-reflective manner.

Supervision is an essential part of working dynamically with patients. Professionals will have their own reasons, conscious and unconscious, for working in the mental health services. Even those persons who have had extensive personal therapy may fall prey to their own unconscious and have their blind spots; supervision should therefore be considered to be an important factor in the maintenance of quality in the therapeutic relationship, and should be an issue of *clinical governance* within psychiatric services. Supervision provides a forum in which to discuss the process of therapy sessions, the atmosphere in the group and the feelings elicited in the therapist. It is distinct from clinical supervision, which is about medical or nursing management of patients, and requires a relationship based on mutual trust and rules about confidentiality. Supervision itself can be conducted in groups, which can provide a useful opportunity for mutual learning. Aspects of patient/therapist interactions and interactions between group members can be looked at in detail and will often provide a new understanding of communications, over which the therapist may have become previously stuck (Sproul-Bolton et al., 1995).

Adequate training is an important part of personal and professional development and needs to be available for individuals working psychodynamically. Decisions will need to be made about the level of regression that can be tolerated. Some patients may find the experience of dependence, one aspect of regression, too painful or threatening (Martindale, 1989). Other people will dissociate into fragmented selves which may be their experience of earlier existence. Understanding of these issues is vital. Patients with fragile egos who have experienced a psychotic breakdown may dissociate once more if their defences are invaded by too analytic a stance; supportive work may be what is required instead to keep people well and out of hospital.

Early on in group treatment, patients may experience a worsening of symptoms, particularly anxiety. Another difficulty that needs to be made explicit to people embarking on psychotherapeutic treatment is that not everyone will be happy with the changes that patients can make in their lives (see Chapter 9). Sometimes partners or family members will find new behaviours threatening. Others may have to re-adjust their image of the person, and families may be a powerful force opposing change. As people age, families may feel they may make decisions on their parents' or grandparents' behalf, and may not appreciate a late-emerging independence.

Boundaries are much harder to maintain in institutional settings; particularly wards and day centres, possibly resulting in a dilution of the group therapeutic potential and putting confidentiality at risk. Interactions between patients outside a group may be extensions of group process which, if not brought back to the group forum, may be lost to analysis. This may hinder progress; worse still it may have a deleterious effect on relationships by complicating alliances, and developing potentially anti-therapeutic subgroups. Confidentiality is also potentially problematic. In units dealing with people with mental illness the risk of suicide is a real one. Disclosing information from the group sessions in a hospital should be at the discretion of the therapist, however disclosures of suicidal thoughts or behaviour will need to be passed on to the relevant people. The therapists will have a duty of care to the patient, and a responsibility to act appropriately in such circumstances. Other group members are under an ethical obligation to maintain confidentiality about their fellow patients, and this should be made explicit at the outset.

SUMMARY

The evidence from work to date indicates that group psychological therapies, cognitive as well as psychodynamic and interpersonal, benefit older people suffering from depression and anxiety disorders (Goodman, 1998; Woods & Fonagy, 1996; O'Rourke & Hadjistavropoulos, 1997; Radley et al., 1997; Reynolds et al., 1999).

More research is required of a practice-based kind (Margison et al., 2001), to assist with treatment models and adverse effects. Since benefits exist, treatment needs to be accessible to all. Professional staff should appreciate unconscious processes and be aware of their own motivation for working with this patient group. Training and supervision must be an integral part of practice in order to achieve and maintain high standards of practice.

REFERENCES

Abrams, R.C. (1995). Personality disorders. In: Lindesay, J. (ed) *Neurotic Disorders in the Elderly*. Oxford: Oxford University Press.

Agazarian, Y. (1994). *In Ring of Fire. Primitive Object Relations in the Group*. Schermer, V. (ed). London: Routledge.

Barnes, W., Ernst, S., & Hyde, K. (1999). *An Introduction to Groupwork: A group analytic perspective*. London: Macmillan Press Ltd.

Bion, W. (1961). *Experiences in Groups*. London: Tavistock.

Bion, W. (1962). A theory of thinking. *International Journal of Psychoanalysis*, 43.

Bion, W. & Rickman, J. (1943). Intra-group tensions in therapy: Their study as a task of the group. *Lancet*, ii, 678–681.

Bollas, C. (1987). *The Shadow of the Object*. London: Free Association Books.

Boyd, J. (1991). Facilitating personal transformations in small groups. In: R. Boyd (ed) *Personal Transformations on Groups: A Jungian perspective*. London & New York: Routledge.

Canete, M., Stormont, F., & Esquerro, A. (2000). Group analytic psychotherapy with the elderly. *British Journal of Psychotherapy*, 17(1).

Dalal, F. (1998). Interlude between Foulkes and Elias. In: *Taking the Group Seriously: Towards a post Foulkesian group analytic theory*. London: Jessica Kingsley.

Elias, N. (1969). Sociology and psychiatry. In: S.H. Foulkes & G. Stewart Prince *Psychiatry in a Changing Society*. London: Tavistock.

Elias, N. (1978). *The History of Manners: The civilising process. Vol. 1*. Oxford: Basil Blackwell.

Esquerro, A. (1989). Group psychotherapy with the pre-elderly. *Group Analysis*, 22, 299–308.

Evans, S. (1998). Beyond the mirror: A group analytic exploration of late life depression. *Ageing & Mental Health*, 2(2), 94–99.

Evans, S. (2000). More disappointing treatment outcomes in late life depression (Letter to Editor). *British Journal of Psychiatry*, 177(3), 281–282.

Evans, S., Chisholme, P., & Walsh, J. (2001). A dynamic psychotherapy group for the elderly. *Group Analysis*, 34(2).

Evans, S., & Katona, C.L.E. (1993). The epidemiology of depressive symptoms in elderly primary care attenders. *Dementia*, 4, 327–333.

Foulkes, S.H. (1964). *Therapeutic Group Analysis*. London: Allen & Unwin.

Foulkes, S.H., & Anthony, E. (1984). *Group Psychotherapy: The psychoanalytic approach*. London: Karnac.

Garner, J., & Ardern, M. (1998). Reflections on old age. *Ageing & Mental Health*, 2(2), 92–93.

Goodman, R. (1988). A geriatric group in an acute care psychiatric teaching hospital: Pride or prejudice? In: B. MacLennan et al. (eds) *Group Psychotherapies with the Elderly*, American Group Psychotherapy Monograph 5. New York: International Universities Press.

Harrison, T., & Clarke, D.J. (1992). The Northfield experiments. *British Journal of Psychiatry*, 160, 698–708.

Hopper, E. (1996). The social unconscious in clinical work. *Group Analysis*, 20(1), 7–42.

Hunter, J. (1989). Reflections on psychotherapy with ageing people, individually and in groups. *British Journal of Psychiatry*, 154, 250–252.

Jung, C.J. (1951). On synchronicity. *Collected Works 8*. London: Routledge.

Kelly, C. et al. (personal communication). The workings of a psychodynamic group in an acute elderly mentally ill unit. Unpublished.

King, P. (1980). The life cycle as indicated by the nature of the transference of the middle aged and elderly. *International Journal of Psychoanalysis*, 61, 153–160.

Lowenthal, M.F. (1965). Antecedents of isolation and mental illness in old age. *Archives of General Psychiatry*, 12, 245–254.

MacLennan, B. et al. (1988). *Group Psychotherapies with the Elderly*. American Group Psychotherapy Monograph 5. New York: International Universities Press.

Main, T. (1977). The concept of the therapeutic community: Variations and vicissitudes. *Group Analysis*, 10(suppl), 2–16.

Malan, D. (1979). *Individual Psychotherapy and the Science of Psychodynamics*. London: Butterworths.

Margison, F., Barkham, M., Evans, C., McGrath, G., Mellor-Clark, J. Audin, K. et al. (2001). Measurement and psychotherapy: Evidence-based practice and practice-based evidence. *British Journal of Psychiatry*, 177, 123–130.

Martindale, B.V. (1989). Becoming dependent again. The fears of some elderly patients and their younger therapists. *Psychoanalytic Psychotherapy*, 4(1), 67–75.

Martindale, B.V. (1995). Psychological treatments II. Psychodynamic approaches. In: Lindesay, J. (ed) *Neurotic Disorders in the Elderly*. Oxford: Oxford University Press.

Moreno, J. (1959). Interpersonal therapy, group psychotherapy and the function of the unconscious. *Psychodrama*, 2.

Murphy, E. (1982). The social origins of depression in old age. *British Journal of Psychiatry*, 141, 135–142.

Murphy, E. (2000). Provison of psychotherapy services for older people. *Psychiatric Bulletin*, 24, 181–184.

NHS Executive (1996). *NHS Psychotherapy Services in England: Review of strategic policy*. London: Department of Health.

Nitsun, M. (1989). Early development: Linking the individual and the group. *Group Analysis*, 22(3), 249–261.

Nitsun, M. (1996). *The Anti-Group: Destructive forces in the group and their therapeutic potential*. London: Routledge.

Ong, Y.L., Martineau, F., Lloyd, C., & Robbins, I. (1987). A support group for the depressed elderly. *International Journal of Geriatric Psychiatry*, 2, 119–123.

O'Rourke, N., & Hadjistavropoulos, F. (1997). The relative efficacy of psychotherapy in the treatment of geriatric depression. *Ageing and Mental Health*, 1(4), 305–310.

Pines, M. (1984). Mirroring in group analysis as a developmental and therapeutic process. In: T.E. Lear (ed) *Spheres of Group Analysis*, pp. 118–136. London: Group Analytic Society.

Radley, M., Reston, C., Bates, F., Pontefract, M., & Lindesay, J. (1997). Effectiveness of group anxiety management with elderly clients of community psychogeriatric team. *International Journal of Geriatric Psychiatry*, 12, 729–784.

Reich, J., Nduaguba, M., & Yates, W. (1988). Age and sex distribution of DSM-III personality cluster traits in community population. *Comprehensive Psychiatry*, 29, 298–303.

Reynolds, C.F., Frank, E., Perel, J.M., Imber, S.D., Cornes, C., Miller, M.D. et al. (1999). Nortrypliline and IPT as maintenance therapies for recurrent major depression: a randomised controlled trial in patients older than 59 years. *Journal of the American Medical Association*, 281(1), 83–84.

Sproul-Bolton, R., Nitsun, M., & Knowles, J. (1995). Supervision in the NHS. In: Meg Sharpe (ed) *The Third Eye*. London, New York: Routledge.

Tross, S., & Blum, J. (1988). A review of group psychotherapy with the older adult: Practise and research. In: MacLennan et al. (eds) *Group Psychotherapies with the Elderly*. American Group Psychotherapy Monograph. New York: International Universities Press.

Winnicott, D. (1960). The theory of the parent–infant relationship. In: Winnicott, D.W. *The Maturational Processes and the Facilitating Environment*. London: Hogarth, 1965.

Woods, R., & Fonagy, P. (1996). Psychological therapies for older people. In: A. Roth & P. Fonagy (eds) *What Works for Whom? A critical review of psychotherapy research*. New York: Guilford Press.

Yalom, I.D. (1985). *The Theory and Practice of Group Psychotherapy*. New York: Basic Books.

Zinkin, L. (1983). The malignant mirroring. *Group Analysis*, 16, 113–129.

Chapter 8

Inpatient dynamics: Thinking, feeling and understanding

Roger Wesby

The child is father of the man

(William Wordsworth, 1802)

This chapter looks at the ways in which psychodynamic ideas can contribute to the understanding and management of patients on any ordinary 'functional' psychiatric ward for the elderly. Psychodynamic factors are always present, affecting to a greater or lesser extent such things as presentation of symptoms and illness, response to treatment, and staff–patient interactions.

THE UNCONSCIOUS

The central concept of psychodynamic thinking is the presence of an unconscious part of the mind that is timeless. The unconscious contains feelings and thoughts that are unacceptable to our conscious minds, parts of ourselves that we do not want. They are kept unconscious by 'defence mechanisms' which are present throughout life (Berezin, 1972) and protect the conscious mind from the intolerable unconscious contents that constantly seek expression. There is, therefore, conflict between opposing forces. (See Chapter 1 for further details on defence mechanisms.) In a therapeutic setting, 'resistance' by a patient to treatment may be evidence of these defences responding to a threat to alter the status quo. In formal psychotherapeutic work, 'interpretation' attempts to make conscious something which was unconscious by linking a thought, feeling or behaviour to its unconscious meaning (Gabbard, 1994).

Also present in the unconscious are representations of experiences from childhood, particularly of the relationship with the mother, that have been internalised ('introjected'). These experiences can be positive (the breast feeding baby with loving mother) or negative (the hungry baby with absent mother who is experienced as rejecting and hostile). These internalised relationships, ever present in the unconscious, continually affect how we relate to others in adulthood. This leads to the phenomenon of 'transference', the experiencing of another person as a significant other ('object') from the past, and of 'repetition compulsion', the tendency to repeat past patterns of behaviour in the present. On a psychiatric ward, the transference of feelings and attitudes from a patient's past will affect how the patient relates to members of staff (and other patients). The complementary term for the feelings that staff have about their patients is 'countertransference'. The unconscious, then, is dynamic: it affects all that we have done, are doing and will do.

PERSONALITY

Central to psychodynamic work is the assessment of personality which develops by a complex interaction between genes and environment. Early environment is crucial to personality development. Bowlby contended that a deeper understanding of the complexities of normal development could only be reached through an integration of developmental psychology, psychoanalysis, biology and neuroscience (Schore, 2001) (and see Chapter 4 on attachment theory). An awareness of the dynamics of the patient's personality helps to understand the ways in which the patient reacts to his or her environment: the origins of symptoms, the response to treatment and reaction to future life events. Excessive use of defence mechanisms caused by a traumatic early life leaves the individual trapped in relating to the world in fixed ways that prevent the necessary adaptation to the changes of old age. Research confirms that adaptation to stressful life events is improved by personality attributes such as extraversion and openness (Headley & Wearing, 1989), attributes that encourage relating to others. Psychiatric illness such as depression, anxiety and psychosis is more likely in a person who is genetically susceptible and whose personality cannot cope with the stress of old age.

DOES AGEING HAVE TO BE STRESSFUL?

A feeling of (subjective) wellbeing embodies feelings of inner and outer security, wholeness and satisfaction with life. It derives largely from personality (Costa & McCrae, 1980) which in younger people is usually cushioned from adverse life events by secure positions within a loving relationship, family, job and society. Self-esteem is nourished further by social status, physical health, sound mind and sexual potency which generate feelings of self-control and mastery. Fears of dependency and death can be put to one side because of an optimistic sense of a future: there is still time to put things right. All this is reinforced by a culture that values achievement, beauty and youth.

As old age advances, many of these external supports fragment: retirement may bring financial insecurity, loss of role and status and altered patterns of relationships with partner and family. Self-esteem may be injured further by loss of physical health, strength, beauty, cognitive ability and sexual potency. With death of a partner and friends, fears of death are difficult to avoid, heightened perhaps by having to move into and be dependent upon an institution (King, 1980). Loss of independence may be the most painful loss of all (Porter, 1991), reverting to that dependent state into which the person was born.

As these outer supports fail, the older person is left to depend increasingly on inner strengths: of 'ego' and 'self' and their defence mechanisms, all contributing (along with genetic influences) to the personality. If inner security is tenuous (maladaptive defences), containment of anxiety will depend necessarily upon external resources whose loss in old age will result in feelings of being 'unwell'. This will be made worse by any organic deterioration caused by a dementing illness.

SPECTRUM OF PERSONALITY VULNERABILITY

Vulnerability of personality, therefore, is relative. 'Normal' personalities have their defences and vulnerabilities too. In psychodynamic work, one is assessing the uniqueness of the personality: its defences and vulnerabilities, and how it is interacting with its current environment. In keeping with this idea, it follows that there is a spectrum of personality vulnerability with 'normal' personality at one end and at the other so-called 'personality disorder', a term that has rather fixed, undynamic connotations. In other words, one is assessing not necessarily whether there is a personality disorder or not, but how much personality disorder or dysfunction there is. So ingrained has the definition of personality disorder become that clinicians may be reticent to diagnose personality dysfunction or disorder presenting for the first time in elderly patients with an apparently 'sound premorbid personality'. In their meta-analysis, Abrams and Horowitz (1996) conclude that the prevalence of personality disorder in the second half of life is approximately 10%, with a range between 6% and 33%. This represents the tip of an iceberg of personality dysfunction that often reveals itself under the stress of old age in the form of psychiatric symptoms such as depression and anxiety – symptoms that may not be completely amenable to treatment.

VULNERABILITY TO PSYCHIATRIC ILLNESS

Whether a person can cope with the stress of old age will depend to a great extent on the vulnerabilities of the personality (including genetic predisposition to psychiatric illness), the frequency and severity of life events, and the meaning (both conscious and unconscious) of such events to the person.

Individuals already sensitised to such things as narcissistic wounds and abandonment will be far more vulnerable to developing depression than those who are better integrated (Sadavoy, 1999). Research into depression concurs with such ideas: most people will succumb to illness when subject to sufficiently high levels of social problems and adverse life events (Goldberg, 2001). Personality dysfunction is increasingly recognised as a component of depression in the elderly and it is not surprising that there are often residual symptoms of depression after treatment, or apparent treatment resistance (Abrams, 1996). This can have important clinical implications.

> *Clinical Illustration*
> *Mrs H, 69, was admitted for a short period of respite after her symptoms of anxiety and depression secondary to a mild CVA became uncontrollable in the community and intolerable to her husband. She was a retired teacher and life had always been ordered. She had prided herself in being very independent and following retirement was on a number of committees and always kept herself busy. Unfortunately following admission her anxiety and depression steadily worsened and she was unable to be discharged until eight months later.*

How many times has one met an elderly patient described as 'very independent'? Jung's idea of 'compensation' can help to understand which unconscious feelings may lurk beneath the surface of the persona: the unconscious compensating for the conscious attitude by holding the opposite feelings. In Mrs H's case, an apparent outer 'independence' defended against unconscious needy dependent feelings. Her defences, already traumatised by the CVA, broke down further with hospitalisation as her increasing dependency and need for medication increased her hopelessness. A psychotherapeutic approach is essential for such patients, in conjunction with medication as necessary. However, if mental health units do not have the capacity for this then it may be in the patient's interest to provide focused symptom relief and rapid discharge (Sadavoy, 1992). Regression is a recognised consequence of hospitalisation, caused by loss of agency (personal autonomy and effectiveness), and the regressive pull inevitable in membership of a large group (Hobbs, 1990).

HOSPITALISATION OR CONTAINMENT

Life events, then, acting on a vulnerable personality structure can lead to a 'nervous breakdown' of defences, presenting in many ways but almost always with an element of anxiety. Patients are admitted to a psychiatric hospital usually in response, at some level, to anxiety that cannot be tolerated by families and carers in the community. The hospital is seen as a safe 'containing' place. Wilfred Bion thought of the mother as a container for her baby's raw intense feelings and fantasies, the baby projecting into her parts of himself in distress (Bion, 1962). Klein called this 'projective identification', a form of communication whereby one person is made to experience or become aware of the emotions of another (Jureidini, 1990). The mother's response (called 'reverie' by Bion) to this primitive communication helps her baby to develop a capacity for thinking and so become able to deal with such experiences himself. She does this by her reaction to his projections, accepting them into her mind without being overwhelmed. If this process does not take place adequately, the baby takes back into himself (introjects) not a comforting containing experience but a 'nameless dread'. Winnicott's 'holding' is a similar concept to Bion's container–contained theory.

Clinical Illustration
A 5-year-old boy falls and badly grazes his back. His mother panics when she sees the blood and the little boy becomes terrified and inconsolable. Later he says: 'When mummy cried I thought there were holes in my back with blood pouring out.'

The baby or very young child needs a containing person who respects and values his anxiety and depression, assesses appropriately their content and consistently conveys understanding, security and tolerability of such experi-ence (Menzies Lyth, 1975). Patients admitted to hospital because of uncontainable anxiety need similar (maternal) reactions from mental health professionals. Old age and physical illness may revive from childhood deep anxieties associated with dependency on others. And, like mothers with their babies, mental health professionals are subject to patients' projections par-ticularly from psychotic and borderline patients who can engender strong countertransference feelings.

COUNTERTRANSFERENCE

Countertransference in its broad meaning includes any feelings experienced by the therapist or health worker towards the patient (Newton & Jacobowitz, 1999). It is a natural emotional response that can be used therapeutically. We all have feelings about our patients but while 'positive' feelings such as com-passion, sadness and concern are felt and acknowledged, 'negative' feelings may be uncomfortable or unacceptable, often because they are incongruous with our professional identities (ego-dystonic). They are then either not talked about or not even felt (repressed). This includes feelings such as anger, resentment, frustration, guilt and hate. Work with the elderly can also gener-ate feelings of inadequacy, emotional pain, loss, dependency and thoughts of death (Katz, 1990). Such feelings, if not acknowledged and worked through, can have significant demoralising effects on staff with consequences such as sickness and absenteeism, as well as direct adverse effects on patient care because of the feelings being 'acted out'. This could include avoidance, becoming impatient, bored or sleepy, arguing, describing a patient in pejorative terms, and wishing to transfer or discharge a patient. Such attitudes contribute to prejudice against disability and ageing (Horowitz, 1991).

Hate is an insidious countertransference feeling that can adversely affect patient management. Winnicott (1949) wrote of the psychiatrist and hate: 'However much he loves his patients, he cannot avoid hating and fearing them, and the better he knows this the less will hate and fear be the motives determining what he does to his patients.' He compares it with the love and hate a mother has for her baby because of the baby's ruthless demands he places upon her, treating her as 'scum'. Patients such as borderline and psychotic have a strong tendency to evoke hatred because of their attacking defences, rendering their carers helpless or 'stuck'. When the treatment team begins to recognise their hate, an internal resistance is dispersed and progress follows (Prodgers, 1991). Such countertransference feelings are one of the root causes of abuse towards older patients (Garner & Evans, 2000). 'Disliking' or 'not liking' a patient may be a subtle indication of hate.

Clinical Illustration

Mrs G, 68, was admitted with depressive symptoms after a threatened overdose and entreaties from her family. She had had a six-month admission for depression the previous year with similar symptoms which had been resistant to treatment and she had finally discharged herself after fifteen sessions of ECT feeling 'exactly the same'. After admission Mrs G settled quickly on the ward but continued to complain of 'depression'. She wanted to stop any medication after a few days, either because of side effects or because the drug had not worked, and continued to demand a 'magic' drug to take away her symptoms. Her family became angry with the treatment team for their lack of progress. Some nursing staff became annoyed with Mrs G, who they felt was inciting other patients on the ward to be troublesome. Others became angry with the consultant for refusing to discharge the patient.

With further assessment, it became clear that what Mrs G referred to as 'depression' was in fact anger and other 'negative' feelings that she found intolerable. Her difficulties originated from a severely disturbed childhood. Her father had died when she was 2 after which she had been separated for six months from her abusive mother who had been hospitalised with depression. Apart from several overdoses as an adolescent, Mrs G's recent history of contact with psychiatric services had begun ten years previously with the death of her mother. This had probably stirred up childhood feelings of anger and hate associated with her original abandonment by her mother. Mrs G had sought help from psychiatric services to rid herself of these feelings. In hospital she was unconsciously using the primitive defence mechanisms of projection and projective identification making her carers feel the 'negative' feelings. Her resistance to treatment was an added frustration to staff who could not feel sympathetic towards Mrs G and wanted to rid themselves of her.

This echoed the abusive relationship Mrs G had had with her mother (repetition compulsion). A better psychodynamic understanding by the multidisciplinary team of Mrs G's behaviour and the reactions (such as hate) being generated in them allowed them to feel more compassionate (loving) towards Mrs G, who then felt more contained and responded by cooperating better with the treatment plan. A long admission, possibly including ECT, was avoided. She continued to feel 'depressed' at times but had a planned discharge with an agreed care plan including work with her family.

BORDERLINE PERSONALITY ORGANISATION

Mrs G meets some of the criteria for borderline personality organisation which is difficult to diagnose in the elderly in the absence of the typical acting-out behaviour of younger patients. Instead there is less physical behaviour such as demandingness, verbal attacks and increased alcohol use. Yet the underlying dynamics remain throughout life with the characteristic need for primitive defence mechanisms. Institutionalisation or hospitalisation with its enforced intimacy is very stressful for such patients. Intolerance of intimate relationships and prolonged or 'pathological' grief reactions are characteristic of borderline personality organisation (Sadavoy, 1992). It may not have been a coincidence that Mrs G had previously received a prolonged course of ECT to 'make' her well. It is always worth considering the role of countertransference feelings in the prescription of treatments such as ECT or intra-muscular medication for the suppression of symptoms which staff (as well as the patient) may find intolerable. Elderly 'institutionalised' patients often display an apparent lack of aggression having 'learned' that their carers cannot tolerate such emotions which are therefore repressed along with other 'vital' emotions leaving a childlike conformity.

SPLITTING

Another characteristic defence mechanism of borderline personality disorder is 'splitting' (Kernberg, 1975). It is a normal mechanism in infancy, allowing the infant to split conflicting opposites, such as good from bad, and love from hate. It is enhanced by the infant projecting the bad qualities and attributing them to another person. In normal development, the infant learns to bring the good and bad together ('depressive position', see Chapter 2). Adverse early life experiences can hinder emotional development and primitive defence mechanisms are then retained into adulthood. Such is the case in borderline personality disordered patients who project various aspects of their inner world onto different staff members, who then behave according to their projected role (projective identification).

Differences in opinion of staff in the ward can reflect these split-off aspects of the patient's mind. As a result, the staff group can be 'split' and care of the patient can suffer. Conversely, the working through by staff of their differences can be therapeutic (Main, 1957). It is recommended that all mental health professionals working with hospitalised patients should understand the concept of splitting and its implications (Gabbard, 1989).

PSYCHIATRIC NURSING

The burden of such unconscious processes makes hospital psychiatric nursing stressful and hard work. By its very nature, it requires staff to give themselves to their patients, like a mother to her baby. If a nurse cannot tolerate a patient's symptoms, it may feed in to the patient's fears that he is dangerous, unlovable or out of control. Staff, themselves, therefore need to feel contained to help them with their difficult job. In her study of general hospital nursing, Menzies Lyth described the development of a social defence system to protect nurses against being flooded by intense and unmanageable anxiety. Social defences included detachment, denial of feelings and preventing nurses developing relationships with patients (Menzies Lyth, 1959).

Nursing methods have moved towards greater intimacy with patients (Williams, 2001) making it even more important to provide nursing staff with more training and understanding of basic psychoanalytic principles (Winship, 1997). It is not surprising that staff defend against such feelings resulting in 'mindlessness' and 'detachment' that can characterise staff–patient interactions (Terry, 1997). Apart from their training and the hospital itself (which can be introjected as 'good' and containing), nurses may look towards other parts of the system to provide containment, such as their senior colleagues, staff support groups, psychiatrists, management and the Mental Health Act. Ultimately, a psychodynamic understanding is containing in itself.

PSYCHOSIS

Psychotic patients can be very demanding to manage, partly because of their excessive use of splitting and projective identification to rid themselves of primitive anxiety. There is also a tendency to concrete transference: the other person, for example a member of staff, literally becoming the person from the patient's past. The patient may therefore be deluded and may act upon this. Such a mechanism can explain apparently unprovoked violent behaviour. Several psychoanalytic theories are useful in explaining psychotic phenomena (see Chapter 2). Bion distinguished between psychotic and non-psychotic parts of the personality, relating psychosis to an intolerance of frustration and mental pain. He also described a mechanism for the production of hallucinations (Lucas, 1986). Considering the content, rather than just the form, of hallucinations and delusional thought is often helpful, not least so that the patient feels listened to and more contained. Psychotic symptoms can also be thought of as the mind's attempt to put something right (Sohn, 1995): they have purpose, and like a recurrent nightmare (also from the unconscious) may continue until the message is understood. On an ordinary unit however, this may be unbearable and antipsychotic medication necessary to reduce anxiety to tolerable levels. Working psychodynamically with younger psychiatric inpatients on a specialist ward, Jackson and Cawley (1992) concluded 'that given an effective containing milieu and the provision of sufficiently skilled psychoanalytic psychotherapy, a high proportion of psychotic patients could be helped towards stability'.

Persecutory delusions in the elderly are sometimes referred to as late paraphrenia (Almeida, 1998) which typically affects socially isolated elderly people with hearing and visual impairments, in other words, cut off from relating to other people and left with their inner worlds. Paranoid ideas can be thought of as the externalisation of an internal threat, such as from a critical superego (see Chapter 1). Fear of being attacked, for example, represents the person's own hostile self-criticisms which he or she projects and then identifies with (projective identification). Intolerable guilt and envy can also be projected, enabling the individual to disown the feelings but then feel persecuted by them.

Verwoerdt (1987) conceptualises paranoid symptoms as a progression from depression through hypochondriasis to psychosis, the bodily self representing a bridge between the inner self and the external world of relationships. Bodily symptoms, in this model, result from failing relationships leading to a greater psychological emphasis on the body. Such physical symptoms may remove responsibility for failure in such areas as intimate relationships, restoring self-esteem. In other words, they are a defence and care should be taken before challenging them. The physical symptoms may also be used to establish a personal relationship with medical staff, the patient being unable to relate emotionally.

SUICIDE

Psychodynamic understanding contributes greatly to the management of patients presenting with suicidal ideation, particularly in assessment of risk.

Clinical Illustration
A 73-year-old man, Mr T, was admitted to hospital following an
attempted hanging which was considered to be a serious attempt to kill
himself. His wife had died three months previously. He had put his affairs
in order, written letters of farewell and had had lunch with two of his
daughters. On admission he was mildly clinically depressed, regretted his
failed attempt, and saw no hope for the future. Exploration of his past
history revealed that Mr T had been born into a close-knit family, living
with both parents and grandparents. When Mr T was aged 3 his parents
left him with his grandparents just before the birth of his brother, Frank.
He described a 'happy' childhood, married at a relatively young age and
had three children. He had a steady working life, largely working from
home. Memories of his early life were sparse but he had vivid memories of
bomb damage during the war and the death of his best friend, also called
Frank. His cognition was normal. On the ward, within a few days he
appeared 'well' but he could not say that he would not try to kill himself
again.

When a suicide attempt and major depressive illness coincide, it is hoped
that treating the latter will prevent the former. Obviously, any clinical
depression should be treated vigorously and appropriately with medication,
especially if there are delusional ideas encouraging death (Roose et al., 1983)
but hopelessness or despair, rather than depression, has been shown to be
more predictive of suicide (Minkoff et al., 1973). In Mr T's case it is helpful to
see both the depression and suicidal ideation as secondary to an underlying
narcissistic disorder of personality.

NARCISSISTIC DISORDER

Stolorow (1975) uses the term 'narcissistic' to denote all mental functions,
activities and relationships by which the self is integrated and maintained,
and infused with positive feeling (see Chapter 5). It is a universal personality
trait which, dependent upon early life experience, will vary in degree from
'healthy selfishness' to pathological. Traumatic early experience can result in
narcissistic personality disorder requiring maximal defences to survive.
Gottschalk (1990) has suggested that narcissism 'pervades most, if not all'
psychiatric disorders. It is particularly relevant in the elderly whose self-
esteem is constantly challenged, for example, by failing physical health.
Patients with narcissistic damage must use external sources to boost their
self-worth. Mr T had never been alone in his life until the death of his wife.
One might speculate that his vague memories of childhood were the result of
suppressing intolerable feelings such as murderous rage felt towards both his
parents and his brother Frank. Such feelings were contained by the secure

relationship with his wife without whom he was prone to 'suicide-inviting affects' such as worthlessness, aloneness and murderous rage (Maltsberger, 1991).

Staff began to become impatient with Mr T's apparent unwillingness to cooperate with his care plan, his refusal to go to the Day Hospital and rejection of offers of help yet constant complaints of helplessness. Plans were made for moving him to a residential home with community follow-up, but the day before transfer he was found cyanosed but alive with a plastic bag over his head.

It can be difficult to bear constant complaints of helplessness. Staff are made to feel helpless, irritated, angry or guilty, which undermines the 'hopefulness' so important in treatment and erodes the loving containment so necessary to patients like Mr T. Watts and Morgan (1994) warn of the dangers for patients who are hard to like, and term the progressive deterioration in staff–patient relationships prior to suicide as 'malignant alienation'. Both staff and Mr T were 'acting out': Mr T by his suicide attempt, and staff by their wishing to discharge him. Acting out is a way of relieving any intrapsychic tension by physical action, the 'internal drama' passing directly from unconscious impulse to action, bypassing conscious thought and feeling. Investigations into any inpatient suicide attempt are not complete until the contributory (unconscious and conscious) psychodynamic factors are understood. This is impossible without some awareness of the true violence of the suicide attempt that is often defended against. Considering it as murder or 'psychic homicide' can help to get in touch with the violence of the act (Campbell & Hale, 1991).

Clinical Illustration
Mr J is a 27 year old man who was referred after he had driven at high speed the wrong way down a motorway, putting himself and others at considerable risk, after his fiancée had suddenly left him for another man. When seen one week later his fiancée had returned to him, wedding plans were afoot and the assessing psychiatrist could detect no psychiatric illness. Mr J declined further psychiatric follow-up and there was no psychodynamic psychotherapy service.

A happy outcome? Viewed psychodynamically, the root cause of this potentially lethal event remains, timelessly, in the unconscious. One might hypothesise that the abandonment by his fiancée somehow revived deep memories of abandonment as a child, leading to murderous rage. Let us hope that they live a long and happy life together. But how might Mr J react should his future wife die before him in 40 years' time? Will he then present to Old Age services with another violent attempt on his life? Such a case highlights the problems brewing for elderly services caused by the similarly poor provision of psychotherapy services for the under 65s.

THE PSYCHODYNAMIC HISTORY

In psychodynamic work one is considering the effects of unconscious processes on the patient, so 'premorbid personality' (so often sidelined in ordinary psychiatric history taking) and family history become central to the assessment, looking in particular for the effects of early life experiences on personality development. What would it have been like for the patient to have been a baby with that mother in that particular family? How are past patterns of behaviour (e.g. relationship with mother) repeating themselves in the present (e.g. relationship with wife)? Behaviour in childhood and adolescence, employment history, and ability to tolerate anxiety give clues to ego strength. Capacity to endure criticism and loss, and to feel worthwhile and loveable when alone, point to the resilience of the self. Choice of lifestyle reflects underlying personality: a racing driver rarely goes train spotting.

Behaviour is guided by underlying, often unconscious, feelings and an assessment should explore the patient's subjective experiences. Assessment of affect in psychiatry is often limited to depression and anxiety but other feelings should not be forgotten, such as anger, which can be the source of depressive and paranoid symptoms; rage, as an indicator of a threat to the self (Wiener, 1998); envy, in relation to siblings and beautiful young mental health workers; and shame and humiliation, caused by the assaults of ageing and which, according to Lazare, often underlie complaints against the medical profession (Lazare, 1987). Feelings are often suppressed by the elderly, having been brought up with 'Victorian' values that encouraged children to be compliant and 'good'.

As in any interview, establishing rapport is paramount. Taking a history can in itself be therapeutic. The patient's choice of memories and the order in which they choose to give the history are significant. Similarly, just as slips of the tongue (parapraxes) are accepted as communications from the unconscious, so choice of words matters. Psychotic symptoms also have meaning, but like dreams, also from the unconscious, this meaning is symbolic and may not at first (or second) be apparent. Taking the content of psychosis seriously is more containing for the patient than questioning simply to break them down into Schneiderian First Rank symptoms. (Asking questions can be a defence against anxiety!) Similarly, when current stressors are noted, the meaning for the patient of such events should be explored to discover what they might be stirring up from the patient's past. An elderly man who develops cancer will be affected more by such a diagnosis had his abusive father died at an early age from a similar illness.

While 'interviewing' it is useful to adopt a fisherman's attitude, watching and listening beyond the words being said (with the hope of catching something from the unconscious). Notice what is unspoken, observe the patient's body language and consider transference and countertransference. How does it feel to be with this particular patient? Such feelings can help guide the interview and offer vital insights into the patient's psyche.

PSYCHODYNAMIC MILIEU

Just as patient behaviour suggests underlying feelings and attitudes, so the behaviour of the organisation (hospital) will affect patients by conveying meaning both consciously and unconsciously about how the hospital feels about them. A crucial therapeutic moment is the welcoming and acceptance of new patients onto the ward (Fagin, 2001). For psychodynamic work, nursing levels should be high enough to allow time not only for patients, but for nurses themselves, so that they may reflect on their patients and consider their own feelings; management should help staff to feel valued and supported by adequate staff numbers, supervision and staff groups; and psychiatrists should have at least some training in psychodynamic psychotherapy with access to a consultant psychotherapist for advice and supervision. All this can create a therapeutic environment in which patients can be helped to 'become' well, rather than be 'made' well. However, much of this can be negated by an adverse physical environment: functional patients having to share the ward with patients with dementia who require more intensive physical nursing; mixed gender wards which can be very threatening to certain patients; and dormitory accommodation which is outdated, disrespectful to the individual and encourages dependency.

RESISTANCE TO PSYCHODYNAMIC WORK

Psychodynamic principles emphasise the universality of mental processes, minimising the difference between patients and staff, breaking down the 'us and them' defence (Hook, 2001), and consequently, staff may feel threatened analysing their reactions to patients. Further resistance is caused by psychoanalytic jargon (e.g. 'object') which can be excluding, and staff may feel disempowered further by lack of training. Management and those who advise them suffer similar blocks to understanding the need for psychodynamic work, not heeding Martindale (1995), who asserts that the capacity for containment of feelings aroused by the needs of the elderly is an important determinant of the quality of a health service's provision for the elderly. The 'us and them' divide among psychiatrists and psychotherapists will gradually be broken down as researchers, such as Solms, continue to work to rejoin psychoanalysis with neurology from which it emerged almost 100 years ago (Solms, 1996), and as psychodynamic psychotherapy becomes a mandatory requirement for doctors training in psychiatry (Royal College of Psychiatrists, 2001). While increased training in psychotherapy for hospital staff is necessary, psychotherapy training should ensure adequate experience in psychiatry. The coming together of these different ways of thinking can be likened to Jung's 'coniunctio', the coming together of opposites: following a period of anxiety ('nigredo') will come new birth, a new way of thinking.

CONCLUSIONS

This chapter has considered just a few of the many ways in which psychodynamic thinking can enrich working with elderly inpatients. To some extent all psychiatric staff are already practising psychotherapy, but with more training and supervision this can be developed to achieve improved communication skills, a deeper, more 'three-dimensional' assessment (Ardern, 1995), and enhanced understanding of patient behaviour and illness. All this, together with a greater awareness of unconscious mechanisms operating in both patients and staff, contributes to formulating the most appropriate management plan for patients, who benefit from feeling more listened-to and contained. Nursing staff benefit from improved morale and prevention of burn-out; and management should be aware that such working could help reduce staff absenteeism, the frequency of complaints and the number of serious incidents such as violence and suicide.

While Old Age services would undoubtedly benefit from more psychotherapeutic input, early intervention is essential (Jackson & Cawley, 1992) and the development of much improved services for younger adults is imperative. Much current distress and illness in the elderly could have been reduced or avoided had adequate psychotherapy services been available in the past.

REFERENCES

Abrams, R.C. (1996). Personality disorders in the elderly: Editorial review. *International Journal of Geriatric Psychiatry*, 11, 759–763.

Abrams, R.C., & Horowitz, S.V. (1996). Personality disorders after age 50: A meta-analysis. *Journal of Personality Disorders*, 10(3), 271–281.

Almeida, O. (1998). Late paraphrenia. In: R. Butler & B. Pitt (eds) *Seminars in Old Age Psychiatry*. London: Royal College of Psychiatrists (Gaskell).

Ardern, M. (1995). Psychodynamic aspects of old age psychiatry. In: R. Howard (ed) *Everything You Need to Know About Old Age Psychiatry*. UK: Wrightson Biomedical Publishing Ltd.

Berezin, M.A. (1972). Psychodynamic considerations of aging and the aged: an overview. *American Journal of Psychiatry*, 128(12), 33–41.

Bion, W.R. (1962). *Learning From Experience*. London: Heinemann.

Campbell, D., & Hale, R. (1991). Suicidal acts. In: J. Holmes (ed) *Textbook of Psychotherapy in Psychiatric Practice*. London: Churchill Livingstone.

Costa, P.T., & McCrae, R.R. (1980). Influence of extraversion and neuroticism on subjective well-being. *Journal of Personality and Social Psychology*, 38, 668–678.

Fagin, L. (2001). Therapeutic and counter-therapeutic factors in acute ward settings. *Psychoanalytic Psychotherapy*, 15(2), 99–120.

Gabbard, G. (1989). Splitting in hospital treatment. *American Journal of Psychiatry*, 146(4), 444–451.

Gabbard, G. (1994). *Psychodynamic Psychiatry in Clinical Practice*. Washington: American Psychiatric Press.

Garner, J., & Evans, S. (2000). *Institutional Abuse of Older Adults. Royal College of Psychiatrists Council Report CR84*. London: Royal College of Psychiatrists.

Goldberg, D. (2001). Vulnerability factors for common mental illnesses. *British Journal of Psychiatry*, 178(suppl. 40), s69–s71.

Gottschalk, L.A. (1990). Origins and evolution of narcissism through the life cycle. In: R.A. Nemiroff & C.A. Colarusso (eds) *New Dimensions in Adult Development*. New York: Basic Books.

Headley, B., & Wearing, A. (1989). Personality, life events, and subjective well-being: Toward a dynamic equilibrium model. *Journal of Personality and Social Psychology*, 57(4), 731–739.

Hobbs, M. (1990). The role of the psychotherapist as consultant to inpatient psychiatric units. *Psychiatric Bulletin*, 14, 8–12.

Hook, J. (2001). The role of psychodynamic psychotherapy in a modern general psychiatry service. *Advances in Psychiatric Treatment*, 7, 461–468.

Horowitz, M. (1991). Transference and countertransference in the therapeutic relationship with the older adult. In: R.J. Hartke (ed) *Psychological Aspects of Geriatric Rehabilitation*. Gaithersburg, MD: Aspen Publishers.

Jackson, M., & Cawley, R. (1992). Psychodynamics and psychotherapy on an acute psychiatric ward. *British Journal of Psychiatry*, 160, 41–50.

Jureidini, J. (1990). Projective identification in general psychiatry. *British Journal of Psychiatry*, 157, 656–660.

Katz, R. (1990). Facing the challenge: Weaving countertransference feelings into the tapestry of our work. In: B. Genevay & R. Katz (eds) *Countertransference and Older Clients*. London: Sage Publications.

Kernberg, O.T. (1975). *Borderline Conditions and Pathological Narcissism*. New York: Jason Aronson.

King, P. (1980). The life cycle as indicated by the nature of the transference in the psychoanalysis of the middle-aged and elderly. *International Journal of Psychoanalysis*, 61, 153–160.

Lazare, A. (1987). Shame and humiliation in the medical encounter. *Archives of Internal Medicine*, 147, 1653–1658.

Lucas, R. (1986). On the contribution of psychoanalysis to the management of psychotic patients in the NHS. *Psychoanalytic Psychotherapy*, 1(1), 3–17.

Main, T.F. (1957). The ailment. Reprinted (1989) in: J. Johns (ed) *The Ailment and Other Psychoanalytic Essays*. London: Free Association Books.

Maltsberger, J.T. (1991). Suicide in old age: Psychotherapeutic intervention. *Crisis*, 12(2), 25–32.

Martindale, B. (1995). Psychological treatments II: Psychodynamic approaches. In: J. Lindesay (ed) *Neurotic Disorders in the Elderly*. London: Oxford University Press.

Menzies Lyth, I. (1959). The functioning of social systems as a defence against anxiety. Reprinted (1988) in: *Containing Anxiety in Institutions: Selected essays, Vol. 1*. London: Free Association Books.

Menzies Lyth, I. (1975). Thoughts on the maternal role in contemporary society. Reprinted (1988) in: *Containing Anxiety in Institutions: Selected essays, Vol. 1*. London: Free Association Books.

Minkoff, K. et al. (1973). Hopelessness, depression and attempted suicide. *American Journal of Psychiatry*, 130(4), 455–459.

Newton, N.A., & Jacobowitz, J. (1999). Transferential and countertransferential processes in therapy with older adults. In: M. Duffy (ed) *Handbook of Counselling and Psychotherapy with Older Adults*. Chichester, UK: John Wiley & Sons.

Porter, R. (1991). Psychotherapy with the elderly. In: J. Holmes (ed) *Textbook of Psychotherapy in Psychiatric Practice*. London: Churchill Livingstone.

Prodgers, A. (1991). On hating the patient. *British Journal of Psychotherapy*, 8(2), 144–154.

Roose, S. et al. (1983). Depression, delusions, and suicide. *American Journal of Psychiatry*, 140, 1159–1162.

Royal College of Psychiatrists (2001). *Requirements for psychotherapy training as part of basic specialist psychiatric training*. London: Royal College of Psychiatrists.

Sadavoy, J. (1992). The aging borderline. In: D. Silver & M. Rosenbluth (eds) *Handbook of Borderline Disorders*. Madison, CT: International Universities Press.

Sadavoy, J. (1999). The effect of personality disorder on axis I disorders in the elderly. In: M. Duffy (ed) *Handbook of Counselling and Psychotherapy with Older Adults*. Chichester, UK: John Wiley & Sons.

Schore, A. (2001). The effects of early relational trauma on right brain development. *Infant Mental Health Journal*, 22, 201–269.

Sohn, L. (1995). Unprovoked assaults: Making sense of apparently random violence. *International Journal of Psychoanalysis*, 76, 565–575.

Solms, M. (1996). Towards an anatomy of the unconscious. *Journal of Clinical Psychoanalysis*, 5(3), 331–368.

Stolorow, R.D. (1975). Toward a functional definition of narcissism. *International Journal of Psychoanalysis*, 56, 179–185.

Terry, P. (1997). *Counselling the Elderly and their Carers*. Basingstoke, UK: Macmillan.

Verwoerdt, A. (1987). Psychodynamics of paranoid phenomena in the aged. In: J. Sadavoy & M. Leszcz (eds) *Treating the Elderly with Psychotherapy: The scope for change in later life*. Madison, CT: International Universities Press.

Watts, D., & Morgan, G. (1994). Malignant alienation: Dangers for patients who are hard to like. *British Journal of Psychiatry*, 164, 11–15.

Wiener, J. (1998). Under the volcano: Varieties of anger and their transformation. *Journal of Analytical Psychology*, 43, 493–508.

Williams, A. (2001). A literature review on the concept of intimacy in nursing. *Journal of Advanced Nursing*, 33(5), 660–667.

Winnicott, D. (1949). Hate in the countertransference. *International Journal of Psychoanalysis*, 30, 69–74.

Winship, G. (1997). Establishing the role of the nurse psychotherapist in the United Kingdom. *Perspectives in Psychiatric Care*, 33(1), 25–31.

Chapter 9

Ethical aspects of psychotherapy and clinical work with older adults

Mark Ardern

The greater the power, the more dangerous the abuse.

(Edmund Burke)

ETHICS AND SOCIETY

In times of national catastrophe, such as war or famine, ethical matters are by and large avoided. When a society's survival is the most pressing concern, ethical questions can seem at best a luxury, and at worst an unwelcome distraction. In these first years of the 21st century, for better or worse, Britain is absorbed in anxious introspection about values. One manifest aspect of this is an acceleration of interest in the ethics of medical practice; reflecting and promoting public scrutiny.

Confidence in health professionals' ability and willingness to improve the quality of their work with patients has been bruised. The causes of this are several. Expectations have increased, but the possibility of meeting these appears to be falling. High-profile tragedies have drawn attention to patients' misplaced trust in particular health professionals such as Beverley Allitt and Harold Shipman, who systematically murdered their patients. These shocking, and fortunately unusual, cases have brought into question the public's hitherto idealising attitude that doctors and nurses can do no wrong. Questions about lack of competence are frequently put to individual clinicians or the systems of which they form part. In reaction to this a wide ranging set of 'safeguards' is in the process of implementation. Doctors must, if they are to continue to practise, be annually appraised and formally engage in continuing professional development. The long talked of registration of psychotherapists is now upon us. While the reasons for these are understandable, it remains to be seen whether patients will benefit, and whether the public is prepared to pay the cost.

In any society ethics are under the influence of the prevailing culture. For example in some a collective drive may diminish self-determination. This was evidenced in Japan during World War II by the extraordinary self-sacrifice of individual citizens and combatants who were ready to die rather than suffer the dishonour of capture. In Nazi Germany eugenics was rationalised as justification for the eradication of the mentally disordered, homosexuals, Jews, gypsies and others. As Goebbels put it, Germany was merely 'weeding the garden of Europe'.

Here in Britain there is no room for complacency. Members of the public who have the misfortune to be diagnosed as being 'dangerous severely personality disordered' may end up being permanently removed from society without having committed a crime (Department of Health and Home Office, 2000). Ethics are concerned, in the political field, between libertarian principles and state control, sometimes with tyrannical consequences.

Practitioners of psychotherapy will have to be mindful of the prevailing laws and prejudices of the day. Those paid by the state may be unwittingly influenced in deciding how to allocate resources at their disposal. Psychotherapists who choose to work with older people may face an uphill struggle in convincing others of the value of their work.

Beauchamp and Childress, in focusing on the individual, have articulated four ethical principles. These are: respect for the patient's autonomy, beneficence, non-maleficence and justice (Beauchamp & Childress, 1994). It is important however to point out that strict adherence to any one of these may hinder the application of a second. For example, an elderly patient with Alzheimer's disease who persists in driving presents the clinician with a conflict about whether or not to breach confidentiality for the sake of the public interest. Even in psychotherapy, where privacy is central to the treatment process, knowledge of risky behaviour occasionally threatens to rupture the therapeutic alliance.

Ethical practice is therefore concerned with the wise consideration of balances. In psychotherapy it is tested by the peculiar nature of the therapist–client relationship. And in work with the elderly there are particular dilemmas to be examined.

SOCIETY AND AGEISM

In a competitive world where capitalism has emerged as the predominant political movement, old people are vulnerable to the influence of market forces. Although forming an increasing proportion of the electorate in democratic societies, the fact that old people are not economically productive will create resentment. For Britain a collective dilemma is the apportionment of wealth to its ageing population.

Back in 1984 the author's own appointment was initially funded from a project called 'The Rising Tide' (Health Advisory Service, 1982). This unfortunate term suggested a malevolent and creeping menace – that is, of the rising tide of old people who, like flood waters, threatened to overwhelm

NHS services. Consciously the abundance of resources given to this service was an example of 'positive ageism', which more recently has resulted in the publication of the National Service Framework for Older People (DoH, 2001). Terms like 'psychogeriatrics' have fallen by the wayside in the search for a language of dignity and respectability. (It may be relevant to ponder why the term 'psychopaediatrics' never evolved.) Unconsciously, however, negative ageism remains. Decisions which on the surface appear to be in 'the best interests' of the older patient may conceal sinister routes of disposal to institutional care or more subtly to remain 'in the community' regardless of what the older person wishes.

One example of an ageist piece of legislation is the continuing existence of Section 47 of the National Assistance Act, 1948. This specifically allows an 'old' person to be taken into institutional care; not on the grounds of mental ill health, but where he is neglecting himself. Here coercion is used in the name of beneficence; and also perhaps to treat the anxiety of others.

Contemporary Britain is preoccupied with independence as a goal to which even the very old are encouraged to aspire. Since many accompaniments of old age (failing mobility, sensory systems, continence, etc.) require external sources of help, a realistic acceptance of ageing will involve the embracing of aspects of dependence. The older patient who presents to psychiatric services commonly has developed a phobic avoidance of dependence. This is a neurotic state of mind, the roots of which are to be found in the patient's early developmental history. Lifelong attachment problems will therefore necessitate special efforts on the part of society, and its health professionals, to reach out sensitively in order to build trust. Staff may themselves be reluctant to encourage dependence where society's doctrine is the converse; that is, of dependence representing some kind of failure. If society's discomfort is manifest by projection of its perceived weaknesses into the vulnerable and needy, attempts at reparation (fuelled by guilt) run the risk of being patronising. This is not altogether surprising given that older people are rarely directly involved in planning services themselves.

Power differentials

In work with older people the dynamics of transference and countertransference will be complicated by the fact that health professionals are likely to be considerably younger than the patients whom they meet. The therapist's relationship with his parents, and the degree to which he has successfully individuated from them, will determine the degree of objectivity he can achieve with his older patient.

Given the prevailing climate of 'independence is all', the older patient may attempt to conceal unacceptable fantasies of becoming a burden on his younger therapist. This may have the effect of falsely reassuring the therapist that only positive feelings towards him exist. The therapist, through his narcissism, may assume that he is sailing in trouble-free waters. He may underestimate the degree of power he has over his patient. In fact the therapist, however inexperienced, holds most of the cards; not least in deciding whether the patient will continue to be seen.

In any clinical encounter between the older patient and therapist, this imbalance of power will be an important determinant in whether a positive experience is achievable. The potency of the 'placebo' effect has long been observed. Here the patient improves solely by his conviction that a therapeutic force exists. It can be tempting for patients to be consciously given a placebo, however unethical. The ends, however, are not justified by the means, which in effect constitute a betrayal of trust. From a theoretical perspective placebo effects work best in suggestible patients. Hypnosis, which Freud witnessed in developing his concept of transference, depends upon a convincing and often charismatic therapist dominating a submissive patient. The effects of hypnosis can be dramatic, but may be short-lived.

The hopes and fears which our vulnerable elderly patients invest in us may be abused in the therapeutic relationship. In psychoanalysis transference reactions are deliberately examined, but in any interaction between an older person and a clinician, transference and countertransference are alive. Ethically all health professionals have a duty to be vigilant to these powerful processes, whether or not they recognise these as transference or placebo effects.

Older people especially are notoriously reticent to complain, but this should not be assumed as evidence that all is well. Lack of complaining on the part of older people has led to the proliferation of advocacy. Sadly many older patients in psychiatric services are at the mercy of what is served up. In poverty, beggars may feel they cannot afford to be choosers.

Boundaries

Foremost in the minds of the public is the potential exploitation of patients in psychotherapy. The most obvious taboo is that of the appearance of a sexualised transference in the relationship, which is then acted upon. Although this is less likely to occur with the older patient, more subtle abuses of power can occur in everyday encounters. It has become increasingly fashionable for younger health professionals to use first names with older patients. Ostensibly this may be done to convey a caring attitude, but is often undertaken without permission and may conceal ambivalent feelings on the part of staff in a process of infantilisation.

Physical contact with the older patient is commonly an ethical consideration. Much has been written about touch in psychotherapy (largely frowned upon) and with older patients generally (often promoted as desirable). Many older people require and appreciate help in assisting their mobility. The danger is that physical contact is not so much given to acknowledge this need, but more to satisfy the therapist's need to be seen as compassionate, in an unconscious 'acting in' of the countertransference. On the other hand a rigid application of a 'no touch' dogma for frail older patients in psychotherapy may be cruel. The importance for the psychotherapist is his reflection of these matters in order to avoid acting compulsively.

With younger patients it is conventional for psychotherapy to be conducted in a familiar, but neutral room. With older patients, however, there arises the possibility that therapy may have to be undertaken in the patient's own living room, with all the problems that this unusual scenario brings. The therapist will need to be even more vigilant that the boundary between professional and social interaction is not lost. This is a particular issue for general practitioners who may be tempted into responding to friendly overtures or even gifts from the patient. Psychotherapists who broaden their horizons to disabled older clients will have to adapt themselves and their practice accordingly.

It is of course up to the therapist to delineate and adhere to boundaries. These will often be tested by the patient, whose unconscious fantasies frequently seek to manipulate the therapist into areas outside therapy. Where money changes hands this can be a severe test of the therapist's ethical resolve (see later).

Confidentiality

Confidentiality is a crucial issue in any psychotherapy. Nevertheless in therapeutic work with older people confidentiality is routinely threatened. In the author's experience the frequency with which older people challenge breaches in confidentiality is rare. So too is the number of occasions on which older patients ask to see their medical case notes.

With this in mind, health professionals, social workers, relatives, home helps or even the next-door neighbour may feel entitled to obtain detailed clinical information. Often this is under the guise of the 'best interests' of the patient. Although some mentally ill older people, particularly those with dementia, lack competence, the overriding principle remains that adults of all ages have a right to retain confidentiality. This can prove inconvenient to multi-disciplinary teams who share information on a day to day 'need to know' basis.

Unwittingly, breaches of confidentiality are evident when visiting a ward for older patients. The names of patients are usually displayed for all to see, including ward visitors. More sinister stars by the patients' names may denote whether or not the patient is for resuscitation.

Group therapy poses an important challenge to patients' confidentiality. Note keeping by group therapists has to be kept separate from patients' individual case notes. During therapy, group leaders will be vigilant not to accidentally divulge personal information gathered during assessment interviews to other group members. By contrast if serious psychiatric symptoms (such as active suicidal intent) emerge, the therapists may be duty bound to report these to the patient's own doctor. These possibilities of disclosure should have been discussed at the beginning of any psychotherapy, and not come as a surprise to patients. In setting the boundaries of confidentiality to the group at the outset, emphasis should be laid on requesting that disclosures in the group are not transmitted outside. Apart from being ethical this will enhance the therapeutic potential of the group process.

RESEARCH AND PUBLICATION

Perhaps more than with any other clinical treatment, research into the efficacy of dynamic psychotherapy has proven problematic. Valiant efforts have been made in this area (see, for example, Roth & Fonagy, 1996). 'When' and 'how' to measure outcome is beset with difficulties in dynamic therapy when compared with more circumscribed treatment interventions such as cognitive behavioural therapy. It has to be concluded that detailed individual case studies are likely to remain the predominant means by which knowledge is advanced.

Unless clinical material can be disguised well enough to prevent patients (and more importantly others) from recognising themselves in print, consent has to be obtained. With careful explanation many patients are happy to provide this. One ethical dilemma for any author, however, is knowing *when* this consent should be sought. If therapy is still in progress its very existence may be jeopardised. Even if therapy is over, the patient's perception of therapy may have been a very different one from that which he reads on publication. This opens up the possibility of retrospective damage. Some patients, not necessarily for the best reasons, will want their therapy published. Others, including the shy, guarded or frankly paranoid, may never agree. This could bias the range of publications in favour of particular types of clinical material.

Reviewers of papers submitted for publication, and journal editors, are faced with ethical considerations. One of these is the decision to publish research demonstrating poor treatment outcome. Journals tend to favour papers which describe something positive or new, and that will appeal to readers. Those papers which are methodologically sound but boring do not enhance a journal's sales. Here we enter the ethics of censorship.

Sometimes it is patients themselves, particularly well informed ones, who teach us most in reporting their experience of psychotherapy. Bruno Goetz, student turned psychoanalyst, reminisced on his own sessions with Sigmund Freud (Goetz, 1975). In this account Goetz demonstrated how Freud forcefully gave him both advice and money. This ex-patient's decision to write about Freud's surprising behaviour reminds us of the personality of the therapist in influencing outcome. Studies into the characterological make-up of psychotherapists are, for obvious reasons, difficult to find.

The publication of mistakes, either in terms of poor selection of patients or incompetence on the part of the therapist, requires courage; not least because nowadays it potentially exposes the therapist to litigation.

INEXPERIENCED AND UNQUALIFIED THERAPISTS

In some quarters ideas are promoted that psychodynamic therapy is only beneficial to patients; or at least that it can do no harm. However this form of treatment can be extremely damaging in its disruption of the patient's defences. Some patients will be driven mad by therapy. The responsibility of embarking on any 'talking treatment' is not to be taken lightly. A patient's reluctance to undergo psychodynamic therapy is often a wise one.

In psychotherapy there is always to be considered the matter of medical responsibility. For non-medical psychotherapists it is routine to clarify medical responsibility (for example with the patient's general practitioner). Consultant psychiatrists automatically assume medical responsibility for their in-patients, even though these patients may be receiving psychological treatments from other members of the team. Here a professional and ethical question is how much the general practitioner or psychiatrist needs to know about the details of therapy. He does have to reassure himself that whoever undertakes this is either appropriately qualified or receives professional supervision from a senior member of that discipline. The doctor who carries medical responsibility should also, in broad terms, be familiar with the patient's clinical progress. In other words the psychotherapy must stay within the limits of the therapist's competence.

In this country it is quite lawful for anyone to undertake a procedure (even surgery) on another person, provided that the latter is not deceived into believing that the 'practitioner' is qualified to do so. Doctors have until now been in a somewhat privileged position of being able to practise psychotherapies of all sorts with their patients. This would not extend to psychoanalysis, though quite normally includes counselling. The contentious area is what might be seen as the 'middle ground' of psychodynamic therapy and defining what this is. The degree to which psychiatrists, who have a limited training in psychodynamic therapy, undertake this with their patients (usually in the absence of any personal therapy for themselves), is a controversial one. The golden rule is to remain within the limits of competence.

CONSENT

For doctors undertaking simple medical procedures, such as removing a blood sample by way of venepuncture, the patient's consent is *implicit* in that the patient offers his arm. The doctor should however satisfy himself that the patient has a reasonable idea of the purpose of the procedure. In more complex procedures, for example where the patient requires an anaesthetic, it is lawful for the surgeon to operate provided he believes the patient has, in simple terms, understood the possible risks and benefits. In practice written consent is usually obtained as a safeguard in any potential future legal dispute. The patient can withdraw his consent at any time whether this is written or verbal.

Where an adult patient has a mental disorder which significantly affects his competence to give informed consent, the surgeon may still proceed if he believes it to be 'of necessity'. No one else can give consent on behalf of the patient. Consulting relatives is often sensible but carries no legal authority. Under certain circumstances, such as during a cardiac arrest or where a patient is about to jump out of a hospital window, the doctor may have a duty to act. Inaction may be later judged in the court to have been negligent.

Psychodynamic therapy poses rather different ethical problems. The fundamental question here is 'to what is the patient consenting?'. Unless the patient is himself undergoing therapy as part of his training, he is unlikely to know about transference, defence mechanisms or details about interpretation. He is also unlikely to be aware of potential harmful effects of therapy, such as psychotic breakdown. In contrast to surgery, the nature of the procedure in psychotherapy and its potential risks and even benefits are rarely spelt out to the patient. Since there are no knives about, the patient may assume that talking is harmless enough.

Patients who are referred for psychotherapy are much more at the mercy of the professionalism of the therapist. They do not enter a written contract but arrive with hope and varying degrees of anxiety. Those who initially idealise the therapist may invest too much hope. Are they looking for symptom relief, personality change, avoidance of future breakdown or even a lover? Once therapy is under way any further questioning by the patient is in danger of being interpreted as 'resistance'. The length of therapy is usually only predetermined at the outset in brief (focal) therapy. But for long-term therapy the end is intangible and could be years away.

In practice few elderly patients are referred for psychotherapy (Murphy, 2000). For these patients the matter of consent is immaterial, since no therapy is on offer. All dynamic therapists should have knowledge of other psychological treatments, such as cognitive behavioural therapy. It would be unethical to only offer dynamic psychotherapy where it was clear that another more suitable form of treatment is available and which the patient prefers. Personal prejudices about other forms of treatment should not be inflicted upon the patient.

RELIABILITY OF THE THERAPIST

In comparison with all other clinical treatments, the reliability of the therapist is paramount. Before any offer of dynamic psychotherapy is made to a patient, the therapist will have to be confident of his available time commitments. This means he must dedicate not only a particular time and place each week (assuming weekly therapy) but one for however long 'the contract' will run.

Although no one can predict the future, any planned breaks, such as the therapist's holidays, will have to be discussed with the patient in advance. Unforeseen emergencies, for example where the therapist falls ill, should also have been anticipated in principle. The patient should have a clear idea of what is likely to happen under these circumstances ahead of time; in other words there should be a contingency plan (Counselman & Alonso, 1993).

Exactly how much should be divulged to the patient about the therapist's absences will in part depend on whether the therapy is strictly analytical or more ego-supportive. Theoretically the withholding of personal information has merits in stimulating the patient's fantasies. However for more vulnerable patients the anxiety provoked may be intolerable. For the older patient in psychotherapy it should be anticipated that the therapist's holiday breaks are often perceived as an escape by an exhausted therapist from a burdensome patient. Unannounced absences are likely to signify serious illness or even death of the therapist.

PRIVATE PRACTICE

Where psychotherapy with older people is practised by a salaried professional, this may facilitate ethical conduct. The therapist does not depend for his living on direct payment from his patients. He is therefore potentially free to do or say things to his patient from which he might otherwise be inhibited. What patients consciously wish to hear might be different from that which is in their therapeutic interest. Selection and termination may be hindered in private practice, especially where finances are no obstacle for the patient.

It is common in private psychotherapy for therapists to determine fees based on an assumption about what the patient can afford. This is an ethical minefield. While it can be argued that payment, especially for 'missed' sessions, might potentially enhance motivation, this can quickly unravel where the older person falls physically ill; an event which is more likely than with younger patients.

Trainee psychotherapists commonly offer their services at reduced costs. Although professional responsibility will largely fall on the supervising psychotherapist, the patient may not be fully aware that this 'low-budget' therapy could be construed as a guinea-pig affair. The alternative, of no therapy at all, is a stark one. Some might argue that not all of us can afford business-class flights, and that charters have opened up air travel opportunities to the wider population.

Occasionally private psychotherapy is made possible for older people by payment from third parties such as adult children. The autonomy of the patient is then threatened. This may become material for therapy itself. Fee-paying relatives might mistakenly assume that they will have access to confidential information on the progress, or otherwise, of therapy. There are some ethical parallels here with private child psychotherapy.

In all private psychotherapy the therapist should anticipate the possibility that the source of his income may dry up. The patient who does not, or cannot, pay places the therapist in a dilemma. Under these circumstances the viability of therapy is in jeopardy. It would be unethical, however, for a therapist to curtail therapy abruptly if he believed that the mental health of the patient was at immediate risk.

PSYCHOTHERAPY WHICH THREATENS THE PATIENT'S RELATIONSHIP WITH OTHERS

Dynamic psychotherapy, by its very nature, is likely to change the patient's attitude to significant others in his social network. This is often exactly what the patient is consciously seeking; for example learning to be more assertive and less willing to 'fit in' with the wishes of others. The patient is experimenting, via the transference, a renegotiation of his place in the world. Some will come to realise that perverse attachments will require termination; for example by divorce or severing of relations with exploitative children. In dynamic psychotherapy the principle of responsibility for these changes is assumed to lie with the patient. The extent to which a therapist exerts influence on this requires examination. Apart from in supportive psychotherapy it will be rare for a therapist to offer direct advice. Tacit approval is more difficult to locate and quantify. However much neutrality the therapist strives to maintain, patients are often all too well aware of what pleases or displeases him. Aspects of behaviour therapy, in the form of modelling or reinforcement, are present too in dynamic psychotherapy. Denial of these influences on the part of the therapist may lead to an overvalued conviction of his neutrality and opacity.

For the older patient an example of this could be the patient's predicament about whether he should move into an old people's home. Unfortunately this decision is rarely possible independent of other realities. Relatives and social workers are frequently involved and usually have strong opinions one way or the other. The therapist, in his countertransference reaction, may find it difficult to avoid being drawn into this. He may be tempted to sway the patient into making what could be an irreversible error of judgement.

CONCLUSIONS

The ultimate goal in psychotherapy in the views of Holmes and Lindley (1989) is that of 'emotional autonomy'. This is no different for older patients, who are nevertheless beset with assaults on their physical autonomy. Successful therapy, and successful living, denote liberation from the ghosts of the past. Harsh internalised figures become replaced by more benign, accepting ones in facing the vicissitudes of old age.

Society has its own perspective on older people and this will strongly influence what is provided for them. Currently there is evidence that Britain is now allocating more resources in the direction of older people. Nevertheless there is a risk that this may be undertaken in a way which reduces 'emotional autonomy' by well intentioned infantilisation. Qualified individual practitioners of psychotherapy with older people are few and far between. Psychological treatments of one sort or another exist but it is not yet clear which of these are of value.

Supervision by dynamic psychotherapists of other health professionals remains inadequate. One consequence of this is that a demoralised workforce in the statutory services may unconsciously enact their frustrations on vulnerable older people who cannot speak up for themselves. The present 'blame culture' may also drive away otherwise caring people from work with the elderly.

Finally the author acknowledges that this chapter has been written in a style which is somewhat superegotistical. The widespread use of 'shoulds' is difficult to avoid when considering ethical matters. In the consulting room and faced with the older patient there exist at least three constituents: the patient, the therapist and his conscience. Psychotherapy can be a lonely business. Its proper progress should be helped by a watchful, internal parent.

REFERENCES

Beauchamp, T.L., & Childress, J.F. (1994). *Principles of Biomedical Ethics* (4th edn). New York: Oxford University Press.

Counselman, E.F., & Alonso, A. (1993). The ill therapist: Therapists' reactions to personal illness and its impact on psychotherapy. *American Journal of Psychotherapy*, 47(4), 591–602.

Department of Health (DoH) (2001). National Service Framework for Older People. Modern Standards and Service Models. London: DoH.

Department of Health and Home Office (2000). *Reforming the Mental Health Act, Parts I and II*. Cm 5016–11. London: HMSO.

Goetz, B. (1975). That is all I have to say about Freud: Bruno Goetz's reminiscences of Sigmund Freud. *International Review of Psycho-Analysis*, 2, 139–143.

Health Advisory Service (1982). *The Rising Tide: Developing services for mental illness in old age*. London: HMSO.

Holmes, J., & Lindley, R. (1989). *The Values of Psychotherapy*. Oxford: Oxford University Press.

Murphy, S. (2000). Provision of psychotherapy services for older people. *Psychiatric Bulletin*, 24, 181–184.

Roth A., & Fonagy, P. (1996). *What Works for Whom? A critical review of psychotherapy research*. New York: The Guilford Press.

Part II

Clinical applications

Chapter 10

Individual psychotherapy in the second half of life

Joan Reggiori

> Glowing coals under grey ashes
>
> (Jung, 1960)
>
> Creativity can emerge from loss
>
> (Storr, 1989)

When does the second half of life begin? Jung and his associates at one time considered that it began at around the age of 35. Freud thought that no one over 50 years old could benefit from analytic treatment. Who is it, today, who decides when we are regarded or designated as being middle aged and when we are seen as being old? To what extent is this culturally or psychologically determined? To what extent are our attitudes determined internally and sub-jectively as opposed to externally and objectively? These factors almost cer-tainly influence our expectations. Many people do not look forward to their own ageing. The ageing process is inevitable but not popular. Generally it is assumed to be associated with a deteriorating process, with perhaps a few compensations, if one is fortunate. Perhaps age is like beauty, as Hungerford (1878) put it 'in the eye of the beholder' – in other words, much is projected by the beholder, whether the latter is an individual or society in general. As with the young, each older person is unique. The author has, therefore, delib-erately moved freely between writing about the middle aged and the old, because there is no clear dividing line. To use the rule of chronological years is too simplistic.

As we age we often comment that we feel just the same inside ourselves in spite of the passing of the years. This can be seen as an inner truth reflecting a timeless sense of self; or it can be seen as a denial of external reality and change. Looked at from a psychological perspective, getting older can be seen as a sense of a primal core of self which integrates and survives superimposed change. However, the process of ageing for the individual includes other factors, social as well as psychological. Being middle aged is generally accept-able but being old is less so. Sometimes the latter represents the shadow side of being young. In other words it carries the negative projection of what is feared and not wanted.

Youth is sometimes indiscriminately over-valued because it carries the enticing attraction of renewal. However there can be a renewal, albeit of a different kind, in the older person if they have a sufficient capacity for reflection and continuing development. Each of us ages differently and at varying rates in physical, mental and psychological processes. As the analytic world ages, it too, as an institution, has matured as a result of experience and reflection. The following quotations are examples of how analytic attitudes have changed over the years.

THE EVOLUTION OF ANALYTICAL ATTITUDES

Freud in 'On Psychotherapy' stated that,

> near or above the age of 50 the elasticity of the mental processes on which the treatment depends, is as a rule lacking – old people are no longer educable.
>
> (1905: 214)

He was then 49 years old. Freud was in many ways ahead of his time in his thinking and in formulating his concepts (see Chapter 1). Therefore, one is led to assume that this particular observation of his was influenced by the culture of the time. Such a comment would be risible in this, the twenty-first century.

This contrasts with the writing of King in 'Notes on the psychoanalysis of the older patient', that there was

> no adequate conceptual framework for considering the possibility that later socio-biological changes would lead to psychological ones, and that changes imposed by ageing could be assimilated and integrated within the personality or that this process could lead to psychological growth.
>
> (1974: 26)

Jung, in 'The Stages of Life' when commenting on transitional periods, observed that we sometimes entrench ourselves in rigid ideals and principles acquired in the first half of life, sometimes at the cost of a diminution of personality:

> many – far too many – aspects of life which should also have been experienced lie in the lumber room among dusty memories; but sometimes too, they are glowing coals under grey ashes.
>
> (1960, para. 772) (See also Chapter 3)

A later quotation from Hildebrand in 'Psychoanalysis and Ageing' is in a similar vein to King:

> because of their preoccupation, in my view, psychoanalytic theorists far too uncritically accepted a hypothesis of continuing psychic and psychodynamic development, with a rising curve of growth from birth to adulthood, a long refractory period, and then a terminal stage of psychic and social withdrawal preliminary to dying and death itself.
>
> (1987: 115)

These quotations illustrate the changing attitudes to the second half of life within the analytic world. Bearing in mind that we are all living much longer and will probably continue to do so, it is essential that we embrace such forward thinking with its emphasis on continuing emotional development and the need for a more comprehensive and imaginative approach to the subject of ageing.

INTERACTION OF THE INNER AND OUTER WORLD

The following pages examine, amongst other important factors, the interaction of the inner and the outer world of the person in the second half of life and how this affects the psyche and individual sense of self. This is, of course, in addition to the crucial experience of the early years which have been, and still are, written about so profoundly and extensively. The term 'inner world' includes personal thoughts, feelings, both positive and negative, phantasies and so on. Whilst certain issues are common to those in the middle stages and later stages of life respectively, as they present themselves during analysis, every analytic process and every analysand or patient is unique and should be respected as such.

Of the many factors which contribute to the complexities within each person, their chronological age is only one. Society tends to group individuals together, often for spurious reasons. A criterion for one group, for example, is the number of their respective chronological years. This is a convenient but reductionist way of relating to a group, thereby ignoring the uniqueness of the individual and their particular stage of development. Cultural expectations of groups are projected into the members; these are consequently introjected by them to an extent which then colours how they view themselves as individuals. Not to conform to this expected image risks feeling isolated or excluded. This can result in feelings of frustration when the process of individuation appears to be in opposition to the expectation of the collective which can include peer and family groups. The term 'individuation' is used as meaning the continuing development of the person's unique psychological potential.

Zoja in 'Working against Dorian Gray: Analysis and the Old' writes:

> analytic work is concerned with old/young as intra-psychic and not
> chronological polarities; when these are emphasized as interpersonal, the
> individual is inevitably regarded as belonging to either one or other; it is
> worth asking if such a rigid separation does not do even more harm to
> the individuality (Latin non divisibility) of the psyche than in the case of
> other archetypal polarities.
>
> (1983: 53)

Zoja's approach to ageing is important because it is imaginative and creative,
and describes how we experience the many parts of a patient's psyche during
the process of analysis. As we live our lives we move back and forth between
the experience of the decades of life, depending on what we are confronted
with as we develop (see Chapter 6). This development evolves as a result of
our experience, often emanating from the interaction of our inner and outer
worlds and the effect this has on us and our openness to change – and no
more so than in this post mid-life period of transitional growth.

Some older people achieve a more 'youthful', in other words, more open,
flexible, tolerant, attitude to life in their seventies than in their forties. One of
the aims of analysis is to help the analysand to understand what is behind
some of their rigid defences and so help them become more accessible to
positive change. When the reason for a rigid defence has been understood and
accepted, then it dissolves of its own accord, for it is no longer necessary.
However, in some cases, intellectual insight alone is not enough and the
symptoms continue. This suggests that there is a secondary gain in their
continuation; for example it could result in the continuation of concern being
received from others.

When referring to the breadth and accumulated experience which
reverberates on the individual's inner world and influences it, one is reminded
of Jung (1960) when he wrote that in treating the problems of psychic life
one inevitably becomes involved in the most heterogeneous branches of
knowledge such as that of the philosopher, physician, historian, etc.:

> for it is out of him and out of his peculiar constitution that man has
> produced his sciences. They are symptoms of his psyche.
>
> (1960, para. 752)

IDENTITY

Throughout our lives we experience various identities, depending on what is
happening in our inner world and what our outer circumstances are at the
time. In Reggiori (1999) 'Who am I? When am I Myself? What's the Time?' an

example is given of the change which occurs in a person's sense of identity
and self when there is a trauma, such as a major bereavement. Other people
treat the bereaved person differently from the way they did before the event.
This serves to reinforce the feeling in that person that they have become a
stranger to themselves – hence 'Who am I?', a new identity has been imposed
upon them and there is turmoil in their inner world as they try to make sense
of this change and try to recover a sense of inner self. We can apply this to the
changes occurring in ageing. When society projects and imposes its expectations on the middle aged and on the elderly, these attributes are then
internalised. As a result a struggle ensues in the inner world of the ageing
person, at whatever time of life, in an attempt to find their own way forward
and embrace, and perhaps retrieve, their own set of values. This is part of the
process of *individuation* (see also Chapter 3).

The middle-aged may fear their loss of youth and feel they have an
uncertain future. The elderly may reminisce and enjoy memories which evoke
a time when they were more certain of having a specific and affirming identity, reinforced by the companionship of others of similar age; those who may
no longer be available. Comparatively few older people are readily regarded
by other persons as having personal creative aspirations. It is as if in moving
towards the end of life they are already regarded as separating from the rest
of us. This is not to say that such individuals do not inspire affection from
others. Jung's attitude (in a BBC interview with John Freeman in 1959) was
that one should prepare for death but at the same time live as if one had
centuries ahead of one.

The middle-aged person who seeks psychoanalytic therapy and presents
with, for example, a psychosomatic condition and depression may well
have suffered from these symptoms for years. What has, not infrequently,
precipitated their seeking analytic help at this time is the breaking down or
potential loss of an important relationship. There are many changes to be
negotiated because they are in the middle years of life. Other potential losses
include the anticipated death of parents and perhaps the moving away from
home of their adult children. The middle-aged woman will be faced with the
end of her child-bearing years. The middle-aged man may begin to have
anxiety about the possible loss of his sexual potency. It is a period of transition and this inevitably involves loss of some kind, including that of a
previous identity, especially when this was heavily dependent on a particular
relationship.

Clinical Illustration I
A middle-aged woman who had lost her partner presented with a long stand-
ing depression, saying that life had lost its meaning. She was unable to value
herself, especially as she regarded herself as being the 'left over half' of a
duo. She projected this view into how she expected society to regard her. She
felt psychologically naked. As a child she had felt that she did not fit in

*with the other school children and tended to withdraw. Exploring with her
therapist the images she had of her depression helped her to feel less isolated with her emotional pain. Slowly there arose moments when she allowed
herself to recognise personal attributes and values which had hitherto
become overwhelmed by society's view of the unattached older woman. This
reverberated with feelings of being unacceptable as a child.*

Clinical Illustration II
*A man came for psychotherapeutic help when he was near the age at which
his father had died. There was a strong identification with his father and a
hitherto unconscious anxiety that he would not be able to surpass his father
in chronological years. There was a looking backwards and a striving to
look forward to the future, accompanied by an inhibition that he would not
be able to be as successful in his work as his father had been in his. In these
transitional stages of life there is a search for an acceptable identity which
includes the question 'Who am I?', at this time.*

The older person may feel that they have little choice other than to remain
primarily identified with the role of an old man or an old woman, with all the
collective connotations of this.

Clinical Illustration III
*Such a patient said, as others have done, 'No one needs me now'. She felt
excluded and patronised by younger people, and so it was difficult for her to
identify with a role other than the one of being chronologically old and of
little value to others and therefore to herself. Consequently there was little
incentive for her to try to get in touch with her own creativity. She used her
years both as an attempt to attract sympathy and help and, at the same
time, as a defence against change – changes which might have come about
from exploring her defences, and her own potential for development. She
remained depressed for some time. However, through listening to her, getting close and being allowed into her inner world, the therapist accompanied
her through her mourning. She grieved over what she had known and
enjoyed in the past, and so became more aware of her own rigid defences
and how these contributed to her sense of isolation.*

Clinical Illustration IV
*Another patient, an artist in her seventies, had given up practising her skill
because she considered that she was too old. She had introjected what she
considered were society's expectations of someone of her age. There was
also a personal element in this attitude, due to her partner's obvious attraction to younger women. Consequently the interaction of her inner and her
outer world had become destructive for her. She needed someone to believe
she still had potential, especially after her husband had left her. She had*

been referred for psychotherapy because of a somatic condition which her doctor considered may have had a psychological component.

Clinical Illustration V
An older patient had managed her life by having her considerable, but unconscious, dependency needs met by others. A crisis in her marriage had dramatically reduced her support system. This had made her feel useless, and unconsciously angry, and had activated her early fears of being left alone. She was gifted in the arts but this played little part in her conscious evaluation of herself. She held her age as being responsible for her unmet emotional needs. Predictably, there arose considerable analytic dependence, which she needed in order to support her when she explored facets of her inner functioning that understandably included a need to control others.

In each of the above examples a new factor, if not a crisis, had arisen which had brought the patient for psychological help at that time. It is always informative to explore and to recognise what this precipitating circumstance is. Whilst none of the above patients was in suicidal despair, it is relevant to bear in mind what Clark (1993) focuses on when referring to such crucial periods in life in his paper. Clark hypothesises that elderly persons who die by suicide have a lifelong character fault which may well remain invisible until life-changes force the issue into the open. He writes that there is a total collapse of a defensive denial (the subject's main coping strategy) and a flooding, overwhelming state of panic and rage.

DEPENDENCY

Reference has been made to a crucial stage, or set of circumstances, which brings a person for analytic help. For the middle aged there is a reviewing of the previous years as well as a wish to look forward to the future, although this may evoke ambivalent feelings. This may include a change of career but more frequently it includes a search for a partner with whom there can be trust, intimacy, companionship and, most of all, a mutual interactive dependence.

The older person often lives alone. If there is a partner, the relationship may be less secure than before because of a loss of sexual intimacy (see Chapter 17). There have been the inevitable losses that are part of a long life. Frequently there is concern, conscious or unconscious, about the number of years left to them. Underlying this is an anxiety about an increasing dependence on someone or some organisation. There is likely to be a physical decline of some kind and perhaps a slowing up of mental faculties. The need for there to be someone special with whom to discuss such anxieties is pressing. Some are fortunate enough to have a close relationship with another perhaps younger person, who is sympathetic to their situation and will allow closeness and who is likely to outlive them. The older man will sometimes marry a much younger woman who will care for him and see him out of this life. However, it is rare for an older woman to marry a much younger man. It is as if woman brings life into this world and then there is an archetypal expectation that she will also see life out of this world in terms of caring for and outliving her partner. In this one respect it would seem that men and women age differently in the collective expectations of this period of life.

During an analysis of any depth it is expected that there will gradually evolve an analytic dependence in the interests of the analysis. It is expected that the analyst will provide continuity of care and create an atmosphere of trust and reliance into which the patient can bring his or her anxieties, as well as loving and hostile feelings. In allowing this closeness, which is experienced in the analytic dependence, there will be an interaction between the two participants which results in some healing of the emotional wounds. A difficulty may arise when it is decided together to work towards an ending of the psychotherapy. In a young or middle-aged person, as a result of the analytic work, a new venture, a new relationship, a new interest, will arise in which the patient can invest some of the psychic energy previously cathected in the analyst or analysis. With the much older person there may have to be a decrease in the frequency of the sessions before the final separation (Reggiori, 2002).

Clinical Illustration VI
An older man presented with depression and anxiety. As therapy progressed it emerged that he had an unconscious fear of loss. He quickly became dependent on the therapist, and when his wife left him, he became markedly more dependent. He wanted to be told what to do but of course, whatever suggestion might be made to him to ease his pain, he always found a reason for not considering it. Exploring new situations meant the loss of the old familiar ones on which he had depended for support and which had contributed to his sense of security and identity.

There are those of us who are dependent solely on other people, with no, or very little, dependence on other interests or creative work, whether these be intellectual, artistic pursuits, or absorbing hobbies. All of these enhance a person's identity and feelings of self worth. The experience of the loss of loved ones in the above circumstances is particularly devastating and it is exceptionally hard to work through the process of mourning without external affirming support. When this patient lost his wife, he became increasingly and clingingly dependent on other people and especially on his therapist. After a period of mourning the therapist tried therapeutically to encourage him to get some of his dependency needs met, by suggesting he involved himself in creative interests which could produce feelings of satisfaction and self worth. These might also relieve him of some of his isolation and his unrewarding demands on other people.

BEREAVEMENT AND CREATIVITY

Storr observes that some well known writers are impelled to develop their imaginative capacities as a compensation for the severance of intimate relationships.

> By creating a new unity in a poem or other literary work of art, the artist is attempting to restore a lost unit, or to find a new unity within the inner world of the psyche, as well as producing work which has a real existence in the external world.

> (1988: 123)

He goes on to state that there can be a creative response to loss (p.132) and gives examples of this. It is not implied that we are all potential writers but, especially in the case of the elderly person who may well have suffered losses of family, friends, colleagues and perhaps ambitions too, there is probably some capacity for creative work, no matter how simple. Creativity can produce a feeling of self worth and so contribute to overcoming the state of helplessness which is part of the depressed state (p.129). In the case of the dependent person who shows no sign of moving on from their state of considerable emotional dependency, it may be helpful, after a period of intensive psychotherapy, to space out the frequency of sessions. In the process of continuing to be 'thought about' by the therapist, they may be able to engage in some creative process, which can be supportive and perhaps lead to other relationships. There may be a parallel with Winnicott's understanding that a child needs first to be able to play in the presence of mother, before being able to play alone (Winnicott, 1971).

Older people can fall into a state of withdrawal or into a clinging dependence with another person which can stifle the creative potential in both parties within the relationship. As Storr observes: 'creative imagination can exercise a healing function' (p.123) (see also Chapter 6). The above approach may well not be seen as classical psychoanalysis. However, in some cases it may be more suitable and helpful to adopt such a modified treatment as a matter of choice. For a discussion of the different definitions of psychoanalysis and of psychotherapy as they are practised see Covington (2002) where the differences between analysis and psychotherapy are explored and the pertinent question is asked as to whether knowledge necessarily produces cure. She quotes and expands on Fairbairn's point that 'technique develops in response to our patient's needs' (p.102), which few therapists could dispute. The theory and practice of working psychodynamically with older patients is still in relative infancy.

Martindale (1989) refers to the situation of younger therapists who find the long-term dependency demands of their older patients rather daunting, because of the needs of their own elderly parents at the time. Elderly patients may decline to acknowledge that there have been some positive changes in their respective lives, for fear that the therapist would then assume that they were beginning to manage their lives without the dependence on the therapist and regular sessions. For the patient this would mean that the therapist might begin to consider terminating the therapy and so one of their support systems would be removed.

It can happen that the most helpful outcome in some cases is that the patient is enabled to accept the external situation which has brought them to psychotherapy in the first place, but cannot be radically changed in the outer sense. An example of this could be crippling anxiety presenting itself in a fear of going out alone after a loved one has died. The dead person cannot be brought back but in the experience of mourning it may be possible to make conscious what other losses have been suffered and are still continuing to affect them. In helping the patient to discover for themselves what they are achieving and what can still be attained, some positive change may come about. Thus a supportive movement can take place within the patient's inner world which can help them to feel less isolated internally, as well as in their external world, and therefore more acceptable to themselves and to others. There can be an inner psychic loneliness as well as an outer loneliness (see Chapter 2).

Some experienced analysts have maintained that a second analysis with an analyst who was much older than the first had a greater depth and a richer quality than that experienced with the younger, middle-aged one. It can be argued that they were each at a different stage in their psychological development (Reggiori, 1999). But the fact remains that a more creative maturity was experienced with the older analyst. There are two main areas in analytic training: the first is concerned with theory and technique; the second is more concerned with the sensitive application, and this skill increases with experience and maturity of the personality.

THE SENSE OF TOUCH

There are occasions when older patients would like to be physically touched by another person but feel their years make them unattractive for this inter-action. Physically touching the patient is not the actual task of the analyst, although essential in a symbolic sense. But to recognise this need emanating from a sense of isolation can be therapeutic. An observation of Margaret Mead (1901–1978) comes to mind here: 'Having someone wonder where you are when you don't come home at night is a very human need'. In other words, to know that one matters to another human being and that one is not totally alone. There are occasions when it is essential and therapeutic to enter into the older, and middle-aged patient's fear of the process of dying and of death, conscious or unconscious, and share with them what the ending of life and separation means to them. Whatever form the latter may take, it must be communicated that it is not an unapproachable subject (Reggiori, 2002). Whatever they have in front of them in the foreseeable future, it will include their death. There are times when discussing the future contains their hopes and fears about how they will feel after the analysis or psychotherapy has ended and they have separated from the therapist.

TRANSITIONS

A factor in one stage of transition can be retiring from paid employment. The retiring person will be wished a 'happy retirement' and for many this will prove to be the case. But it is often not what one is retiring from that is the determining factor in the change – rather it is what one is retiring to. Some people will find the loss of a work identity very disabling. Others will feel supported by a loving close family including perhaps an extended one and the enjoyment of grandchildren. Others will not be so fortunate. For some there will be a feeling of shame about growing old, and retirement will confirm this state. Hultberg writes that:

> loss of control, one of the deepest causes of shame, lies behind the general fear of ageing and illness. . . . Behind shame is a fear of being excluded from society and implies a fear of total abandonment. . . . One type of shame ensures membership of human society through conformity.
>
> (1988: 117)

The author would add to this comment, a fear of 'not belonging' and of not being valued by others. This militates against a conscious sense of self, which in turn includes being unsure of one's identity. All this may happen at a time when the ageing process may have already made one feel vulnerable. Shame can emanate from a lack of self-esteem. The shame of 'not belonging' causes a person to move between feelings of anger and depression. It often brings relief when the therapist interprets that anxiety and anger are often interactive, and legitimises the anger they feel in the circumstances. Consequently having these powerful emotions becomes less shameful.

We are not only who we appear to be on the surface at any given time, for we are a composition of all the many 'selves' we have been before which are still dormant within us (Redfearn, 1985). The stooping, slightly deaf old man we see before us, is also the popular Head Boy. Other identities and experience inside him have contributed to the person he is today. Yet all too often, all we see is just a slow old man with some memories. We project a lot of our fears of loss, including a loss of potency, into the elderly, and they therefore come to represent a threat to us. This can include an anxiety about the extent of their future dependency demands on us.

We may be distressed at the inevitable change we perceive in ageing parents, not least because it reminds us of what is in store for us. We may have fantasies, as we had as young children, that parents do not indulge in sexual intercourse for example. Yet Hildebrand (1995) observes that older people can enjoy a very active sex life, when he refers to the intimacy between older people which can produce an exchange far richer than in the younger person (p.29) (see also Chapter 17). Freud (1917) stresses the central factor of loss in causing depression. There are many losses to integrate in the process of ageing in the second half of life. As the adolescent sees in the middle aged the loss of his youth, so the middle aged sees in the elderly the loss of active life and frequently his or her independence as well. Some times a middle-aged person may refer a parent to a psychotherapist. It is not unknown for the parent to subsequently cancel the appointment. One is then left wondering whether the referrer has a problem which he or she has projected into the elderly parent and with which they hope the therapist will deal, or whether there is a family problem which is better addressed with them as a unit. A comprehensive assessment is important before taking a patient on for long-term therapy.

The psychotherapist often receives the projections from the older person needing psychotherapeutic help, of all that they fear. This can include feeling worthless, unwanted and depressed. The psychotherapist may introject these feelings and sometimes risk feeling impotent with the patient as a result of this, and especially so if many patients of this kind are being seen. It is important to bear in mind that the later years can be creative and there is frequently a successful search for renewal. This is dependent on the movement of the 'inner psychic time' which is different from the 'outer chronological time'.

POSITIVE ASPECTS OF AGEING

Reference has been made previously to the fact that the second half of life may represent the shadow side of youth. The latter searches for a freedom from being dependent and longs for independence. Those in the second half of life are usually searching for someone on whom they can reliably depend and with whom they can feel close. Both may be searching for an identity. However, there are those persons of mature age who are extremely successful in their work and find one expression of identity in that area.

Creative artists like Tippett and Solti in the music world, painters such as Picasso for example, and many writers in their seventies and eighties, have been, and still are, producing impressive works and are acknowledged and valued world wide. Age and experience seem to have enhanced their creative abilities. It is often a matter of rising to the occasion whatever the person's age. Churchill was made Prime Minister in 1940 at the age of 64 years and proceeded to lead the nation through the Second World War. He was then at an age when others would have been forced to retire from paid employment because society considered them to be too old to function adequately. Churchill might not have been so successful if he had been younger at that time, because he would not have had the necessary experience and maturity. (Whether the situation produces the man, or the man creates the situation is open to debate.) We need outstanding figures such as those mentioned, with whom we can identify in our inner private worlds, in order to satisfy our own ambitions and narcissistic needs. Thus the admired and the admirer are closely interdependent.

In his paper of 1965 Jacques maintains that the mid-life crisis begins around the age of 35 years and that the 'process of transition runs on for some years'. He also states that another crisis or period of rapid transition occurs at 'full maturity around the age of 65 years' (p.502), thus supporting the concept of progressive development. He considers that the mid-life crisis is a depressive crisis, and calls for a re-working through of the infantile depression but with mature insight into death and the destructive impulses. Can it be argued that Churchill's periods of depression were an ingredient in his creativity as was his advancing age?

It is not being suggested that anyone should embark on psychotherapy or analysis solely with the purpose of becoming more creative. However, there is evidence to show that persons entering the analytic process principally for relief of unwanted symptoms find that after a while new skills emerge from within themselves. This can lead to an expression of a new identity. As Jung has written: 'The afternoon of life is just as full of meaning as the morning; only its meaning and purpose are different' (1953, p.74).

CONCLUDING OBSERVATIONS

Whether or not one chooses to adhere firmly to the classic psychoanalytic approach, should be decided by what is most helpful for the particular patient one is treating. To use a psychoanalytically informed understanding of the situation and explore the early years with such a patient without necessarily making a great many interpretations is invaluable, and may well be the most facilitating method of healing in a given situation. In other circumstances a more classic approach is appropriate. If the analyst can get close to the patient and value what they are bringing to the encounter, then the patient can take into their inner world a positive image of a validating inner therapist, which will help them gradually to value themselves. This will reduce some of the inner loneliness from which so many older patients suffer. When their outer world begins to diminish, partly through the inevitable loss of some of their lifelong friends, a person's inner objects may be depleted also, leading to feelings of isolation.

Hildebrand's words are relevant here:

> an approach which does not insist on the rigidity of a formula in which everything is related to the Oedipus complex, to defences, to drives and their derivatives, but which can listen to the patient and what the patient brings, is far more appropriate to working with older people, far more comfortable, than one which forces everything into an infantile metaphor.
>
> (1987: 118)

In the same paper he challenges any concept that old people are passive during psychotherapy and observes that 'Countertransferentially old people, with their vivid and often enormously strong sexual and aggressive fantasies, make enormous demands on us' (p.120).

Jung makes a similar comment to Hildebrand on the subject of the use of interpretations when he writes:

> The one sided reductive explanation becomes in the end nonsensical. . . The sense of boredom which then appears in the analysis is simply an expression of monotony and poverty of ideas – not of the unconsious, as is sometimes supposed, but of the analyst who does not understand that these fantasies should not be taken merely in a concretistic reductive sense but rather a constructive one.
>
> (1960, para. 146)

This attitude is expressed in Jung's teleological approach – an orientation which maintains that the symptoms of the neuroses contain the purpose as well as the roots of the problem. Zoja suggests that the conception of analysis or initiation (meaning a beginning) aims at viewing old age 'not simply as a loss of youth but as a psychological state attained gradually and with difficulty but worth entering into . . . and points to the importance of a psychological preparation for death' (1983: 64).

Perhaps we need to look more closely at what we can learn from the older person and their special experience and creativity. It must be acknowledged that, as with the young, some are not particularly reflective whilst others are rich in their contemplation. Renewal and creativity can still be achieved during the second half of life, if defences against change are not too rigid and cultural prejudices are not too powerful. Intellectual insight alone does not necessarily produce change; there needs to be an emotional understanding as well, as to why the individual may need to continue with his or her symptoms.

REFERENCES

Clark, D. (1993). Narcissistic crises of ageing and suicidal despair. *The American Association of Suicidology*, 23(1).

Covington, C. (2002). The myth of pure analysis. *Journal of Analytic Psychology*, 47(1).

Freud, S. (1905). On psychotherapy. Standard Edition 7. London: Hogarth.

Freud, S. (1917). Mourning and melancholia. Standard Edition 11 (p. 214). London: Hogarth.

Hildebrand, P. (1987). Psychoanalysis and ageing. *The Annals of Psychoanalysis*, 15.

Hildebrand, P. (1995). *Beyond Midlife Crisis*. London: Sheldon Press.

Hultberg, P. (1988). Shame: A hidden emotion. *Journal of Analytical Psychology*, 33(2).

Hungerford, M. (1878). Molly Bain. In: *Oxford Dictionary of Quotations*. Oxford: Oxford University Press.

Jacques, E. (1965). Death and the mid-life crisis. *Journal of Psychoanalysis*, 46, 502.

Jung, C.G. (1953). Two essays on analytical psychology. *C.W. 7*, p. 114.

Jung, C.G. (1960). The stages of life. *C.W. 8*.

King, P. (1974). Notes on the psychoanalysis of older patients. *Journal of Analytical Psychology*, 19(1).

Martindale, B.V. (1989). Becoming dependent again: The fears of some elderly patients and their younger therapists. *Psychoanalytic Psychotherapy*, 4(1), 67–75.

Redfearn, J. (1985). *Myself, My Many Selves*. London: Karnac Books.

Reggiori, J. (1999). Who am I? When am I myself? What's the time? *Journal of the British Association of Psychotherapists*, 37.

Reggiori, J. (2002). Analytic dependence. In: *Contemporary Jungian Practice*. London: Karnac Books.

Storr, A. (1989). Bereavement, depression and repair. In: *Solitude*. London: Flamingo Fontana Paperbacks.

Winnicott, D. (1971). *Playing and Reality*. London: Tavistock Publications.

Zoja, L. (1983). Working against Dorian Gray: Analysis and the old. *Journal of Analytical Psychology*, 28(1).

Chapter 11

Brief psychodynamic therapy with older people

Siân Critchley-Robbins

Time has an important resonance to older adults, with the concept of limited time taking on a new meaning, as older people face their own mortality in more immediate ways. Brief therapy can be said to recapitulate the central dilemma of late life: time, mortality and loss. The 'last chance' phenomena observed by Pearl King (1974) can serve to mobilise creative capacities and desires. Brief therapy can provide the patient with the opportunity to review their life, reworking their story to enable them to embrace the life they have lived, to mourn and to accept. As Gorsuch (1998) comments, such reflection takes courage when time is short and opportunities are steadily closing down.

This chapter focuses on brief psychodynamic therapy with older people. Currently, the literature on the application of brief therapy with older adults is limited. The initial sections of the chapter provide an overview of brief psychodynamic therapy concepts and models from the general literature, before moving on to specific issues in later life.

LONG-TERM VERSUS BRIEF THERAPY

A number of studies in the United States have indicated that regardless of the type of treatment, the setting or the patient, the great majority of patients are seen for between 6 and 12 sessions (e.g. DeLeon et al., 1991). Both Levenson (1995) and Messer and Warren (1995) conclude that most mental health professionals are conducting brief therapies, if unintentionally. Levenson (1995) suggests that most patients choose to leave therapy during the time they are experiencing the greatest rate of clinical improvement. She emphasises the difference between what Stern (1993) calls 'naturally occurring brief therapies' (where clients have dropped out of treatment) and therapies that are planned from the start to make the most of limited time.

Long-term therapy hopes to produce sustainable characterological change and increased emotional maturation. Brief therapy has a different emphasis, taking instead a focus on a particular critical moment in a patient's life, often a time of crisis. The aim is to enable the patient to understand and resolve the crisis, helping them to 'get back on track' with life. It concentrates on the detail of this critical moment, whilst deliberately excluding the bigger picture (Mander, 2000).

What makes brief therapy different from long-term therapy is the specificity of goals, the active role of the therapist and the expectation that the therapy will be short. The therapist brings a sense of confidence and optimism, symbolised by the time limitation, which indicates to the patient that the therapist hopes that a great deal can be achieved in a short period of time, actively working through the core conflict. The hope is that understanding change in the area of focus will have a ripple effect to produce understanding in other areas (Mander, 2000).

The remit of the therapist consists of insistent adherence to the central focus, actively discouraging digressions, persistent confrontations and interpretations, and by means of these interpretations, discouraging regression and avoiding dependency. Instead, the therapist places an emphasis on keeping the therapeutic process more reality-based, concentrating on the here-and-now relationship between therapist and patient. Rather than taking the long-term therapy stance of 'evenly hovering attention', the brief therapist practices 'selective attention, selective interpretation and selective neglect' (Malan, 1979). Brief therapy aims to provide a 'corrective emotional experience' (Alexander & French, 1946), where emotional change is based on the re-experiencing of old conflicts within a new context: the therapeutic relationship. Whilst the brief therapist is alert to the transference, the emphasis on its use varies between models. It is used sparingly within some models of brief therapy and generally only when it enables the work to be moved on decisively. In other brief therapies, the positive transference needed to maintain a supportive and encouraging atmosphere is used. Other important attributes of brief therapy include the selection criteria, the therapeutic alliance, the optimism of the therapist and the agreed contract with the patient, which includes the planned termination. The setting of a time limit is a therapeutic tool in itself.

The duration of brief therapies may vary, from as little as one session to as many as one or two sessions a week for a year. Therapists such as Mann (1973) insist on the maintenance of the therapeutic boundary through adhering to the contracted number of sessions, using this as a therapeutic tool in itself. If a patient seems to need more therapy, therapists such as Malan (1979), refer the patient on to a different therapist. Other therapists convert brief contracts to longer contracts, and others practice successive contracting (Mander, 2000).

MODELS OF BRIEF THERAPY

Modern brief psychodynamic therapy began with the work of Michael Balint and David Malan in 1955, who pioneered a workshop at the Tavistock Clinic in London to develop and research a model of brief focal psychotherapy. They developed a model of working with a carefully selected dynamic focus in order to resolve unconscious conflict interfering in the patient's psychic functioning and leading to symptom formation. At around the same time, Habib Davanloo was developing his model of intensive short-term dynamic psychotherapy (ISTDP) in Canada, and Peter Sifneos was working in the United States developing his model of short-term anxiety-provoking psychotherapy (STAPP). Messer and Warren (1995) describe these as 'Drive or Structural Models' of brief therapy, viewing them as being rooted in the classic tradition of Freud's drive theory. Davanloo, Malan and Sifneos all regard unresolved Oedipal conflicts as the core focus for their models of brief therapy.

Malan

The Malan (1979) model explained the basic principles of brief dynamic psychotherapy in terms of the interpretation of two 'triangles of insight': the triangle of conflict and the triangle of person.

The 'triangle of conflict' helps the therapist to identify the anxieties, defences against these, and the hidden feelings that create the patient's unconscious conflict. The 'triangle of person (or time)' enables the hidden feeling to be related to three categories of person: Other (significant people in the patient's current or recent past), Transference (the therapist in the here-and-now) and Parent (significant people in the distant past, typically parents, other caretakers or siblings). The aim in therapy is to reach beneath the defence and the anxiety to the hidden feeling, and then to trace this back from its origin in the past, usually in the relationship with parents. A distinctive feature of this model is the use of repeated follow-ups to monitor whether the achieved therapeutic changes are maintained. Malan's approach is based on selective listening and interpreting of the focus. Malan's style has been described as gentler and less confrontational than either Davanloo or Sifneos (Messer & Warren, 1995; Mander, 2000).

Davanloo and Sifneos

Davanloo's model (1978, 1980) also employs the two triangles, but places emphasis on the original conflict being generated within multiple relationships in the early environment. Davanloo's technique is based on the repeated confrontation of the patient's defences in order to expose the hidden feelings and conflicts. Sifneos' (1972, 1992) therapy is characterised by direct confrontation of the impulses/hidden feeling, without necessarily confronting the defences first, as well as assisting patients in learning to understand their dynamic patterns.

Molnos

Molnos (1995) outlined a model which expands Malan's two triangles into four, and drew on the 'strong but fair challenge' approach of Davanloo. This approach combines psychic holding with confrontation. Molnos described the importance of the patient being able to be in touch with and repeatedly express anger towards the therapist, describing this as 'a moment of separation within a good relationship'. This approach requires a certain amount of strength on the part of both patient (to bear the pain) and the therapist (to maintain the challenging style) (Mander, 2000).

Luborsky; and Strupp and Binder

Messer and Warren (1995) describe the approach to brief dynamic psychotherapy therapy by Luborsky (1984) (Supportive-Expressive Psychotherapy), and Strupp and Binder (1984) (Time-limited Dynamic Therapy) as the second main trend in brief psychodynamic therapy, referred to as 'Relational Models'. Messer and Warren (1995) see these approaches as being more closely aligned with the object relational tradition.

These models suggest that difficulties originate from an individual's maladaptive patterns of interacting with others, which are construed in the context of their past relationship experiences. The concept of the focus within Luborsky's model is the core conflictual relationship theme (Luborsky, 1984; Luborsky & Crits-Christoph, 1990). Conflicts are between interpersonal wishes and feared or anticipated outcomes. The therapeutic approach is based on 'supportive' and 'expressive' interventions. The focus within Strupp and Binder's model (Strupp & Binder, 1984; Binder & Strupp, 1991) is the cyclic maladaptive pattern. The model views the way individuals place themselves and others in relationships as resulting in 'maladaptive interaction sequences, self-defeating expectations, negative appraisals, and unpleasant affects'.

Mann

Mann (1973) proposed a model of brief therapy that draws on the ego, drive, object and self, which Messer and Warren (1995) describe as an 'integrative' model. The central issue is separation, framed in developmental terms. Time and termination are core to the therapeutic task. This model of time-limited psychotherapy employs a specific structural framework of 12 weekly sessions, with a precise, predetermined goal, and focuses on ending. The incorporation of a developmental perspective is helpful in working with individuals experiencing difficulties in negotiating the transition from one life stage to another, such as retirement or facing old age.

DEVELOPMENTAL THEORIES IN RELATION TO BRIEF THERAPY

As people age, so they are exposed, as individuals and as part of a cohort, to myriad life experiences. These experiences shape how they adapt and respond throughout life. Our understanding of age-specific notions should therefore include a lifespan developmental perspective, such as Erikson's (1966) theory of the life cycle (see Chapter 6). More recently, Joan Erikson (1998), drawing on her own and her husband's experiences of ageing, has suggested that there may be a ninth stage to address the challenges of extreme old age. She emphasises that there is the potential for psychological growth and personal development throughout the life cycle, regardless of age.

Budman and Gurman (1988) describe the notion of 'developmental dysynchrony', referring to the intrapsychic impact of failing to negotiate a developmentally defined objective. For example, a woman in her mid-seventies who had married but never had children described in her therapy her wish to have had a large family. This highlighted the divergence between her expectations (defined in terms of her peer group and broader cultural norms) and her actual life situation.

Mander (2000) described the importance for the brief therapist of assessing where the patient is in the life cycle, and how well they have achieved the various life tasks, such as acknowledging the onset of old age. The therapeutic task may then become one of facilitating the developmental transitions. Where there are multiple failures at various life stages, brief therapy may not be appropriate. Knight (1996) discussed the need to be aware of the difference between socially defined age-graded roles and developmental tasks. For example, retirement is often presented as a developmental milestone but, as Knight argued, it is a socially created role, which is being continually redefined.

ASSESSMENT AND SELECTION CRITERIA FOR BRIEF THERAPY

In brief therapy, careful assessment and selection of clients is crucial to ensure maximum benefit from the therapy. It is essential to gain a picture of the patient's personal and social history, some evidence of how the patient relates, their ability to self-reflect, their internal and external functioning and how they manage anxiety. Messer and Warren (1995) suggest that consideration should be given to whether a medical assessment would be helpful. This may be particularly pertinent with older clients, where medical conditions may be contributing to the presenting difficulties. The therapist also needs to evaluate the forces in the patient for or against improvement. It is important to make an assessment of the most disturbed the client has ever been, as

Malan's (1979, 1995) 'Law of increased disturbance' suggests that psycho-therapy may make a client as disturbed as the client has ever been in the past. This means that previous breakdowns need to be noted. Throughout, it is important to remain aware of the possible effects of assessment: increased hope, disturbance and attachment.

Analysts and psychotherapists have given long consideration to exclusion and inclusion criteria, and opinions differ. Mander (2000) emphasises the importance of rapport in making an overall judgement. Malan and his col-leagues offer a useful system of guidelines. An important inclusion criterion is psychological-mindedness, which Colthart (1988) discusses eloquently, and incorporates a capacity to reflect on oneself, and to perceive relationships between events in one's life and feelings, and a sense of curiosity about oneself. Further inclusion criteria include: motivation to engage in therapy (seeking change, not just symptom relief), and the ability to form and sustain a relationship. An assessment of the patient's ability to make use of interpret-ative therapy is deemed crucial, and can be gauged through the use of 'trial interpretations' in the initial assessment.

Issues potentially leading to exclusion include chronicity (including depres-sion,) obsessiveness, acting out or self-destructive behaviour (including ser-ious suicide attempts). An inability to self-reflect and to form relationships would be negative factors, as would paranoid conditions and rigid defences where dismantling could lead to breakdown. Messer and Warren (1995) sug-gest that all brief treatment methods 'require a minimum of reality orienta-tion, facility with language, affective presence, and alertness' (p.318). Thus, they suggest that patients with organic problems, severe depression, or other medical problems that limit cognitive and affective functions are not likely to benefit. Whilst it is appropriate to consider the suitability of patients with cognitive impairment, the author has experience of applying brief therapy to individuals with dementia, where the focus for the work has been on the very losses occurring as a result of the dementing process. The losses are often the reality for the client, and as such may be more easily accessed and worked with in the therapy. However, careful attention needs to be given to the adap-tive function of the client's defences in this situation. Sinason (1992) provides a moving account of one year of psychodynamic therapy with a man who had Alzheimer's disease.

SELECTION ISSUES FOR BRIEF THERAPY WITH OLDER CLIENTS

Hildebrand (1982), based on his experience of short-term therapy with older clients, has drawn attention to the greater emotional strength and self-reliance of older people. He suggests that they can be motivated and can more readily use briefer therapy than younger clients. Their life experience enables them to take a longer-term view and affords them a certain resilience. The awareness that time is running out brings a sense of urgency to working on emotional problems (Terry, 1996). Pollock (1982) highlights the older person's capacity for self-reflection and self-observation. Bateman and Holmes (1995) suggest that: 'The elderly person who remains active, able to form meaningful relationships and to seek new experiences, is at least potentially able to show the psychological flexibility needed for psychotherapy.'

It is important to acknowledge that there may be obstacles within the older patient to therapy. These may include a reluctance to explore sensitive issues with seemingly young and inexperienced workers. Some older people may employ particular defence mechanisms such as denial, somatisation, and a focus on the practical; also in some cases 'an inability or lack of desire to confront the vulnerable, the undiscussable, the irresolvable' (Stern & Lovestone, 2000). Maintaining the brief therapy focus requires skill in the face of such resistance.

There may be real practical problems of poor mobility, difficulty in hearing and declining memory. However, it is important for the therapist to give consideration to whether these are real external problems that need to be attended to, or whether either patient or therapist is employing them as a defence. For example, it is necessary to consider whether the difficulty in hearing something is a physical hearing problem, or a difficulty for both therapist and patient to appreciate what is being said. In considering the practical problems, Nordhus and Nielson (1999) argue that the therapist sometimes needs to be more flexible about the duration and frequency of sessions.

ISSUES IN WORKING WITH OLDER PEOPLE

Issues bringing clients to therapy

Many of the issues faced by older clients focus on actual loss, the threat of loss or anger at loss. They may face disappointments over their achievements in life, and eventually face death itself. Ruth Porter (1991) described how psychotherapy can help elderly patients make new internal adaptations in five areas: loss, anger, discontinuity (from earlier parts of their lives), disorder and chaos, and sexuality. Knight (1996) reminds us that negotiating death is a task of late middle age, and that older people have often come to terms with their own mortality. Losses in later life may stimulate memory and emotion associated with earlier losses, perhaps previously unattended to. This in turn may affect an individual's ability to adapt to ageing. Brief therapy, with its time limitation, and its selection of a core focus places issues of tolerating loss and separation at the centre of the therapeutic process.

Evans et al. (2001) suggest that some older people may need to renegotiate life, and may need assistance in rediscovering a purpose in their lives. Pollock

(1982) stated that older people wish to be useful and to maintain their dignity. Messer and Warren (1995) suggest that brief therapy can help older people not only with their enduring pain around core issues, but also to consider the possibilities for new outlets and pursuits in life. Brief therapy may be a primer into a new willingness to seek help as and when the need arises. This may be particularly important for clients in later life, when, as noted by Cohen (1982), one must be able to recognise one's own sense of dependency, to allow environmental help to be sought.

Evans et al. (2001) demonstrate how group therapy can help people who have been emotionally isolated for years to take the risk of establishing new relationships. Nordhus and Nielson (1999) suggest that brief dynamic therapy, such as the Strupp and Binder model, can be usefully implemented with older clients who are experiencing conflicts in current, close relationships.

Experiences of time

King (1980) describes older people as operating within various time-scales: the chronological time-scale, a psychological one, a biological time-scale, and alongside these, the time-scale of unconscious processes which are paradoxically timeless. King states that such an understanding of the time-scale for an older person within a session is an important key to understanding the transference phenomena of the patient. The critical principle underlying Mann's model of time-limited therapy is the unconscious and conscious meaning and influence of time. Mann suggests that time-limited therapy requires clients to deal with the dread of time and its implications for losses. The age of the therapist may also need to be taken into consideration, including their own perceptions of the passage of time and its meaning.

Transference issues

Whilst the transference may be used more sparingly within brief therapy, the therapist must still be alert to it. The transference may include the therapist as parent, grandparent, contemporary, a lover or an authority figure. The therapist may represent the patient's children or grandchildren. The therapist is treated as the repository of hopes and fears, shame or delights, aspirations or guilt, but in terms not only of the past but also the future. As Hildebrand (1986) states, this is a future that may or may not include the older patient, for whom personal death is a far more concrete reality than for the younger patient. Orbach (1994) emphasises that transference may be stronger if a person is experiencing an increasingly bleak life, where friends and relatives frequently die. The brief therapist needs to be alert for signs of regression and dependence, which are discouraged within brief therapy, and thus need careful management.

Countertransference issues

The therapist must also consider the countertransference issues in work with older people, which might include distaste for the physical and cognitive losses of the older person, and pessimism about the opportunities for change. The therapist may feel helpless, frustrated, angry, resentful, or depressed in response to the older, frailer person's dependency needs. Martindale (1989) writes that if the therapist is currently experiencing demands from their own ageing parents, demands for the therapist's time and attention from their client may feel more burdensome. This can lead to guilt over termination, especially when the client has little other emotional or social contact. There may be veiled expressions of concern as to whether the therapy was really of any value to the older client in the face of their real problems.

Martindale (1989) reminds us of the importance of the therapist acknowledging any wish that might exist for their older patient to be a substitute for the parent or grandparent who would admire or praise them for their work, and that this wish would not be gratified if the therapist recognised the infant in the elderly patient. Porter (1991) highlights the fear of failure in the presence of an older figure.

The therapist's own wish to 'cure all' can be challenged by the focused work of brief therapy with older people. There may be a fear that unconscious issues have been opened up without sufficient time to work them through. This may leave the therapist concerned about potential harm the therapy may have caused. Given the need to socialise some older clients to therapy (Nordhus & Nielson, 1999), there may be a concern that the real issues have not been addressed because they came to light too late. The volume of material can lead to a sense that if a little more could be offered, the patient may be cured. It is important for the therapist to be able to reach their own tolerance of life's imperfect solutions, and still view themselves as 'good enough' therapists, or negativity about the therapy may be conveyed to the patient. The therapist, as well as the older client has to face the painful reality that ageing is not reversible (Bateman & Holmes, 1995). Mander (2000) reminds us that focusing and containing the area of therapeutic exploration to a clearly identifiable nuclear conflict through an assessment and brief intervention can be beneficial.

Separation and termination

Brief therapy uses the ending as a core therapeutic technique. Placing the issue of separation and individuation at the forefront of the therapeutic technique reflects a basic respect for and encouragement of the patient's capacity for autonomy. This can counter the older client's beliefs about themself as helpless, inadequate and in need of support. Addressing the ending from the beginning reinforces the client's confidence in their ability to resolve the current complaint in a limited time, and thus accelerates the therapeutic process.

Brief therapists need to be aware of their own separation issues, in order to avoid emotional withdrawal from the patient, with little exploration of the meaning of the ending. This is crucial for maintaining the focus of the work and not slipping into dependency. Mander (2000) discusses how the therapist's knowledge that there is the possibility of further brief therapy in the future can help brief therapists to let go. However, brief therapists working with older people have to tolerate the anxiety that further work may not be possible because their older patients may be facing death.

Power and authority

Brief therapy requires the therapist to take a more active stance, which can engender conflict in the therapist over power and authority (Messer & Warren, 1995). This needs to be reflected on as both a transference and countertransference issue. The patient may view the therapist as an authority figure or 'magical expert' (Knight, 1996), and may expect the therapist to provide solutions and instruction on how to solve problems, or to make major decisions on their behalf. Knight (1996) highlights the dual role therapists may have in working with older people, acting as both therapist and case managers or assessors of mental health status, further complicating issues of power and authority. The therapist's belief in their own authority within the therapy can be an issue. The therapist may also wish to hold on to a notion of an older adult as developmentally stable, to be 'all grown-up', devoid of issues which they themselves may be grappling with (Crusey, 1986)

Orbach (1994), in discussing the issue of the focus within brief therapy, cautions against therapists simply focusing on issues they feel comfortable confronting in working with older people. Orbach describes a particular kind of resistance within the younger therapist: that of crossing the generation boundary, probing into what may seem like parents' secrets. This may include confrontation of parental and transgenerational sexuality. Particular kinds of countertransference may also hinder therapists in perceiving the real client problem. For example, the therapist may feel overly protective of their older client, perceiving them as the archetypal grandparent, which may prevent them perceiving particular problems (e.g. dementia, substance abuse, psychosis, etc.). Porter (1991) suggests that a tendency towards sympathy in work with older clients can get in the way of 'correct' but seemingly 'cruel' interpretations.

An important aspect of brief therapy is encouraging clients to be empowered, to have confidence in their own curative abilities. In working with older people, therapists are confronted with issues which are beyond the control of the client: the fact of chronic disability, clients forced into dependency against their will. The brief therapist working with older people needs to be able to recognise the value of improvements in terrible situations and the importance of psychological factors in undeniably physical disabilities (Knight, 1996).

IMPORTANCE OF SUPERVISION AND TRAINING IN THIS WORK

It is important for therapists to understand the specific nature of problems of later life. Attention needs to be paid to generational or cohort effects (for example, years of formal education, differences in word usage). Knight (1996) described the importance of therapists being aware of the different historical backgrounds and value systems and the distinctive social milieu of older adults. Therapists need to be informed about the way physical health problems and their treatment impact on psychological and social wellbeing in later life, and to be able to recognise and work with grief when it occurs. Martin (1992) discusses the impact of being attuned to the older person's pain whilst being aware that one cannot alleviate their distress, suggesting that this can lead the therapist to question their image of themselves as 'an effective, caring professional'. Therapists need to be supported in understanding these issues, through appropriate training and ongoing supervision.

CONCLUDING COMMENTS

The various models of brief psychodynamic therapy share many key characteristics. The models have been well developed, with manuals explaining the theory and techniques of the approaches. Brief psychodynamic therapy has an extensive outcome literature. The outcome literature pertaining to older people is more limited, but indicates that brief therapy can be successfully applied to work with older people. Consideration of the pertinent issues in later life highlights the suitability of brief psychodynamic therapy for some older clients. In particular, placing loss and separation at the core of the therapeutic technique allows these issues to be addressed, and encourages the client to feel empowered in tackling their current difficulty. The attributes required of a brief therapist are also important for therapists working with clients in later life. Of particular relevance is the ability to mourn, a willingness to bear uncertainty, and the capacity not to expect perfect results. Practising brief psychodynamic therapy with older people requires skill, an appropriate knowledge base and ongoing supervision and support.

Case Illustration
The following illustrates some aspects of brief therapy and issues representative of those likely to be addressed with patients in later life, including physical health problems, family issues and a developmental lifespan context.

A Malan approach to brief therapy with Mr P

Mr P was 72 years old and presented to the psychology service six months after the death of his dog. He reported various symptoms of depression, and commented that both his son and daughter worried about him.

Mr P never knew his father, who was killed shortly after he was born. He was evacuated, age 7, and was away from home for 3 years. He was billeted with a loving foster family, who cried when he left. On his return, he found his mother had remarried and had another child. She later had a third child. Whilst the rest of his childhood was fairly straightforward, he described feeling slightly outside of his family, and as though his step-father never accepted him. At the age of 18 he joined the army. He described this as a very happy time, stating that he felt he 'truly belonged' somewhere for the first time in his life. He described 'seeing some terrible things' during his army service, which he had never spoken about to anyone.

Shortly after leaving the army, he met and married his wife, and had two children. He was married for 45 years, and reported that they were very happy during the early years of the relationship, describing how they would often go to dances together. Shortly after the birth of his eldest daughter, he started work-ing as a lorry driver to earn a better salary. He reported that his marriage changed after this. He and his wife argued about his job taking him away from home for days at a time. Eventually, the arguments lessened, but he felt they drifted apart. He hoped that when he retired, they would be able to enjoy doing things together, 'growing old happily together'. Shortly after he retired, his wife had a series of strokes, culminating in a stroke that left her paralysed. For the last year of her life, Mr P provided intensive personal care for his wife. He described his relief at being able to care for her to the end, but his disappoint-ment that they had not been able to return to the closeness of the initial years of their marriage. He wondered if she would have looked after him in the same way.

Following her death, he played bowls, took his dog for long walks, and attended his local club. He saw his children occasionally, and appeared to be coping well.

Assessment and formulation

*In the assessment, Mr P reported that following the death of his dog, he stopped all of his activities, and withdrew from his son and daughter. He described missing taking his dog for walks. The therapist commented on how much care Mr P had given to his wife in the year prior to her death. Mr P looked tearful but said he had to 'stop moping and get on with life'. The therapist suggested that Mr P had thrown himself into activities after his wife's death (*defence*), to avoid being overwhelmed (*anxiety*) by grief (*hidden feeling*). The death of his dog had triggered his unexpressed grief. Mr P agreed with this, and said he felt* *his wife had been neglected by services before she died, going into some details about a particular instance that had distressed him. The therapist commented that he was angry about events connected to his wife's death, and had not been able to give voice to this.*

Therapeutic focus and contract

The therapist suggested that the focus for their work together would be Mr P's unexpressed grief about his wife's death. Mr P readily agreed to this. A contract of 16 weekly sessions was agreed.

Early resistance: Physical disabilities as a defence

During the initial sessions of therapy, Mr P did not wear his hearing aid, avoided eye contact with the therapist and spoke at length. The therapist interpreted his avoidance of contact with the therapist as being due to his fear of recognising his painful feelings and also fear of becoming attached to the therapist as a consequence of her understanding his pain. Mr P stated that his hearing aid was uncomfortable, but he began to wear it in the next session, and a two-way dialogue slowly emerged. He described aspects of his current (rather empty) life, but continually referred back to his 'happy time of belonging' in the army.

Breaking through the defence against grief and anger

Mr P's use of avoidance as a coping strategy manifested itself in the therapy. He missed the eighth session, leaving a telephone message to say he wished to end the therapy. In supervision, the therapist discussed the many losses Mr P had experienced, and also her concern about whether she had chosen the wrong focus, contemplating whether Mr P needed to talk more about his wartime experiences, with the focus on the 'terrible things he had seen'. Having established in supervision that the missed session was further evidence of Mr P's avoidant coping defence, the therapist wrote to Mr P asking him to attend their next appointment. This session, which he attended, was an important breakthrough session.

The therapist interpreted Mr P's avoidance of intimacy. Mr P's response was to acknowledge the pain of talking about his experiences. He spoke at length about his regrets about his life, and how he had avoided family life by becoming a lorry driver. He began to speak about the complexities of his marriage and childhood. He described feeling displaced by his 'new' family when he returned from his evacuation billet, recognising the anger and sorrow that he had never before acknowledged or expressed. He was able to make links between these early experiences, and his avoidance of family life because of his feeling of being displaced in his wife's affections by his children. He expressed sadness and regret at what he called his 'missed years' with his family. This opened up his grief at the loss of his wife, and the loss of the retirement he had hoped to spend with her. He wondered who would care for him, should he become unwell. He began to contemplate how he could enjoy the time he had left with his family, and grandchildren.

Ending of therapy

As the end of therapy approached, Mr P began to distance himself, and stated his belief that he had much to say that his young, female therapist could learn from to use with her 'new' patients. The therapist interpreted Mr P's anger and sense that he was being displaced by the therapist's new patients. [This interpretation of feelings of displacement in relation to the therapy represented a completion of the triangle of person – therapist (T), other (O), past (P) – link in relation to this theme.] *Mr P acknowledged this, describing his disappointment 'at what had not been said'. He described a walk he had taken with his daughter, when they had spoken at length about his wife, and his daughter had spoken affectionately about her childhood. He commented on the warmth, compassion and understanding of his daughter.*

Outcome

Mr P expressed anger and sorrow in relation to the loss of his wife, and other, earlier losses. He had begun to see his children regularly, and had taken up bowls. At six-month follow-up, he spoke of the pleasure he gained from time with his grandchildren. He was planning a holiday with one of his brothers, and was considering a move to sheltered accommodation. He appeared to have re-engaged with life as a result of grieving (Freud, 1917) and had overcome an impulse to retreat from life (Steiner, 1993). Whilst many issues had not been addressed, this had been openly acknowledged (which can be regarded as a key factor in a successful brief therapy; Mann, 1973).

Commentary

This case highlights some of the issues discussed earlier in the chapter. Mr P's cohort-specific experience as an evacuee and in the army illustrates the importance of this knowledge for the therapist. An awareness of stroke disease, and the range of age-related services Mr and Mrs P may have had contact with was helpful in understanding Mr P's reports of events in caring for his wife. Mr P presented with various issues pertinent to later life: experiences as a carer, adjusting to retirement, and many recent losses (his wife, his pet, his hopes for retirement, his role as a carer), which had stirred up memories of earlier losses (his father's death, his home and family when he was evacuated). Mr P had cared for his wife as she became increasingly dependent, which had led to him considering his own future dependency needs, and who would care for him if he was faced with disability or illness.

This was Mr P's first experience of therapy and part of the assessment focused on socialising Mr P to thinking and talking about issues in a way that included a psychological or emotional perspective. Given the complex history Mr P presented, the therapist was concerned whether the focus selected meant that other important issues were neglected. Supervision was crucial in understanding the transference relationship and his avoidance of intimacy with the therapist. The case illustrates how real practical problems, such as Mr P's hearing difficulty, can be used as a defence within therapy. The therapist needed to be sensitive to the real difficulty, whilst interpreting its use as a defence. Part of the therapy included an aspect of life review, and the nature of the transference changed throughout this. The therapist noted that at times Mr P identified her with his mother, such as when he spoke about the therapist's preoccupations with her other patients (linking to the theme of displacement). He later seemed to identify the therapist with his daughter.

REFERENCES

Alexander, F., & French, T.M. (1946). *Psychoanalytic Therapy: Principles and application*. New York: Ronald Press.

Bateman A., & Holmes, J. (1995). *Introduction to Psychoanalysis*. London: Routledge.

Binder, J.L., & Strupp, H.H. (1991). The Vanderbilt approach to time-limited dynamic psychotherapy. In: P. Crits-Christoph & J.P. Barber (eds) *Handbook of Short-term Dynamic Psychotherapy*. New York: Basic Books.

Budman, S.H., & Gurman, A.S. (1988). *Theory and Practice of Brief Psychotherapy*. New York: Guilford Press.

Cohen, N. (1982). On loneliness and the ageing process. *International Journal of Psychoanalysis*, 63, 149–155.

Colthart, N. (1988). Diagnosis and assessment for suitability for psychoanaltyic psychotherapy. *British Journal of Psychotherapy*, 4(2), 127–134.

Crusey, J. (1986). Short-term dynamic psychotherapy with a 62-year-old man. In: C. Colarusso, & R. Nemiroff (eds) *The Race Against Time*. New York: New York Press.

Davanloo, H. (1978). *Basic Principles and Techniques in Short-term Dynamic Psychotherapy*. New York: Spectrum Publications.

Davanloo, H. (1980). *Short-term Dynamic Psychotherapy*. New York: Jason Aronson.

DeLeon, P.H., VandenBos, G.R., & Bulatao, E.Q. (1991). Managed mental health care: A history of the federal policy initiative. *Professional Psychology: Research and Practice*, 22, 15–25.

Erikson, E.H. (1966). Eight stages of man. *International Journal of Psycho-Analysis*, 47, 281–300.

Erikson, J.M. (1998). In: E.H. Erikson *The Life Cycle Completed*. [Extended version with new chapters on the ninth stage by Joan M. Erikson.] New York: Norton.

Evans, S., Chisholm, P., & Walshe, J. (2001). A dynamic therapy group for the elderly. *Group Analysis*, 34(1), 287–298.

Freud, S. (1917). Mourning and melancholia. In: J. Strachey *Standard Edition of the Complete Works of Sigmund Freud 11*. London: Hogarth.

Gorsuch, N. (1998). Time's winged chariot: Short-term psychotherapy in later life. *Psychodynamic Counselling*, 4(2), 191–202.

Hildebrand, P. (1982). Psychotherapy with older patients. *British Journal of Medical Psychology*, 55, 19–28.

Hildebrand, P. (1986). Dynamic psychotherapy with the elderly. In: I. Hanley, & M. Gilhooly (eds) *Psychological Therapies for the Elderly*. London: Croom Helm.

King, P. (1974). Notes on the psychoanalysis of older patients. *Journal of Analytic Psychology*, 22–37.

King, P. (1980). The life cycle as indicated by the nature of the transference in the psychoanalysis of the middle-aged and elderly. *International Journal of Psycho-Analysis*, 61, 153–160.

Knight, B.G. (1996). Psychodynamic psychotherapy with older adults: Lessons from scientific gerontology. In: R.T. Woods (ed) *Handbook of the Clinical Psychology of Ageing*. Chichester, UK: John Wiley & Sons Ltd.

Knight, B.G. (1996). *Psychotherapy with Older Adults* (2nd edn). Newbury Park, CA: Sage.

Levenson, H. (1995). *Time-Limited Psychotherapy: A guide to clinical practice*. New York: Basic Books.

Luborsky, L. (1984). *Principles of Psychoanalytic Psychotherapy: A manual for supportive-expressive treatment*. New York: Basic Books.

Luborsky, L., & Crits-Cristoph, P. (1990). *Understanding Transference: The CCRT method*. New York: Basic Books.

Malan, D.H. (1979). *Individual Psychotherapy and the Science of Psychodynamics*. London: Butterworth.

Malan, D.H. (1995). *Individual Psychotherapy and the Science of Psychodynamics* (2nd edn). London: Butterworth.

Mander, G. (2000). *A Psychodynamic Approach to Brief Therapy*. London: Sage Publications.

Mann, J. (1973). *Time-limited Psychotherapy*. Cambridge, MA: Harvard University Press.

Martin, C. (1992). The elder and the other. *Free Associations*, 3(27), 341–354.

Martindale, B. (1989). Becoming dependent again: The fears of some elderly persons and their younger therapists. *Psychoanalytic Psychotherapy*, 4(1), 67–75.

Messer, S.B., & Warren, C. (1995). *Models of Brief Psychodynamic Therapy, A Comparative Approach*. New York: Guilford Press.

Molnos, A. (1995). *A Question of Time: Essentials of brief dynamic therapy*. London: Karnac.

Nordhus, I.H., & Nielson, G.H. (1999). Brief psychodynamic psychotherapy with older adults. *JCLP/In Session: Psychotherapy in Practice*, 55(8), 935–947.

Orbach, A. (1994). Psychotherapy in the third age. *British Journal of Psychotherapy*, 11(2), 221–231.

Pollock, G. (1982). On ageing and psychopathology. *International Journal of Psycho-pathology*, 63, 275–281.

Porter, R. (1991). Psychotherapy with the elderly. In: J. Holmes (ed) *A Textbook of Psychotherapy in Psychiatric Practice*. London: Churchill Livingstone.

Sifneos, P.E. (1972). *Short-term Psychotherapy and Emotional Crisis*. Cambridge, MA: Harvard University Press.

Sifneos, P.E. (1992). *Short-term Anxiety-provoking Psychotherapy*. New York: Basic Books.

Sinason, V. (1992). *Mental Handicap and the Human Condition: New approaches from the Tavistock*. London: Free Association Books.

Steiner, J. (1993). *Psychic Retreats: Pathological organizations in psychotic, neurotic and borderline patients*. London: Routledge.

Stern, S. (1993). Managed care, brief therapy, and therapeutic integrity. *Psychotherapy*, 30, 162–175.

Stern, J.M., & Lovestone, S. (2000). Therapy with the elderly: Introducing psycho-dynamic psychotherapy to the multi-disciplinary team. *International Journal of Geriatric Psychiatry*, 15, 500–505.

Strupp, H.H., & Binder, J.L. (1984). *Psychotherapy in a New Key: A guide to time-limited dynamic psychotherapy*. New York: Basic Books.

Terry, P. (1996). *Counselling the Elderly and their Carers*. London: Macmillan Press.

Chapter 12

Art therapy with older people

Clinical illustration in a case of post-traumatic stress disorder

Kimberley Smith

For you our battles shine
With triumph half-divine;
And the glory of the dead
Kindles in each proud eye.
But a curse is on my head,
That shall not be unsaid,
And the wounds in my heart are red,
For I have watched them die.
('To the Warmongers', Sassoon, 1917)

A HISTORY OF ART THERAPY

Art therapy with older people as a specific client group appears to have emerged a little later than other areas of art therapy practice. Moreover art therapy with the elderly has remained less visible in general within the profession than with younger patients until more recent years. There is, for instance, much more literature on art therapy with adults and children. This is partly due to the channels that art therapy developed, which are clearly outlined in Waller's (1991) book *Becoming a profession, the history of art therapy in Britain 1940–1982*. The first art therapy research conference *per se* was in 1949. Waller wrote that the need for research was: 'essential if the art therapy movement is to continue and flourish both in theory and practice, as a radical form of psychotherapy'.

The importance of writing about art therapy with older people is that it attempts to make the practice visible. The profile of art therapy can be encouraged through recording its effectiveness with older adults. Elderly services have long been thought of as Cinderella services within psychiatry in general. The art therapist working with elderly patients has to find confidence within herself, to work in an under-recognised specialist area of psychotherapy, and to add to the literature. In the fields of art therapy in general in the past it seemed there was little by way of evidence-based practice. Research and a demonstration of positive outcomes are required in order to develop status in the world of psychiatry and other health service disciplines.

There is a need to build and communicate a framework that allows us to understand how best to utilise our practice with older patients. Waller (1991) wrote about art therapists who contributed to the beginning of the art therapy profession and the formation of the British Association of Art Therapists which grew from links with the National Union of Teachers. BAAT was formed in 1963 with 32 members and art therapy became a recognised profession in 1964.

Rita Simon is the first British art therapist identified by Waller. Simon originally worked as a commercial artist, but got involved in art therapy in the 1940s. Simon appears to be the only art therapist specifically working with the elderly amongst a large number of art therapists involved in the formation of the BAAT.

In the mid 1970s there were possibilities for art therapists to work in the psychiatry of old age services, due to greater awareness of the needs of an ageing population. In the late 1970s BAAT increasingly established links with a health service union, in order to be more incorporated in to the health service as a profession that was separate from occupational therapy. The development into a profession in its own right was a difficult one, and even today art therapists are still mistaken for occupational therapists (many of whom traditionally worked with the elderly). Despite that, many positive alliances have been made between the two professions. Art therapy has successfully gained a place in the Health Service as an autonomous state registered profession (1997). Consultant art therapy posts are being negotiated for the first time.

Although our now elderly patients were not involved with these early movements of art therapy, the profession began at a time that is embedded in many of their memories, particularly the time of the Second World War, which itself opened up opportunities for therapists, psychiatrists and psychologists. The beginnings of art therapy in this area have been developed from the use of art as therapy for the shell-shocked soldiers during the many experiments going on at the time, such as those that occurred at the Northfield Clinic. Laurence Bradbury, a young sapper in the Royal Engineers with artistic ability, was recruited as an instructor for therapy. In his own way he conducted a mini 'Northfield experiment' (see Chapter 5).

> I had this little hut of mayhem. It was really a sort of anarchy, . . . There was no rank in there . . . people could do as they liked . . . I was just one of them, painting with them, there was no instruction given . . . the general attitude in the hut was that they could be themselves and god knows they needed to be. Many of them still trying to cope with the guilt of killing or of not being killed if their chums were. All these things came out in pictures.
>
> (Holden, 1998)

THE EMERGENCE OF ART THERAPY WITH OLDER PATIENTS

Unconsciously professionals working with the elderly can often be subject to the same feelings as their patients. This can occur to such an extent that these feelings can manifest in the profile of that profession. Therefore counter-transference to older people with mental health problems might include feeling invisible, lonely, isolated, and having poor self esteem.

Angela Byers (1995) comments that there is 'a need for an element of faith' when working with elderly patients. She continues with comments on the countertransference felt by the art therapist:

> It is often hard to keep aware of the value of this work. Our clients convey a sense of futility and helplessness which makes us feel helpless in countertransference. I think this is one reason why the care of elderly people with severe memory loss is often seen by professionals as one of the least attractive areas of work.
>
> (Wilks & Byers, 1992)

Byers described countertransference feelings of frustrated anger, confusion, disintegration and feelings of loss, which if not realised can be directed at other professionals. Jane Harlan (1990) further describes the importance of 'autonomous functioning' for patients with dementia and the fear of being regarded as failures. She includes a description of art therapy in long stay wards. The wards are 'often socially and culturally impoverished, a factor which can exacerbate the already fragile capacity a resident may have in maintaining vital links with other people'.

These factors are further elucidated in the latest art therapy book on dementia care *Art Therapies and Progressive Illness: Nameless Dread* (Waller, 2002). The long stay ward may also be 'the last port of call, and will have a terminal quality which cannot help but influence the ability or inclination of the residents to interact with others' (Wilks & Byers, 1992:100). Other professionals working in this area can also experience these feelings and may in turn experience a sense of failure. As in all work in this area, supervision is essential for the art therapist, particularly to find the ability to remain separate from the patients' feelings and confident in their work.

THEORETICAL DEVELOPMENTS IN ART THERAPY WITH OLDER PATIENTS

The role of art therapy is separate and distinct from leisure activities, and from that of other professions such as occupational therapists using creative work and art teaching. These arguments were put forward by BAAT during the establishment of the profession. Several art therapists have been identified by Waller (1991) as having made important contributions during the early years of the profession. These therapists broadly represent two theoretical approaches; the first being the importance of art making as a therapeutic activity. Adrian Hill, who was a pioneer in this area, practised in the 1940s and used art techniques as therapeutic and enjoyable art activity in his practice. Marie Petrie, like Hill, 'focused on the healing "integrative" aspects of art'. Edward Adamson was another influential art therapist at this time who focused on the idea of being an artist who assisted patients through art, rather than through a transference relationship with the therapist.

The second theoretical approach comprised art therapists who worked on a more psychoanalytic level, using the art object as part of a dynamic between patient and therapist, which could then be interpreted. Waller (1991) stated that the focus of art therapy is the image, but that the therapeutic process occurs between the creator (the patient), the artefact and the therapist. Bringing unconscious feelings to a more conscious level is seen as an important goal, as is the exploration of these feelings. The latter approach has become more dominant in the art therapy world today and provides a clear separation from the more diversionary forms of art practised in occupational therapy and art teaching. Generally 'aesthetic standards' have been regarded as unimportant in the context of art therapy. This is reassuring for patients who are daunted by the art-making process. The expression and condensation of unconscious feelings which production of a work engenders, are the essential elements of a therapeutic transaction. The psychoanalytic model has been successfully utilised in art therapy work and in art work with older patients.

The American Naumberg (1958, in Waller, 1991) was a psychoanalyst who pioneered art therapy. Champernowne (1963, in Waller, 1991), a Jungian psychotherapist, was influenced by Naumburg's work and by art therapy. She and her husband were founders of the Withymead Centre, which ran some of the first art therapy training schemes in Britain. Dalley (1984, in Waller, 1991), a contemporary art therapist, has upheld the psychoanalytic approach in art therapy.

Other psychoanalysts have used art effectively in their work, such as Winnicott (1971) with his use of the 'Squiggle'. The squiggle game involved the therapist making a line on paper and inviting the child to make an image out of it. Although most of Winnicott's patients were children, in more recent years approaches to working with children have been usefully employed with older people. Winnicott also focused on the use of objects between mother and child to which he applied the term 'transitional object'. Art therapists have made use of this term for the production of images and other art works made between therapist and patient.

There exist other newer, valuable models of art therapy which are being explored today by art therapists. Some are not curative. Their aim is to provide a better quality of life, moment by moment, experienced by the elderly person who may be suffering from a chronic or deteriorating condition, such as dementia. At times the aim is to enable a patient to come to terms with a deterioration; this includes coming to terms with the ending of one's life (Sheppard, Rusted & Waller 1998). It can be of particular benefit where there is a state of deterioration, such as when people cannot articulate their distress due to loss of ability, or when the emotional state becomes fragile due to fear of a future which cannot be named or contemplated.

THE ADVANTAGES OF ART THERAPY WITH OLDER PATIENTS

By the early 1990s art therapists working with elderly patients had become more visible due to their employment in newly formed services within psychiatric hospitals. Roger Wilks and Angela Byers (1992) wrote about their work in statutory services and elderly wards in psychiatric hospitals. They concentrated particularly on treating elderly people with severe memory loss. Byers' (1995) paper was called 'Beyond Marks'. Due to cognitive decline the patients could no longer mark the paper. The title relates to the difficulty which might conceivably be felt by the dementia sufferer in making an impression on others.

Byers created a technique which employed the use of objects, which is even closer to the use of *transitional object* (Winnicott).

> In art therapy many elderly people with severe memory loss lose interest in making marks, but become absorbed in the process of arranging and playing with the materials themselves in a way which indicates that this has meaning to them. It is an activity which takes place in the space between the client and the therapist, just as the process of making images does.
>
> (Byers, 1995)

The fact that art therapists can work on a non-verbal level often enables them to treat patients who cannot be reached through verbal communication. The art object, whether it is an actual object or image, can give form to a fragmented inner and outer state of being.

There have been various papers published in the *American Journal of Art Therapy* such as 'Alzheimer's disease and the role of art therapy in its treatment' by Wald (1983), in which she illustrates striking drawings by the elderly suffering with dementia demonstrating the fragmentation, decline and emotional impact of the disease. She also gives a moving case study in 'The graphic representation of regression in an Alzheimer's disease patient' which she describes in phases through the progression of the disease. In the early stages she describes a bright lively woman whose main difficulty appeared to be 'an expressive aphasia'. The patient's drawing at this time had minimal distortion, but later in the second phase the distortion can be seen to be greater along with fragmentation and sexual preoccupation. Wald also used images made by patients in art therapy to assist in the medical diagnosis. In the third phase she refers to the patient's awareness and terror of death demonstrated in angry outbursts and feelings of loss and depression: 'she worked in a small space and produced a tight little drawing with many eyes and colours and staccato broken lines'. Wald followed her patient through her deterioration to the last weeks when she could no longer attend the program, and appeared to be in despair. The therapist seemed to contain the obvious terror experienced by the patient both by her presence and through the artwork.

Byers and Wilks predict a future rise in the need for care of the elderly, in which art therapists can play an important role; not only as a resource in the psychodynamic understanding of the elderly people within the multidisciplinary team, but also as individual therapists fostering some greater understanding for the elderly themselves.

PROFESSIONAL GUIDELINES

There are guidelines for professional art therapists working with vulnerable patients. The formation and maintenance of the profession BAAT has ensured professional codes of practice and support for individual art therapists. This includes a code of ethics and registration board. BAAT created regional groups which also provide important links for therapists who even now often work in isolation as the profession remains relatively small. An ongoing development in BAAT is also the creation of subgroups in specialist areas, such as old age (ATOLL).

THE PRACTICE OF ART THERAPY WITH OLDER PEOPLE

Art therapy practice is increasing. Referrals may now be received from a broad area; acute inpatient wards, day hospitals and the community. Art therapy services cater for elderly patients with both organic and functional illness. The author and her colleagues utilise a variety of approaches in art therapy according to the patient's diagnosis and their setting. Most sessions are for one hour a week; these include open and closed groups, and individual work. The approaches vary from psychoanalytic models to more directive models that may focus on group paintings, which have themes that help to orientate the confused elderly patient. Object play is also utilised with groups and individuals. The descriptions of art therapy with the elderly so far in this chapter have focused on elderly patients suffering from dementia. The following case study, however, is of a man who was referred with a diagnosis of a 'functional illness'; post-traumatic stress disorder.

CLINICAL ILLUSTRATION

Individual art therapy with a patient in later life: death or glory

The following case study is to give the reader an illustration of the actual process of individual art therapy with an 87-year-old man who was referred with a diagnosis of post-traumatic stress disorder (PTSD). It has been written up with his express permission and full cooperation. He also had a history of depression and anxiety that had led to several breakdowns, and had been thought to have mild cognitive impairment.

Albert had been a Signal Sergeant and Grenadier Guardsman who fought at both Normandy and Dunkirk. His PTSD followed his active service in the war. When Albert was referred he had been having flashbacks from the war during the day. He was also physically active during his nightmares which caused his wife to have to sleep in another room.

Two elements have been essential in working with Albert. First, listening to and understanding his traumatic memories of the war and other events in his life, and second, the encouragement of an acceptance that these traumas occurred in the past. This was in order to achieve a moving on from trauma to gain a more peaceful emotional experience in the present. This was achieved verbally and more importantly through images which had to change intrinsically in order to enable a positive shift in Albert's psyche. The verbal and visual interaction had been part of a developing relationship between therapist and patient which had enabled Albert to enjoy a healthier relationship with himself and with those around him.

The beginning

Albert commenced art therapy in April 2000. He arrived at his assessment interview with a detailed manuscript of his active service experiences which was filled with intricate line drawings. Albert thought his art therapist could help him give colour to his drawings, which was understood on an unconscious level that he wanted to be given back his emotions.

Consciously Albert was afraid of exploring himself in depth, but at a different level he had a need to understand his emotions in order to resolve his nightmares, depression and anxiety.

An important focus in the art therapy is that of the transference. Schaverien (1995) has described this transference relationship between patient and therapist in art therapy well and states, 'Sometimes the pictures embody transference desire.'

Albert had always been able to discuss his feelings openly, which gave the opportunity for them to be understood rather than simply acted upon. One strong feeling Albert had in relation to seeing a younger therapist was the joy of 'feeling alive again', to see and be with someone younger. Another issue in the transference was to do with power and a need to keep control of the proceedings. Albert attempted to maintain control through chivalry. He would pull out the chair for the therapist to sit down on arrival.

Rather than challenge Albert for authority, attempts were made to reflect on this with interpretations in order to create space for comments and different kinds of activity. For instance in an early session during which there was such a potential struggle for control, Albert began to talk about playing chess. He and his therapist mused on which pieces each would be. Albert thought the therapist would be the queen, who could be viewed in two ways, one as a chess piece which can be moved about easily – the potential for manipulation or the desire to manipulate could be great – or the queen could be threatening to Albert as she could move quickly and penetrate his defence easily, and open up the painful areas he was trying to avoid.

There was often a humour that emerged between them at those times which helped defuse tension and allowed understanding of serious issues. One of the most frightening areas which the 'queen' may have opened up could have been old age and depression. Feelings of persecution would even have been preferable to the feeling of depression.

A typical interaction that was gradually worked through in many sessions is described by the following. Albert always arrived with a bag bursting with files documenting the war, recent sleep activity and his own art materials, all symbolic of a life packed full with detail, and to a level that at times felt un-containable. The therapist picked up this feeling from the process of countertransference, finding it difficult to 'unpack' Albert's kitbag of a life.

Albert was reluctant to move on from the descriptions of the traumata, but the therapist invited him to think about his need to bring material to the session. He had felt it would interest the therapist; referring to a previous session when they had spoken about spontaneity. At the same time as inviting a movement away from Albert's usual use of his traumatic past, it was important to acknowledge it. For the elderly, reminiscence has another level of importance beyond recall of events with younger patients.

> Many elderly people are surprised at the clarity with which they can remember things, and that their minds so often wander to certain events of a long time ago, even when their short term memory is poor. This process is recognised as 'the life review process'.
>
> (Birren, 1964)

The therapist continued, 'The way we often look at your experience is by referring to the manuscript and I'm wondering about looking at it in a different way.' The therapist decided to invite activity and asked: 'Well how would it feel to make a painting using paper and art materials from this room?'

Albert responded: 'Could you get something of what you are looking for from the experiences I have spoken about?'

The therapist held on to the idea of creativity by asking: 'I wonder what feelings you might have been having when I mentioned using the materials?'

Albert said, 'My ability to paint, I'm more of a copier than a painter. On the other hand one can paint in one's mind eventually.' Opening his bag, he took out his own materials. The therapist commented: 'I think this is what we have gone over already and you're going to show me documents prepared out of the session when I am asking how it would feel to paint with the materials in the room in the session, and I am aware this is sidestepping.'

Albert said, 'Yes we have gone my way.'

The therapist asked him if it would feel things were not going his way if he were to use the art materials in the room. A way to resolve the impasse might have been to think about Albert's feelings about painting in the art therapy room with the therapist's materials. At that moment Albert decided he was going to paint in the session. However as he walked over to the art materials the tension appeared to increase and Albert had to return to his bag and attempted to take his own art materials again.

His ambivalence continued for some time during which the therapist encouraged him to talk about how he was feeling until finally he was able to paint without preconceived ideas from home. Albert painted a tree and then two more which he entitled Youth, War and Peace.

Gradually as this process was re-worked again each week, Albert was able to be more spontaneous and less involved in the remembered trauma he had been carrying with him for so long.

Albert had a great ability for story telling and a vivid imagination which allowed him to create an impressive manuscript, filled with detailed accounts and line drawings of his active service. He brought images of his nightmares which were also line drawings and had been made with precision and a regimented intensity in their detail.

The post-traumatic stress had been connected to aggressive masculine feelings which had an important energy, but which became out of proportion. There had been a working through of Albert's potentially violent thoughts as a male patient in therapy with a female therapist which had been manifested as a fear of contaminating her. Albert's trust and faith in the therapy process was built over many sessions. The permission to hold and understand violent thoughts was useful in allowing Albert to have an experience of containment both verbally and through his art work. This demonstrated to him that his feelings were not so explosive that they would destroy his therapist or his therapy. Albert claimed to have felt a reduction in anxiety and relaxation as a result.

The painting in the session of the exploding rainbow has been one of the very successful uses of art in a spontaneous manner within the sessions, where these more unconscious thoughts could have space (see Figure 12.1).

Figure 12.1 Exploding rainbow.

Albert reported feeling affected by his actual experience in the war. Apart from the brutality in battle he also mentioned 'the barrack room' which was the place that soldiers socialised and expressed the 'low' masculine attributes. Albert took time to recount these experiences as they expressed his darker side. The acceptance by his female therapist of these experiences, and the maintenance of boundaries, encouraged Albert to contain rather than repress these memories. The greater Albert's repression of this experience of the violence of war and in himself, the stronger the desire of the unconscious to express it; and it would emerge in his nightmares. Albert's fear of harming women had been exacerbated by the fact that he had lost several significant women in his life. Albert had expressed this successfully both in writing and with images.

Rehabilitation

In considering Albert's fear of depression; if he were to move beyond his experience of trauma and aggressive feelings, Albert had to have a realisation of why he recalled the war and the brutal aspects. He said with passion 'Maybe that's what's keeping me alive'. The fear of depression was connected to a fear of losing momentum and of coming to a halt, of dying and of old age.

Albert was introduced to another possible energy, the spontaneous moments of creativity in the fusion of therapist and patient in art therapy, and consequently in his masculine and feminine aspects which were held symbolically in the image making. For instance Albert spontaneously painted two daffodils which he said represented himself with his female therapist. Albert worked through fear of losing control to messy and depressive feelings which may have been attached to the feminine.

The packed intense colour of Albert's images reflected his state of mind. Albert often spoke about the intensity of horror during the war and the intensity of joy following the war which can be seen in Figure 12.2. They illustrate two extremes that left the therapist wondering about a neutral territory in between. Albert could proudly place himself as the soldier and he worked at recognising himself as an ordinary man. Most importantly he began to understand that being good enough is better than only being good by being a glorious man. 'In the light of claims for compensation for Gulf War Syndrome. The cap badge says, "Death or Glory" not "Compensation"' (Holden, 1998).

The argument is that people who volunteer to fight have done so with the understanding of the risks involved. However in terms of the male psyche the seductiveness of glory is the bait and death is the risk. An extreme state of mind has to be adopted and one that has effects even after the battles are over. It is therefore also difficult to reach peacetime, in terms of regaining a balanced state of mind. The illustration of the exploding rainbow symbolises the intensity with which Albert had his experiences. This had a volatile capacity; as a *double entendre* and described the concept of death or glory in the soldier's mind. Albert wrote below the second illustration of the rainbow (Figure 12.3), 'Peace and hope to a golden gate to golden corn heavenly peace over the rainbow'.

In art therapy, the therapist tried to offer an ordinary experience, for Albert the man rather than Albert the soldier. It was the finding of the place that had

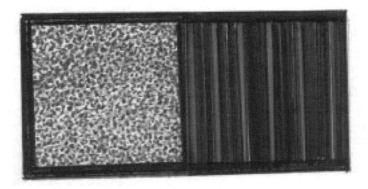

Figure 12.2 How can I illustrate my today and yesterday?

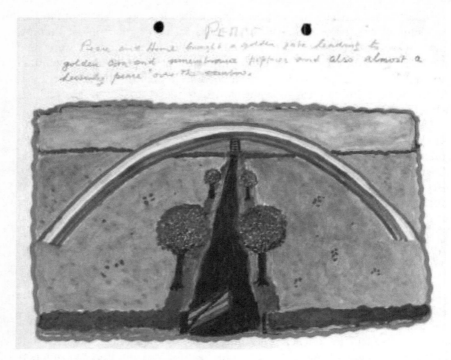

Figure 12.3 Peace and hope to a golden gate to golden corn heavenly peace over the
    rainbow.

been lost between the polarities of death and glory of war that was
important. As the images developed, they became more prosaic and more
spontaneous, such as Figure 12.4. On reflection it has become apparent that
this question could be unconsciously referring to the search for neutral
territory in which to rehabilitate. On the right side of the image there is a
harsh, bright, empty field, but on the left there is a field that is dull and even
has a few shadows which could even symbolise patches of depression.

Resolution

Albert was able to employ playfulness in his images and between himself and
his therapist. The therapy seems to have had the effect of changing his state of
mind quite directly. Albert had the experience of shouting out 'I'm happy' in
one session after experiencing such a moment, and said he felt fortunate to
have such an experience at his age. The spontaneous playful moments
which took Albert into a different healthier state of mind appeared to occur
in a kind of no man's land where there was a meeting between therapist
and patient.

Figure 12.4 Could there ever be a better site to rehabilitate?

Figure 12.5 Look down on no man.

Albert drew an image (Figure 12.5) which he said was important to him as it was about humility. It reminded him not to look down on or to forget anyone in the overwhelming history of the war hero.

No man's land is an area where Albert and his therapist attempted to meet, which was not about possession but freedom. Following treatment, his anxiety and PTSD greatly reduced. Albert wrote about this change in the two reports he voluntarily wrote describing the reduction of his anxious preoccupation regarding the troubling nature of his nightmares. This demonstrated a shift from the obsessive recalling of past trauma to an ability to enjoy his present.

As the therapy progressed, Albert indicated a coming to terms with old age in his description of a wonderful meeting with an 'old man' in the day centre he used to visit. The old man could hardly hear or see him but had told Albert that it had meant much to him that Albert had taken time to speak to him. It seems that Albert was not only talking about the benefit of taking time to speak to this elderly man but also to confront what the old man symbolised; that being old, which often brings deterioration, also provides the spirit and humour and capacity for intimacy. The essence of the art therapy work involved the reviewing of life whilst simultaneously liberating the individual from trauma towards a more peaceful future during the concluding years of his life.

Notes

Sadly Albert died of cancer during the writing of this chapter. The author would like to thank him and his widow for their cooperation in the writing of this clinical study in order to help other people learn about the process of art therapy.

The author would also like to thank Dr Sandra Evans; Dr Nicola Blandford; Professor Diane Waller; Val Huet; and arts therapists from Fulbourn Hospital for listening to this work in progress and giving valuable feedback.

ACKNOWLEDGEMENT

Extract from 'To the Warmongers' © Siegfried Sassoon by kind permission of George Sassoon.

REFERENCES

Birren, J. (1964). *The Psychology of Aging*. Englewood Cliffs, NJ: Prentice-Hall. Quoted in: D. Waller & A. Gilroy (eds) *Art Therapy: A handbook*. Buckingham, UK: Open University Press, 1992.

Byers, A. (1995). Beyond marks. *Inscape*, 1, 16–22.

Champernowne, H.L. (1963). Art therapy in the Withymead Centre. *American Bulletin of Art Therapy*, Spring. Quoted in: D. Waller (ed) *Becoming a Profession, the History of Art Therapy 1940–1982*. London & New York: Tavistock and Routledge, 1991.

Dalley, T. (ed) (1984). *Art as Therapy*. London: Tavistock. Reprinted in: D. Waller (ed) *Becoming a Profession, the History of Art Therapy 1940–1982*. London & New York: Tavistock and Routledge, 1991.

Harlan, J. (1990). Beyond the patient to the person: Promoting aspects of autonomous functioning in individuals with mild to moderate dementia. *American Journal of Art Therapy*, 28.

Holden, W. (1998). *Shell Shock*. Channel 4 Books.

Jacques, A. (1988). *Understanding Dementia*. Edinburgh: Churchill Livingstone. Quoted in: D. Waller & A. Gilroy (eds) *Art Therapy: A handbook*. Buckingham, UK: Open University Press, 1992.

Naumburg, M. (1958). Art therapy: Its scope and function. In: E.F. Hammer (ed) *Clinical Application of Projective Drawings*. Springfield, IL: Thomas. Quoted in: D. Waller (ed) *Becoming a Profession, the History of Art Therapy 1940–1982*. London & New York: Tavistock and Routledge.

Schaverien, J. (1995). *Desire and the Female Therapist*. London: Routledge.

Sheppard, L., Rusted, J., & Waller, D. (1998). *Report of a control group trial to evaluate the effectiveness of art therapy with older people with dementia*. Brighton, UK: Alzheimer's Society.

Wald, J. (1983). Alzheimer's disease and the role of art therapy in its treatment. The graphic representation of regression in an Alzheimer's disease patient. *American Journal of Art Therapy*, 22.

Waller, D. (1991). *Becoming a Profession, the History of Art Therapy in Britain 1940–1982*. London: Tavistock and Routledge.

Waller, D. (2002). *Art Therapies and Progressive Illness: Nameless dread*. Hove, UK: Routledge.

Waller, D., & Gilroy, A. (2001). *Art Therapy: A handbook*. Buckingham, UK: Open University Press.

Wilks, R., & Byers, A. (1992). Art therapy with the elderly in statutory care. In: D. Waller & A. Gilroy (eds) *Art Therapy: A handbook*. Buckingham, UK: Open University Press.

Winnicott, D.W. (1971). *Playing and Reality*. London: Routledge.

Chapter 13

Music therapy

Rachel Darnley-Smith

> She has almost fallen asleep. From the kitchens, a gentle rhythmic croon-
> ing, like an ayah's lullaby for a baby. But there is no ayah and no baby, it is
> the cook's old blind grandmother, who sits outside all day rocking herself
> and alternately dozing and singing.
>
> (From *Air and Angels* by Susan Hill)

The significance of music as an expression of ourselves, and as a non-verbal link to others, does not seem to decrease in old age. A familiar scene in a hospital setting is of the elderly woman, who is blind and suffers from advanced Alzheimer's disease, sitting in the corner of a ward. Music replaces the 'chatter' on the television. She begins to tap her foot and after a moment to smile. The musical sounds have provided her with a means to link to the outside world and with the potential for someone else to join her. This is not surprising. From the very moment we are born we make and respond to sounds in communication with those around us. We use our innate musicality as 'part of our earliest engagements, part of our ongoing expressive and communicative life' (Pavlicevic, 1997: 118). Indeed, music is part of our very being, our emotional and physical selves throughout our lives. As Robarts writes:

> The impulses of walking, breathing, heartbeat, autonomic processes, and indeed all kinaesthetic or motion sensing aspects of expression through movement, with the tonal inflections of our voices (whether in laughing, crying, or speaking) form a musical hierarchy or orchestration of self regulation and self-organisation, all directly linked to feeling states, and to their emotive transmission towards others.
>
> (1998: 176)

It may be through the creating and making of sound and music that we have the most visible evidence of a person's emotional life and need for connection to others that continues to exist in extreme old age. It is certainly an assumption upon which music therapy has developed as a valuable resource in the provision of psychological care of elderly adults with mental health problems.

WHAT DO MUSIC THERAPISTS DO?

The modern practice of music therapy in the UK as developed since the 1950s spans various models of improvisational music therapy (Bruscia, 1987). The method of clinical practice focuses upon unplanned live music making, generally using free improvisation, but also the spontaneous use of pre-composed music. This is in contrast to some other parts of the western world, particularly the USA and Australia where styles of music therapy have largely developed within a medical model with a focus upon planned pre-composed music making, and planned listening to recorded music (see Standley, 1995: 3). In improvisational music therapy, clinical practice involves the making of music through which a therapeutic relationship, both verbal and musical, is formed. The music therapist is required to be a skilled musician, but the patient may or may not be. Instruments are generally used with which the patient is likely to be familiar in cultural terms, and upon which sounds can be made with the minimum of skill.

EARLY INFLUENCES ON PSYCHODYNAMIC MUSIC THERAPY IN THE UK

It is likely that some of the pioneering music therapists during the 1950s and 1960s were much influenced by the developments in both individual and group psychotherapy which had flourished with the intense need for psychological care in post-war Britain. Juliette Alvin, who in 1968 founded the first music therapy training course at the Guildhall School of Music and Drama, London, frequently referred to a relationship between music and psychoanalysis. For example, in her first book *Music Therapy* she writes (Alvin, 1974: 77) 'Music works at id, ego and superego levels. It can stir up or express primitive instincts and even help to let them loose . . .' However it was her students and music therapists from other training backgrounds who later began to actually absorb psychoanalytic ideas and practice into their everyday work (Priestley, 1975; Streeter, 1999a, 1999b; Darnley-Smith & Odell-Miller, 2001). Alvin was given strong support in her teaching at the Guildhall by the composer and Professor of Composition Alfred Nieman. As part of his work, Nieman also taught free improvisation to instrumental students, who were sometimes reluctant to learn about the twentieth-century sound world of atonal music (Nieman, 1968: 5). His method of free improvisation was intended to free classically trained musicians from the musical conventions of the past into which they would inevitably fall if asked to improvise.

Most significantly he believed that this was a way of contacting one's own self in musical sound and that to play freely was to engage with and express our inner emotional world, in a manner not unlike that envisaged by Jung (1957) in his formulation of the concept of 'active imagination'. Jung postulated that the free use of art forms stimulated the imagination actively in such a way that the unconscious could be directly apprehended. The free creation of art forms could be used as a way of 'dreaming with open eyes' and as such could function as collaboration between conscious and unconscious factors (Samuels, Shorter & Plaut, 1986: 9). Mary Priestley (1975: 31), who developed the first psychodynamic method of music therapy in the UK during the 1970s called 'Analytic Music Therapy', wrote of her training with Nieman, quoting him as saying:

> Music faces us with the realisation that there are two worlds: the inner and the outer. The inner is often incommunicable, a spiritual world which is difficult to enter from the outer world where we normally speak to one another. Music is a bridge for us by which we can reach this inner world. That is why this free expression is so vital for music therapy.

Nieman's teaching of music therapists continued for many years up until the early 1990s, and his particular approach is a reminder that clinical improvisation in music therapy was developed within a context of a twentieth-century sound world. Bartram (1991: 7) commented that 'improvised music offers a language in which the therapeutic relationship can express itself on the moment by moment time scale which a therapeutic relationship requires. It can be open and without pre-designation ... often it is the language of experimental and avant-garde music which makes this openness possible.' Peregrine Horden (2000: 317) comments that the free improvisatory sounds made in music therapy sessions are a contemporary phenomenon unprecedented in historical accounts of music therapy. He writes that such sounds are acceptable to our modern conception of music as 'a vulgarization of Cage or Stockhausen' but in Europe before 1950 would have been considered symptomatic of a disease or disability, rather than part of a musical method for cure.

MUSIC THERAPY AND PSYCHOANALYSIS[1]

There is a long tradition within psychoanalytic literature which has examined and sought to understand the nature and function of music (Bryce-Boyer, 1992: 56). The work of music therapists could in part form a body of empirical evidence for such theorising, and as some music therapists have chosen to undertake additional training in psychotherapy there is at present a growing interest in mutual exchange.[2] There is also mention in the same psychoanalytic literature, and music therapy literature, of practitioners' use of musical forms and images as a way of thinking about verbal work (Brown, 1999; Powell, 1983; Strich, 1983). For example Andrew Powell relates the classical structure of Sonata Form in music to the process of participation in an analytic group:

> The third and final section of the sonata is the recapitulation. There is a return to the tonic key, often following a struggle with quite remote keys. The subject is restated, gathered together again, yet heard differently because it has been understood at a deeper level in all its aspects during the course of the exposition and development.
>
> (Powell, 1983: 16)

Music therapy in Europe, parts of the USA and also notably Argentina, has been strongly influenced by psychodynamic theory and practice, and practitioners have sought to understand the co-improvised music making in terms of the patient's 'internal world and pattern of relating in relationship with the therapist' (Stewart, 1997: 30). In the UK since the 1990s there has been a plethora of new writing which has reflected this tradition. For example, many music therapists, following on from the pioneering work of Mary Priestley, have begun to describe and understand their musical responses to their clients in terms of transference and countertransference. Odell-Miller (1999: 120) writes of the intense experience of 'here and now' provided in a music therapy where 'interactions are played out often within improvisations'. Her definition of countertransference is where 'as the therapist you realise that you are playing in a certain way in response to the patient, which previously you had been unaware (or unconscious) of. You then are able to subsequently make use of this musical experience' (1999: 121).

Streeter (1999b) provides a detailed musical analysis of two improvisations with a patient as a way of analysing the emerging process of the transference. She writes of one section, 'By the time the therapist pianist realized she had taken the lead (. . .) the client's input had become a shadow in the background. Then the music stopped. An obstacle appeared to have been put in the way of the life of this music. It had lost direction. There was an awkward pause' (1999: 93). Streeter shows us how in music the patient actually is relating to the therapist, and how the musical interactions become a manifestation of transference and countertransference dynamics.

John (1992: 12), writing about the function of music, emphasised the importance of the role of words in music therapy. He wrote that 'it is as if the music acts as a bridge between the unconscious and conscious, but . . . that the traffic of unconscious "things" needs to be thought about and become words in order to prevent it returning to the unconscious'. Using Freud's early topographical model of the mind, he characterises the music as having a 'pre-conscious' function of connection between unconscious and conscious.

Heal (1994: 290) adapts Bion's clinical concept of 'maternal reverie' in her case study of work with a young woman with Down's syndrome. She writes of how the improvised music was used intuitively, without any conscious planning, and how she would use her own emotional experience of the client to create an improvisation which she hoped would reflect her client's feelings but 'in a digestible way'. These are just some of the ways in which music therapists have begun to think about the psychodynamics inherent in their work with clients and to inform the process of music therapy as a whole.

MUSIC THERAPY AND PAVLICEVIC'S CONCEPT OF DYNAMIC FORM

Music as a therapy is not new; as many historical accounts of music therapy explain, 'At various times and in various cultures over the past two and a half millennia – and probably still further back in time – music has been medicine' (Horden, 2000: 1). On the other hand as a 'profession allied to medicine' music therapy is new. Music Therapy was recognised as a Health Service Profession in 1982, and achieved state registration as recently as 1997. It is written elsewhere of how a knowledge base began to develop out of the early pioneering work of Alvin, Priestley, and Nordoff and Robbins[3] during the 1980s in the UK (Darnley-Smith & Patey, 2003: 12–15). In recent years the music therapy literature has begun to draw upon the 'body of knowledge of non-verbal communication as one of the theoretical paradigms underpinning music therapy' (Pavlicevic, 1997: 118). In particular extensive reference has been made to the observational work of child development researchers Daniel Stern and Colwyn Trevarthen (Bartram, 1991; Pavlicevic, 1990, 1997; Robarts, 1994, 1998, 2000; Rogers, 1994; Stewart, 1997).

Pavlicevic's concept of dynamic form (1990, 1997) provides what might be regarded as the cornerstone of an emergent indigenous theory of music therapy (Ansdell, 1999: 73) in the description it offers of the 'interface between human emotion and clinical improvisation'. Here Pavlicevic shows, by reference to observational studies of early mother–infant communication (Stern, 1985), that 'the significance of clinical improvisation is that it is an *interpersonal* event rather than being only a *musically* interactive event' (Pavlicevic, 1997: 121, author's italics). She describes how feelings can be signalled through the qualities of our expressive acts, and how through clinical improvisation in music therapy this happens in a musical way. As human beings we express ourselves in many different ways or modalities, for example, through tone of voice, gesture and facial expression. 'Dynamic form' in Pavlicevic's terms refers to the abstracted meaning we make of the emotional signals contained in these modalities of expression. Within a clinical improvisation the same innate process is mobilised. The therapist and client experience the expressive quality of, for example, the tempo, dynamics or modulations of timbre or pitch in the music, and understand the sounds as emotional or relational. Trevarthen and Malloch (2000) support this view. They write of the human capacity for 'communicative musicality' which can be observed as 'an intrinsic organising principle in healthy parent–infant interactions' (2000: 6). They describe how parents and infants make use of pulse, pitch and timbre

> to form vocal narratives of shared emotion and experience. When parent and infant are communicating in a way satisfying to both, they are sustaining a co-ordinated relationship through time. In a similar way, we believe, when music therapist and client are communicating with sounds in a way satisfying to both, they too are creating a co-ordinated relationship through time.
>
> (Trevarthen & Malloch, 2000: 6)

Pavlicevic distinguishes between the workings or mechanics of clinical improvisation and individual psychodynamic meaning or 'what happens "around" the improvisation' (1997: 138) between client and therapist. It is to the nature of relationships in music therapy that I shall turn next.

AN EXTRACT FROM A SINGLE SESSION

Sean was a 70-year-old Irishman who had lived in London for about 50 years. He was married with no children. He lived with his wife who was suffering from the early stages of Parkinson's disease. Two years previously, he had suffered a stroke and become increasingly dependent upon alcohol. He was referred to a day hospital to try to help him to control his drinking, and as respite for his wife. Here he appeared depressed in his mood, with few words, and only the minimum of interaction. His reluctance to communicate with staff, or other patients, was the main reason for his referral to a music therapy group. The group ran for two years on a weekly basis. The other group members had a range of problems associated with the most common diagnosis in the group, mild dementia. They differed from Sean in that, as the months progressed, they gradually became more curious about each other, more attached to the group and interactive with each other. Sean mostly remained detached and was sometimes uncertain as to whether he wanted to attend. At one session, two months after Sean had started the music therapy group, due to illness and absences from the day hospital, he was the only group member present.

At the start of the session the therapist explained the reasons for the absence of the rest of the group, and encouraged Sean to choose an instrument. He chose three instruments, the drum, metallaphone (a metal xylophone) and the cymbal, and arranged them closely round himself. The therapist speculated to herself that the physical presence of the instruments possibly made him feel more comfortable. Sean began to play and the music therapist played the piano. The music was entirely improvised – they did not discuss what they were going to play beforehand. Sean started to create a musical pattern by making regular individual sounds on each instrument in turn and always ending with a crash on the cymbal. The sequence was repeated over and over again, for about four minutes, at a slow pace and a soft volume. Although the music was uncomplicated in rhythm and melody, the therapist struggled to meet Sean's pace and to find ways of making musical links with his sounds. She tried different ways of accompanying his music from the piano, at first with single notes, followed by experimenting with different chords before adding some simple melodic ideas. The therapist felt sleepy, and a need to glance at her watch. She reflected afterwards that she was probably wanting to escape from the great heaviness in his music, and the feeling that Sean was discouraging her from joining him. It is possible that he also wanted to escape, maybe from some anxiety about playing music on his own with her, without the group and whether he was good enough to do so.

After the music the therapist asked Sean how he felt about the music. His response to her question was that the music was 'all right', and that she was 'good'. After some silence he asked her, 'When are you going back to college?' The therapist explained that she was not at college, and feeling the need to convey some stability, added that she worked here all the time. Sean then asked about other patients whom she might work with in this room, and commented that it was a big hospital. After another pause he said that he 'missed the people'. The therapist responded that she felt their absence had had a big effect upon this session. Sean said that it had, 'yeah', and after another pause he said 'very different'. There was another silence. Soon afterwards he suggested that they play once more.

Discussion

Upon listening back to this work later on audio tape, the therapist wondered why she had felt so uncomfortable and disconnected from Sean during this improvisation. In fact she could hear a musical dialogue, even if, at the time, it had been painful to be part of and hard to hear. In retrospect the therapist felt that the slow pace at which Sean was playing was a musical manifestation of her experience of being 'shut out'. With the aid of a metronome, it was possible to hear on the tape recording of the session that throughout this extract she was frequently trying to speed him up. She was at times actually playing slightly faster than him, although there were moments where she rested in the music to 'wait' for him.

This example demonstrates that it is not only the musical skill of the therapist which is required here. The therapist's subjective experience of the session strongly suggests that her difficulty in meeting the tempo of Sean's music was not just technical, but rather connected to the difficulty she felt in meeting

Sean himself. The musical dialogue had provided her with a direct way of knowing him, from which countertransference meaning could be extracted. She experienced him as lonely and isolated but also felt that he had the need to shut her down, to keep her at a distance. In particular, the ability of music to reflect time and individual speed with flexibility is very significant. It is often observed and much researched that in old age life slows down. Any professional who has tried to engage with an elderly person in a hospital setting at the pace of a younger person will have come up against this difference of tempo all too sharply. In this case it was the difference in tempo which signalled the feel of the relationship between the client and therapist. Although Sean found interacting in words difficult, and possibly undesirable, through music he was able to convey much about himself.

MUSIC THERAPY AND WORK WITH ELDERLY PATIENTS

Music therapists frequently work with elderly clients in mental health settings, with clients who might have a broad range of needs. In particular music can be an invaluable tool in work with patients with dementia, where communication via language has become limited or incoherent. It is common knowledge amongst those who live with and care for adults suffering from dementia that even where the dementia is in final stages, musical sounds still evoke responses. Brotons (2000: 62) notes that *why* this occurs is currently not clear although the phenomenon is extensively documented in research literature. She makes two suggestions: first is it the 'aesthetic nature of music that in turn activates preserved brain structures, thereby allowing these people to connect with the outside world for certain periods of time'? Second she questions whether it is the 'interpersonal, caring relationship established with a therapist [which is] responsible for eliciting the responses' (2000: 62).

Aldridge (2000) writes that 'the [musical] responsiveness of patients with Alzheimer's disease to music is a remarkable phenomenon (Swartz et al., 1989). While language deterioration is a feature of cognitive deficit, musical abilities appear to be preserved. This may be because the fundamentals of language are musical, and prior to semantic and lexical functions in language development' (Aldridge, 2000: 140). As Brotons (2000: 62) comments, this is certainly an area that warrants further research. Whatever the reasons for such responsiveness to music however, the use of the medium enables music therapists to work with emotions, evoking memories, relieving some loneliness, and engaging with the individual on both a personal and culturally specific level.

Case Study[4]
This case study illustrates how some patients use music as a means of intense interpersonal contact, but also come to music therapy wanting to talk, showing how the therapy sometimes happens in both words and music. Harry was a 78-year-old Jewish man who had grown up in Glasgow. He had a diagnosis of mild dementia, mostly manifested through short-term memory loss, when he was referred to a mental health elderly day hospital music therapy group. He presented as a very articulate man, but partly due to his memory impairment there were large gaps in his history.

Six months previously he had been found wandering lost in the streets and was taken in to hostel accommodation by a charity organisation for the homeless. The day hospital was working with the charity organisation to help to find him long-term accommodation and also to assess his other needs. His referral to the music therapy group was based upon his expressed enthusiasm for music and his often dismissive attitude to the talking and activity groups which created a feeling amongst other staff of not knowing what to do with him.

Harry came to two individual assessment sessions and sang with unusual gusto and confidence in response to a couple of songs the music therapist played on the piano. He spoke nostalgically of having played the harmonica but felt unable to do this any more. The therapist also played the percussion instruments with him and they improvised musical sounds. He improvised vocally with great ease and feeling around melodies of tunes that he knew, or in a style with which he was familiar, for example the blues. The therapist realised in this first session what a strong attachment he had to music, his playing and singing was full of energy and feeling, by which in response she felt moved and musically inspired, but also a little overwhelmed.

In his first group session Harry obviously found the experience of having to share her attention extremely difficult, and for the first time she had a sense of his emotional fragility. He rejected any offers of music making and expressed a complete lack of interest in the other members of the group. Instead he began to talk with some tearful distress about his wife's death, and the subsequent conflict and estrangement with his niece. Having gained the attention of the therapist and the group, he launched into a medley of songs, simply by beginning to sing them. 'Night and Day', 'Let's Face the Music and Dance', 'The Lady is a Tramp', 'It was a Fine Romance but now it's Over', 'You are so Easy to Love' followed each other in quick succession. The therapist and the rest of the group joined in as well as they could by playing along, or where they knew the tunes and the words, by singing also. Soon after this, as it was summer, the therapist went on annual leave and the group had a break for three weeks. When she returned she learnt that Harry had been expressing strong feelings about her to other members of the day hospital staff. It was as though he had needed to keep the therapist alive during the break by professing his wish to marry her.

During the first music therapy session after the break, he seemed extremely distressed. He didn't want to sing or play, and just kept asking her personal questions about her life and holiday. She felt some guilt, that in engaging him in music therapy she had invited him to connect with an emotional part of himself that was vulnerable, intensely lonely and in need of contact with another human being. She felt that involving him in music therapy had aroused feelings with which he could not cope. He made her feel on the one hand extremely powerful, but at the same time rather overpowered, as she felt unsure as to how to respond and indeed felt flattered by his attentiveness and praise for her musical abilities.

The sessions continued into the autumn during which time a pattern emerged. Harry would attend sessions regularly, sitting in the same chair each week and rejecting instruments which were offered to him. Sessions always included a mixture of pre-composed and freely improvised music, sometimes including special music to begin and end sessions. The contents were never planned, always in themselves improvised. Where there were pauses Harry would always fill them saying 'Come on, let's sing something', or he would simply start singing. He had a wide repertoire of British and American romantic songs from the 1940s, which he would sing in the form of a medley, leaping from one song into the next.

If the therapist tried to encourage him to join the group in playing the instruments to improvise, he would usually refuse, saying 'I'm no good with my hands, I keep telling you'. If she tried to ask him about how he felt about his participation in the group, his relationship to her, or his relationship to others, he would retort 'talk, talk, talk', as though they were embroiled in a lover's row, and he was needing to defend himself. He became stuck in a pattern of interrupting other group members with his songs, and dominating the sessions. At the same time the therapist kept trying to find a way of responding to his need for special contact with her, and the powerful sense of loss and rejection he continued to convey both in terms of his talking about life experiences, and also what she came to feel she was acting out through the guilt she felt in not agreeing to his demands. That is to say, as she worked hard to process feelings of flattery and of being seduced, she felt unconfident in her attempts to set boundaries around his domination of group sessions.

Other group members had by now also begun to contribute songs such as 'What shall we do with the Drunken Sailor', 'Autumn Leaves', 'Amazing Grace', 'La vie en Rose', 'Danny Boy' and 'Summertime'. As if in response, Harry's music no longer felt alive with energy and feeling, but was instead like an angry demand for individual attention which in turn made the therapist feel angry with him. She felt that while he was singing in the group nothing else could happen – the other group members simply had to wait. Everything was on his terms and the relationship was one-way.

This impasse lasted with varying degrees of intensity for about eight months, during which time he moved into permanent accommodation in a residential home. The following autumn a series of events leading up to Harry's discharge from the day hospital and from the music therapy group, affected the relationship, allowing her to provide more containment for him. He began to suggest new songs, sometimes sung in different languages, and some-times in response to the nationalities and languages of other members of the group. There was a German song that he began to sing one day which seemed to prompt him to talk about his terrifying experiences during the 1939–45 war of watching friends being blown up in front of him, and of running for his life: 'I had 10 seconds to get out' he would frequently say. He would speak of the nightmares he still had. It was as though he was becoming more trusting of the group space. This also coincided with a series of concerts being organised in his residential home, from which he brought the programmes to show the therapist, and this provided the focus for some conversations about music which he liked.

At about the same time, during one session, the therapist suddenly found a new way to respond to his regular medley of songs, which were still a feature of sessions. Instead of simply trying to sing with him, she now improvised around the melodies. That is to say, instead of just singing the tune, she improvised harmonies and counter-melodies, whilst he continued with the original. Impro-vising around tunes is quite a usual way for music therapists to improvise music in a music therapy session, but it had not occurred to her before as a way of integrating Harry's songs into the group sessions. It was as though the idea for making music in this way had been unconsciously blocked off in the mind of the therapist whilst Harry recreated in the music therapy sessions his previous experiences of rejection and isolation. This he had done by expressing his long-ing for closeness, and subsequent angry rejection of the therapist, the other group members and their music. It seemed that Harry had needed this length of time in order for him to trust that the therapist could survive the different manifestations of his feelings of longing and rejection and before he could allow himself to occupy the same musical space as the rest of the group. He now readily accepted the new musical ideas which the therapist instigated, and took an active part. It also had the simultaneous effect of involving the other group members.

It seemed remarkable to the therapist that through this music making they were beginning to be able to link together as a group. She felt that she had at last found the musical meeting ground where Harry could sing his songs in relationship to her and the rest of the group, and at the same time feel some attention and nourishment. Furthermore she perceived that he could now relate to her as a therapist.

Discussion

Denis Carpy (1989: 292) in his paper 'Tolerating the Countertransference' writes of the effect on the patient of experiencing the therapist's acting out as confirmation that they are communicating feeling: 'The analyst's partial act-ing out allows the patient to see, consciously or un-consciously, that [they are] affecting the analyst and inducing strong feelings in him, and it allows [them] to observe him attempting to deal with these feelings.' Carpy writes of how through this process the patient is gradually able to 're-introject the pre-viously-intolerable aspects of himself that are involved. He is also able to introject the capacity to tolerate them which he has observed in the analyst.'

Something of this process possibly occurred with Harry. He experienced the music therapist's ambivalence in both rejecting his advances and also seeming pleased at his attention, and then subsequently finding a way of changing the musical interaction between them. It also exemplifies the hold-ing or containing function of music, in that the therapist after a period of time was able to find the way to give Harry his music back in a digestible form.

CONCLUSION

In this chapter some aspects of music therapy as practised within mental health settings in the UK have been outlined, together with the historical context from which the discipline has emerged since the 1960s. Some psycho-dynamic concepts which have been developed in music therapy have been described together with reference to how the establishment of a therapeutic process based on musical communication draws upon our innate musicality. Making music is a living dynamic activity which engages innate human drives to express feeling and to make relationships. Furthermore, although the process of free music making may at times involve verbal intervention, the benefit of music therapy with older adults is that a psychotherapeutic process can take place in the non-verbal realm of music making. This allows for the possibility of a meaningful psychological intervention for clients who may be verbally inarticulate, or unused to considering themselves in terms of their feelings, in addition to it having benefits for those who may be too organically impaired for other kinds of therapeutic activity.

This chapter began with an allusion to the particular relevance of this work for older adults with severe dementia in order that a more general point might be emphasised. For some individuals in old age, engagement with music may provide the only meaningful link with the world and a means of self-expression where words may not be possible, not enough, or simply not the point.

ACKNOWLEDGEMENTS

Thanks are due to the patients whose participation in music therapy is portrayed here, Ruth Berkowitz for her supervision, and to colleagues Helen

Patey and Helen Loth for their additional suggestions concerning the final text.

NOTES

1 For the purpose of this chapter the term psychoanalysis is used in its broadest sense to refer to the analytic traditions of Freud and Jung, together with the more recent schools of Klein and Winnicott, and others (see Frosh's 1999 definition in *The New Fontana Dictionary of Modern Thought*. London: Harper Collins).
2 In December 2001, The Confederation of Analytical Psychologists held a one day conference, entitled 'Imagination Bodies Forth the Forms of Things Unknown' to examine the relationship between Jungian psychology and the arts therapies, including music therapy.
3 A second training course was started by Sybil Beresford-Peirse in 1974 based at Goldie Leigh Hospital, South London. The focus of this second training course was the work of Paul Nordoff, an American composer, and Clive Robbins, a teacher of children with special needs. They had collaborated in developing a specialised model of improvisational music therapy with children. They had met in the late 1950s at a children's home run along the principles of Rudolf Steiner, 'according to which great emphasis was put on the importance and relevance of music and the other arts in the lives of people, even the most severely damaged' (Tyler, 2000: 387). There are now seven music therapy training courses in the UK.
4 I have written elsewhere about this case material in Darnley-Smith (2002: 83–86).

REFERENCES

NB: *Journal of British Music Therapy* changed its name in Volume 11 to *British Journal of Music Therapy*. They are the same publication.

Aldridge, G. (2000). Improvisation as an assessment of potential in early Alzheimer's disease. In: D. Aldridge (ed) *Music Therapy in Dementia Care*. London: Jessica Kingsley Publishers.

Alvin, J. (1974). *Music Therapy*. London: Hutchinson, 1966.

Ansdell, G. (1999). Challenging premises. *British Journal of Music Therapy*, 13(2), 72–76.

Bartram, P. (1991). Aspects of psychodynamic music therapy. Unpublished paper. Presentation given at the Scottish Music Therapy Council Conference, *Music Therapy and the Individual*, November 1991.

Brotons, M. (2000). An overview of the music therapy literature relating to elderly people. In: D. Aldridge (ed) *Music Therapy in Dementia Care*. London: Jessica Kingsley Publishers.

Brown, S. (1999). Some thoughts on music, therapy and music therapy. *British Journal of Music Therapy*, 13(2), 63–71.

Bruscia, K. (1987). *Improvisational Models of Music Therapy*. Illinois: Charles C. Thomas.

Bryce-Boyer, L. (1992). Roles played by music as revealed during countertransference facilitated transference regression. *International Journal of Psychoanalysis*, 73, 55–70.

Carpy, D.V. (1989). Tolerating the countertransference. *International Journal of Psychoanalysis*, 70, 287–294.

Darnley-Smith, R. (2002). Group music therapy with elderly adults. In: A. Davies & E. Richards (eds) *Group Work in Music Therapy*. London: Jessica Kingsley Publishers.

—— & Odell-Miller, H. (2001). Historical perspectives interview series: Helen Odell-Miller interviewed by Rachel Darnley-Smith. *British Journal of Music Therapy*, 15(1), 8–13.

—— & Patey, H.M. (2003) *Music Therapy*. London: Sage Publications.

Heal, M. (1994). The development of symbolic function in a young woman with Down's syndrome. In D. Dokter (ed) *Arts Therapies and Clients with Eating Disorders*. London: Jessica Kingsley Publishers.

Hill, S. (1998). *Air and Angels*. London: Arrow Books.

Horden, P. (ed) (2000). Introduction. In: *Music as Medicine*. Aldershot, UK: Ashgate Publishing Company.

John, D. (1992). Towards music psychotherapy. *Journal of British Music Therapy*, 6(1), 10–12.

Jung, C.G. (1957). The transcendant function. In: *The Structure and Dynamics of the Psyche. C.W. 8*. London: Routledge and Kegan Paul.

Nieman, A. (1968–1969). A fresh look at Webern. *Composer*, 30, 1–9.

Odell-Miller, H. (1999). Investigating the value of music therapy in psychiatry: Developing research tools arising from clinical perspectives. In T. Wigram and J. De Backer (eds) *Clinical Applications of Music Therapy in Psychiatry*. London: Jessica Kingsley Publishers.

Pavlicevic, M. (1990). Dynamic interplay in clinical improvisation. *Journal of British Music Therapy*, 4(2), 5–9.

—— (1997). *Music Therapy in Context. Music Meaning and Relationship*. London: Jessica Kingsley Publishers.

Powell, A. (1983). The music of the group. *Group Analysis*, XVI(1), 3–19.

Priestley, M. (1975). *Music Therapy in Action*. London: Constable.

Robarts, J.Z. (1994) Towards Autonomy and a Sense of Self. In Ditty Dokter (ed) *Arts Therapies and Clients With Eating Disorders*. London: Jessica Kingsley Publishers, 229–246.

—— (1998). Music therapy and children with autism. In: C. Trevarthen, K. Aitken, D. Papoudi, J.Z. Robarts *Children with Autism: Diagnosis and interventions to meet their needs*. London: Jessica Kingsley Publishers.

—— (2000) Building a theory of poietic processes in music therapy relating to research-in-progress. In Robarts, J.Z. (ed) *Music Therapy Research: Growing Perspectives in Theory and Practice*. London: BSMT Publications.

Rogers, P.J. (1994). Sexual abuse and eating disorders. In: D. Dokter (ed) *Arts Therapies and Clients with Eating Disorders*. London: Jessica Kingsley Publishers.

Samuels, A., Shorter, B., & Plaut, F. (1986). *A Critical Dictionary of Jungian Analysis*. London: Routledge.

Standley, J. (1995). Music as a therapeutic intervention. In: Wigram, T., Saperston, B., & West, R. (eds) *The Art and Science of Music Therapy: A handbook*. Amsterdam: Harwood Academic Publishers.

Stern, D. (1985). *The Interpersonal World of the Infant*. New York: Basic Books. [Cited in Pavlicevic (1997).]

Stewart, D. (1997). The Sound Link: Psychodynamic group music therapy in a therapeutic community setting. *Psychoanalytic Psychotherapy*, 11(1), 29–46.

Streeter, E. (1999a). Finding a balance between psychological thinking and musical awareness in music therapy theory: A psychoanalytic perspective. *British Journal of Music Therapy*, 13(1), 5–20.

——(1999b). Definition and use of the musical transference relationship. In: T. Wigram & J. De Backer *Clinical Applications of Music Therapy in Psychiatry*. London: Jessica Kingsley Publishers.

Strich, S. (1983). Music and patterns of human interactions. *Group Analysis*, XVI(1), 20–26.

Swartz, K., Walton, J., Crummer, G., Hantz, E., & Frisina, R. (1989). Does the melody linger on? Music cognition in AD. *Seminars in Neurology*, 9(2), 152–158. [Cited in Aldridge (2000).]

Trevarthen, C., & Malloch, S. (2000). The dance of wellbeing: Defining the music therapeutic effect. *Nordic Journal of Music Therapy*, 9(2), 3–17.

Tyler, H.M. (2000). The music therapy profession in modern Britain. In: P. Horden (ed) *Music as Medicine*. Aldershot, UK: Ashgate Publishing Company.

Chapter 14

Dance and movement therapy for people with severe dementia

Marion Violets-Gibson

> Don't isolate
> if you see someone not dancing
> it's your fault
> never is too late
> and a dance short lived or long
> is all that's needed . . .
> ('Never is too late', Joan Armatrading, 1977)

Older people who have been given the diagnosis of dementia have to face major issues of loss and mental health problems. People with dementia may have specific communication and language difficulties. Dance and movement therapy offers non-verbal and verbal communication within a psychotherapeutic framework.

This particular method of working was developed to support psychotherapy for people in the later stages of the illness. There had been little awareness previously that this could be necessary or possible. (The method has been adapted and used with success for people in earlier stages of the illness, and with people with mixed ability; the author knows of no other examples of this work with this particular patient group to date.)

The model is eclectic, incorporating influences from dance movement therapy, developmental psychology, neuropsychology and body movement theory. There is a potential for a long-term application of the method in group psychotherapy for those with dementia. It was also seen as possible that certain aspects could be adapted for use in a training programme for care staff, to improve communication skills with patients with dementia. In addition, a person-centred approach could assist a broader understanding of the condition.

THE PERSON IS ALWAYS THERE

Deep anxiety is frequently expressed by the person with dementia. The person struggles with their confusion, memory loss and disorientation (see Chapter 15). The presentation of distress, in what seems to be a hopeless situation, is often so overwhelming for staff working in this setting that we are frequently tempted to use practical methods to distract the client and deny that anything is wrong. This can reinforce the feeling of nightmare for them, and is often deeply unsatisfactory. It does not explain to them why they are being kept against their will and why they have lost control over their own life and contact with their loved ones. These loved ones may or may not be still alive but may remain constantly in the present, in their memory. Residents often express the feeling that they are being ignored and treated as though they have no relevant thoughts or feelings; that they are no longer a person at all (Sinason, 1992).

During the whole period of this work and through direct contact with many clients within this home and other residential settings, the author received frequent confirmation that the core self (Stern, 1985) of each person with dementia always remained intact, until the point of death (Violets, 2000). In the aims behind the development of the movement therapy group was the preoccupation with how this group of clients would be able to find a means of expression for their human concerns and their specific psychosocial needs (Yalom, 1995).

It was felt that stereotypical attitudes towards the elderly in general, and towards dementia in particular, needed to be taken into consideration. Dependency, loss of autonomy and bereavement are often viewed in a negative light and are frequently interpreted as behavioural issues. Feelings of worthlessness and disgust are consequently internalised within these individuals (Stockley, 1992). The aims in this programme were directed specifically towards enabling each individual to access their own physical and creative skills, which they had acquired during their lifetime. Through the use of movement and rhythm they would be able to access their procedural memory, enabling them to express feelings and connect with others who not only had an illness in common, but also full, complex and unique life histories.

ECLECTIC MODEL

This model of working incorporated concepts and techniques from several disciplines. The interactive movement circle has been used extensively in what could be described as a classical dance movement therapy method, which was developed originally by Marian Chace (Chaiklin, 1975), working with unmedicated psychiatric patients in the 1940s. This model was adapted for these clients by using a chair circle, so that they could work in a seated position, as many of them had mobility and balance problems. Within this circle, interaction was developed by the interventions of the therapist who worked with and extended the group members' own movements. The session had a prescribed structure using warm-up, theme development and closure. There is significant evidence that this would help to create a safe 'holding' environment (Leventhal, 1992). In the warm-up section, any of the following dance movement therapy techniques could be used: for example, mirroring, which has also been described in the mother–infant interaction by Winnicott (1971). This technique also has been paralleled in the verbal psychotherapy process, rephrasing what the client has said (Stanton-Jones, 1992). Rhythmic expression and physical 'warm-up' are used at this stage of the session. The next stage develops the theme for the day, broadening, extending and clarifying actions. The use of verbalisation and imagery, role playing and symbolic action are all encouraged. The form of people in a circle is often emphasised during this section, with the use of synchronous rhythm, using 'props' (equipment such as two-way stretch lycra ropes). This is reinforced again during the closure, when there is an emphasis on slowing down the activity, working with the group cohesion and enabling discussion and sharing of feelings.

For this group of people, who have difficulty in locating and remembering where they are in time and space and whose body image and integration of sensory experience is fragmented, these methods of group process are fundamental in helping to contain their memory at least for the duration of the session. The familiar movements and rhythms, which enabled each person to re-discover a sense of their own whole body self, also appear to access memory and re-establish connections with others, eventually enabling them to identify as a group. For people whose whole sense of self is severely impaired at an organic as well as a psychological level, the need for a strong reference in the form of a structured, therapeutic container is essential (Erfer, 1995a).

BUILDING A PSYCHOTHERAPEUTIC FRAMEWORK FOR GROUPS OF PEOPLE WITH VERBAL DIFFICULTIES

The author has been involved in the setting up and running of a 'dance movement' therapy group in a secure residential unit. This is an NHS provision for people with severe dementia and challenging behaviours, who would not have secured placement elsewhere. Although some of the residents did go out with volunteers, family or staff, had home visits and received visits from family or friends, they were not able to leave the unit on their own.

Because of the advanced stage of their illness, the residents were unable to make many choices or decisions about how they would spend their day. They were all in need of personal care. The age group ranged between 50 and 90.

There was no confidential therapeutic space in which to run the group, nor was there any tradition of psychotherapeutic group work within the setting.

The advantages and disadvantages of using a structured, contained psychotherapeutic space for these residents, working specifically with movement, rhythm and communication, were considered. From these observations, this model of group work and how it appeared to change people's relationships with each other and staff, was assessed. An evaluation from these findings was made from:

1　Movement and interactive observations looking at video footage of the session.
2　Therapist's detailed notes and assessment sheets.
3　Feedback from care staff and key workers.
4　Feedback from nursing staff, management and doctors.
5　Feedback from family and friends.
6　Detailed assessments by post-graduate movement therapy students.

The intention was to view these outcomes in long-term psychotherapy with these residents and to take an overall view of this intervention in terms of quality of life. There were also observations made on the training programme and its effect on the wellbeing and communication of both clients and staff.

A need for person-centred care

Outside the group, residents tended to sit in isolation, not engaging with each other or the external environment. Others wandered anxiously and incessantly, searching for 'home', family or former employment. There were frequent outbursts of anger between residents or with members of staff. This appeared to focus on misunderstandings in communication and the perceived feelings of frustration and despair which followed. There was often a pervading sense of deep sadness and helplessness underlying these exchanges, which seemed connected to a sincere desire to help but an inability to find a common 'language'.

People with advanced dementia often lose their ability to communicate verbally. They may not be able to describe the terrifying experiences they appear to be having. An example of this can be seen in the exchange between a therapist and a very anxious client who called her over and tried to explain her concern about something that she could see going on in the corridor. The therapist sat with the client, leaning in the direction of her gaze, and described what she could see, which was a person vacuuming the carpet. There was a long flex trailing about from the noisy machine. This work was going on in the doorway of the client's own room. She had very anxious and often paranoid thoughts about people doing horrible things to her in her room. She was making agitated and jumbled sentences about bad things going on in the corridor. The therapist moved close and in rhythm with her, as a confidante. She attempted to explain the scene, describing household activities. Suddenly the patient looked into the therapist's eyes and said with a note of sad recognition in her voice, 'You can't see it can you?' The therapist acknowledged that this might be true, but added that she could sense that what the client was seeing was making her feel very anxious. At this the resident squeezed her hand and said, 'Never mind dear, you are doing your best.' This was very clear and appropriate, in contrast to her usual dysphasic mode of speaking. After this she relaxed her stiff, anxious posture. It seemed more important that someone was making the attempt to acknowledge her experience and validate her feelings as legitimate. It is essential for those who work with people with dementia to acknowledge the emotion behind the confusion, even if the details are hard to decipher and perceptions not always shared (Kitwood, 1997).

Building the therapeutic container

There was a need to find a concrete sense of group, through using the physical dynamic of the circle of chairs. This built the core of the group around the central 'potential' or 'transitional' space in which they could experiment and play together in the presence of the caring 'other'. In this case, the 'good enough' therapist (Winnicott, 1971). For people who were losing their orientation in space and time, where they might not recognise that the object floating in front of them was their own hand, this physical sense of containment was effective. The therapist was also a container, especially during the early stages of the group. Within it she had a physical contact role, using touch specifically as a tool (Levitt, 1995) to increase the appreciation of proprioception. For example, by lightly tapping or pressing the limb in a specific way and naming it (Spotnitz, 1971). She also used direct gaze to establish trust and acted as the primary object in relation to the transitional objects (the props).

In this way the therapist embodied the group physically and contained, in her person, their memory of themselves as a whole, while they were in the 'nascent' group stage (Sandal & Johnson, 1987). Patients appeared only to understand and remember the group when they saw the therapist who used familiar movements and songs to remind them. They would register no recognition if another member of staff merely announced that they were going to the group. When the group became a memory over time, the prompt was the sight of the circle of chairs with people sitting in them, the sound of the familiar songs or watching someone mimicking movements. The ball was a powerful tool in this respect. It was a memory prompt, alerting the emotions of joy, interest and pleasure or sometimes annoyance.

The interaction with the ball was able to connect a reflex response with a sense of self-agency. The patient was able to physically experience receiving the ball with their own body; their movement in relation to the eye gaze and the mirroring movements of the therapist. Initially the ball was not necessarily identified as such. This was clear from the surprise, sometimes confusion or anxiety, with which the ball was held. The person might query it, misname it and also mistake its function. The therapist would build a movement interaction with the client, which might be worked on over several sessions, naming and also verbalising feelings that might be implied by the patient's reactions. This would be done with synchronous rhythm and mirrored movements which might involve touch. The physical block, which often occurs in the motor response in the process of dementia, was also eased through this work. This neural block can present as jerky stuttering, contained in a pre-movement, which is not able to flow to complete the task; like the festinence associated with Parkinson's disease.

The ball could be seen as the transitional object (Winnicott, 1953) which would enable the group to experiment with their own autonomy. It was instrumental in the first contact with the therapist, enabling the person to reform an image of themselves in relationship to another. The members were then able to move on from their dependence upon her and identify with each other as a social group. It is particularly helpful at this stage for the person with dementia to use movement to define a definite relationship to the outside world and to objects; keeping them connected to everyday reality and a sense of themselves in relationship to the rest of the world (Schilder, 1950).

It was through the closed circle form, and the physical interaction with the ball and the therapist, that the members of the group were able to connect with each other in a transitional play space. The residential setting where individuals have to a large extent lost their autonomy, and rely on a carer to attend to all their intimate needs, produced a similar environment of dependency to that experienced in childhood. The container here represented the play space, redolent of latency, when children would still be dependent upon parents but where they would experiment and adventure together, trying out social relationships. Of course these patients were not children. The parallel was the quality of the environment and the individual's position within it. We have often 'overlooked the fact that it was through movement that we were first socialised to our cultural group' (Moore & Yamamoto, 1998).

It is interesting to note that people of this age group would be very familiar with circle interactive games which often also used movement and singing (Opie & Opie, 1985). In this particular group, the therapist needed to find a solid base in the shifting layers of perception, by going down through the levels of development. This might include tactile communications and a smile as with the primary carer. This was often the point where the therapist could make contact and work, re-connecting the layers of experience and relationship through the game itself. The Kestenberg scale (1967), which relates psychosocial stages of development to rhythm patterns, was used to inform the therapist's observations during this process.

It was often quite clear to see dysfunction in a client's attachment patterns (Bowlby, 1988) by observing their rhythm sequences. Attachment difficulties often appeared to affect the behaviour and responses of the clients to each other in the group (Mahler et al., 1975). It was frequently demonstrated that for older people, early attachment issues often re-emerged. For example searching anxiously for the lost parent. This presented clearly when faced with a threat to their survival, particularly with this kind of degenerative, life-threatening illness, embodying fear of abandonment by loved ones and loss of self-agency (Wadell, 2000).

Procedural memory and neuroscience in dementia

Working with this structure therapeutically required patient attention and creative repetition. As the capacity for verbal and abstract thought disintegrated within the person with dementia, it appeared to be possible to make connections to memories through body sensation and the experience of movement. It was found to be essential in this client group to work with their procedural (skills) memory (Squire, 1987). Recent research from the field of neuroscience shows clearly that as humans we have highly complex, interdependent neural networks, which make it possible for us to use different cognitive methods for accessing and assimilating memories. Much of our mode of communication in modern society is based on 'declarative' memory, which involves the ability to receive verbal instructions. This requires the neural ability to make internal representations of images. The associated pathways may be amongst the earliest to be damaged in the dementia process, robbing a person of the means to understand a direct verbal communication. Consequently they have no reference point to integrate the information given. For most members of the group their ability both to receive and to impart verbal information was seriously impaired. This does not mean, however, that this person is not 'present' or that there are no other means of communication, which is often the assumption. For people with dementia, the procedural memory which remains in the musculature and rhythms of the body, often remains intact throughout the illness. Skills that the person has learnt throughout life are there to be accessed.

> There are other types of knowledge. One is the perceptual and motor knowledge that enables us to ride a bicycle; this does not rely on fact but skills. The retrieval of procedural knowledge requires motor output rather than internal representation.
>
> (Damasio, 2000)

The author thinks that people with dementia should be encouraged to move and sing. This enables them to contact stored knowledge and memories remaining in the complex memory patterns of motor co-ordination with which they can develop new systems and pathways (Hannaford, 1995).

During the work in this group, it became evident that people, even in the advanced stages of brain damage through a dementing illness, were able to acquire new memories, from the creative repetition of movement interaction and song. From about the twelfth session, individuals were able to recognise the group when they saw the familiar circular form, or when they saw the therapist make certain movements or sing a phrase of a well-known song. This newly acquired memory of the group, and the members in it, was demonstrated when one of the group members, on entering the building, heard the group singing from a distance. He began to sing his special song, which was known to the group. The group stopped their own singing and joined in with him, with smiles of recognition. All this occurred at a distance, without them being able to see each other. Considering the severity of the short-term memory loss in this group of people, this example of the development of a new memory would not have been thought possible.

> The correct perspective relative to the oncoming car is important to design the movement with which you escape it and the same applies to the ball you are supposed to catch with your hand. The automatic sense of individual agency is born there and then. Integral to the learned movement response is the connecting emotion, which instigated that particular movement response.
>
> (Damasio, 2000)

So it would seem that through the changes and developments in body movement, the clients in this group were also able to re-invoke the emotions, which were integral to the memory of the movement itself (Kaplan-Solms & Solms, 2000). '[T]he sense of self is intricately related with the object, the emotion and the movement response' (Damasio, 2000).

The development of the psychotherapeutic work

In the preliminary sessions, clients were often encouraged to engage in a relationship with the therapist, as though with the primary carer. The positive transference made initially was essential for the client to feel safe enough to make links to other members of the group. The therapeutic work at this stage was to observe and extend the clients' responses to a phrase of a song or movement, which could then be used to link one client with another. Work was partly structured using objects and tools, for example soft balls, bean bags, stretch fabrics of varying weight and texture. Other specific techniques were used, such as mirroring movements and re-phrasing dysphasic clients' words. The therapist spoke directly to and called people by name, using a mnemonic rhyming song, which became the embodiment of the group memory. She would name the body part which was making the movement and described how this might be happening, e.g. light, heavy, strong, gentle etc. Later when the group had been able to construct its own memory, using these techniques of creative repetition (Richards, 1985), the therapist was able to retire and to assist in the 'orchestration' of the movement and dialogue between group members. This was psychological as well as physical, in the sense that the therapist was able to become more participant observer, rather than the primary object in the transitional space. Once this level of group cohesion and identity had been reached, the anxiety and often paranoid feelings of group members were then able to find expression and possibly resolution. They were able to begin exploring the underlying issues of abandonment and self-loathing.

One concern for people was not to be seen as 'crazy'. This often appeared to make them feel anxious about committing themselves to a group where others behaved in a bizarre way. They had to confront themselves in the illness of others, in the mirroring effect of group dynamics; something that may be thought of as frightening. The deeper sense of personhood and social identity remained intrinsic within the sense of the core self, even though many other functions were noticeably disintegrating and causing ostensibly odd behaviours.

The therapeutic value in flexible boundaries

A porous boundary was an important feature of the physical structure of the chair circle and the containment of the group. If the circle was too tightly closed, this created a potential conflict. People having a choice about whether to come or go from the circle had a positive therapeutic effect. A group member might suddenly feel the need to leave, or a person from outside might wish to investigate and to experience what was happening in this group.

Having the choice to come and go was confidence building. For people who had so little autonomy, having freedom in this respect established a strong group identity. The therapist and the group supported the person's need to leave, which might have come from a feeling of anxiety about a missed husband, wife or child, or the need to perform a familiar task. The fact that the partner may have been long dead or inaccessible was not the point. Both the therapist's and the group's recognition of the need gave an authenticity to the deeply remembered feeling, for this person to come back 'home' to the group, after the necessary 'mythical journey'. This support system was reinforced by asking the person to return again soon when they said that they needed to leave. Each time they would be told that they were valued in the group. The therapist also found that if the group's 'doors' were open to other residents, whose wandering or preoccupations made them resistant to joining, they would often come in to 'visit'. This became part of the group culture, to recognise and welcome a wanderer. Some of these 'guests' eventually found the confidence to become permanent members of the group.

Clinical Illustrations
Ruth was the first to come into the group that day. She complained of pain and how she could not move at all. She sat looking at other people around the circle and began to mutter 'Let me die, please let me die . . . God help me . . . they're all mad.'

One second later, as the Dance Movement Therapist turned to her and said 'catch', throwing her a soft ball, her body lifted up and her eyes sparkled, she smiled mischievously and threw the ball back with ease and grace. Almost instantly her body had remembered the game and with it her identity, as a capable, autonomous person. With this alert and interested response, she engaged Harry by tossing the ball to him lightly, with a warm smile. The sight of him only the minute before had invoked anger and despair for her. For both, their previously slumped, disengaged postures and expressions of despair and loathing had lifted into the appearance of much younger people, more vibrant and full of life.

Once there was a structure for memory and cohesion in the group, it felt safe enough to express difficult and angry feelings. Harry had problems with being able to physically moderate his movements between strong and direct and slow and sustained. This also applied to his singing between loud and soft. Every movement was jerky. However as work began in the group, catching and throwing soon revealed his considerable skills. Once these were accessed and he had begun to regain his confidence, his interest and motivation helped him to interact with others in more complex patterns of relationship. There was a clear improvement in his ability to extend his movement, following its flow right through without jerkiness. His singing moderated, no longer shouting.

He had previously experienced problems due to his inappropriate expression of sexuality towards women residents and staff. He would suddenly grab at body parts which people found offensive. The intensity of the expressed desire seemed to have a direct relationship with the increasing disintegration he was experiencing in the progression of his illness. He became very distressed when he provoked anger in staff and clients. Everyone would be in a state of agitation and discomfort. The therapist worked upon this issue in the group. Through the erotic transference he made with her, she linked his feeling of autonomy through the expression of his sexuality, to his skill and mastery with throwing and catching the ball. This game demonstrated his strength, flexibility and co-ordination and could include others.

There was an intensity and also humour which enabled other patients to create wider patterns of relationship, which also included sexual reference, in the form of play and flirting. This became evident both in pair work and in the wider context of the whole group, but particularly with Dawn who had been venomous towards Harry over his inappropriate behaviour. She made a cutting gesture across her throat towards him which made him cower, using a characteristic, defensive movement. This gesture had been observed previously as a defence, possibly against physical blows earlier in his life. There were layers of meaning contained in Dawn's gestures, particularly because she had a considerable sense of dramatic humour.

In the next session she was up and dancing with the therapist while Harry sang and drummed. Suddenly she turned on him and said that he was bad and she wanted to kill him. He drew himself up and there was a moment of 'stand off'. The group was suddenly very alert, would there be a fight? The therapist had asked him if he thought Dawn had meant what she said. He rarely used words but he had looked at Dawn and then directly at the therapist and said 'yes'. The therapist was lightly supporting Dawn in a standing position, as her balance was quite impaired, and asked her what she had really meant. Suddenly Dawn responded with a smile.

'He's not so bad really . . . give us a kiss.'

At this point they were able to give each other a reconciliatory kiss of friendship, which had previously been unthinkable. It seemed that with the therapist as mediator, Dawn had been able to find her capable self in her dancing movement. From this position of strength she had been able to meet Harry as an equal partner and reconcile her feelings of anger towards him.

In a following session they had chosen the maracas to make rhythm for the songs. Suddenly they had turned on each other, sparring with the instruments like clubs, their movements contained and rhythmic like flamenco dancers. The therapist mirrored the quality of their movement dialogue. She verbalised to the group what she thought might be happening. She had suggested that Dawn and Harry were angry with each other, and had used her own body movement to emphasise the flow of the dance rhythm (Laban, 1960/1992). In this way, the movement language became a dialogue. Dawn had developed her words into a song, 'you are a naughty, naughty boy'.

Harry joined in with his own, 'you are a stupid, nasty woman'. This was chanted with the clashing rhythm of the maracas. The feeling in the group had been quite electric. The therapist had contained the movements and dialogue within a framework of serious play, to reduce the anxiety of the other group members. Outwardly expressed anger was often seen as frightening and symbolised 'bad behaviour' for this client population, within the residential setting. Consequently there had been a stillness within the group, like people gathering around a fight, where everyone was able to project their fantasies. The clashing and chanting grew in crescendo and had suddenly exploded quite surprisingly into laughter, when the duelling pair had thrown the wooden instruments onto the floor with a crash.

Ruth's eyes had registered a keen interest. She had experienced her own issues around Harry's acted out sexuality. She had complained about him grabbing her, and had shouted that he was a disgusting, ugly old man. Again Harry had been mortified. Ruth had spoken about herself to the therapist, in earlier sessions, about how she might like to be with a man. She had not been able to see herself as the same age as Harry and wanted to deny that she was 'losing her mind'. She had only wanted to remember herself as attractive. The full horror of the slowly dawning recognition of her own fate, had been deferred through her acerbic verbal attacks against the others. This was the projection which Harry had invoked through seeing himself as the desirable male. They had both been filled with rage and grief at the image of an old and disgusting person; neither wanted to see themselves in this way and had projected the ugliness onto the other.

After this incident between Dawn and Harry, Ruth had also became much more relaxed and ready to engage in skilful and often flirtatious play together, with the ball. Mutual admiration developed between them, during these engagements. It seemed that the opportunity to make a physical expression of these internal drives had given a context and framework for a wider and more social exchange between these three people within the group dynamic.

Working individually to enable group participation

During the period of establishing the group, the author worked individually with Nia, a patient whose illness was so advanced that she had not been able to attend groups. One of the main factors in the grief and fear presented by dementia sufferers in the advanced stages of the illness is isolation. The therapist planned a series of sessions with Nia to try to enable her to come to some reconciliation within herself of the tragic loss of her family and her own autonomous life. Nia was considerably younger than many of the other residents. She had lost her speech. She was suffering such severe physical disorientation that she could not locate herself in space. Her eyesight was poor. She was in danger of falling and crashing into objects and so she had to have 24-hour observation. Her shouting and desperate vocal attempts to communicate, distressed and frightened other residents, who often told her angrily to 'shut up'.

She had been especially fond of dancing and still responded very positively and rhythmically to music. In these sessions the therapist had begun to move around the room with her, speaking and humming and mirroring her movements. Nia had been very angry initially, expressing her rage by trying to get out of the door, which was difficult for her to locate. The therapist had encouraged her to express this anger towards her, as the object which stood between her and the door. While they had been moving together in this time and rhythm, she had spoken aloud to Nia, suggesting how difficult this might be for her and how angry she might feel. At the end of the session Nia seemed to have accepted this situation as the status quo and returned to her carer. The therapist clearly explained when she would work with her again.

The second session began while Nia was sitting in a chair. She was shouting very loudly. Residents and staff had both been expressing agitation. The therapist began by singing and holding Nia's hands, encouraging her to stand and move in rhythm. She mirrored her patterns, allowing space so that Nia was moving separately but still connected in the dyadic relationship. Nia began to follow the therapist's clapping and then initiated her own rhythms, which the therapist was able to follow. At a change in the rhythm of the tape, the therapist began to tap both hands against her thighs. This was a style which held a specific dance memory for Nia, who suddenly looked up and gave direct eye contact for the first time and laughed warmly. The therapist felt that this was a completely appropriate and congruent response, which did not have any of the former ambivalence. There was a feeling of mutual understanding, which marked the beginning of a different level of communication (Malan, 1979).

In view of the positive transference that Nia had made with the therapist, it was proposed that she should try to work with the group. At first this was very difficult for her, because although she was able to move with the rhythm and music, the work with the ball was outside her range. It also brought up issues for others in the group, especially Ruth who had gone into panic at the sight of Nia's disability. Ruth had always projected her fear of her own loss of autonomy and person-hood particularly onto Nia, who so visibly presented the severe stages of the illness. Nia's skill had always been an impeccable sense of rhythm, so she was invited by the therapist to be the rhythm and pitch keeper for the group. They began to look to the tapping of her toe to see if they were singing in tune or dancing out of rhythm. On one occasion after playing Celtic harp music, which had been spoken about several times before, Nia looked directly at the therapist and clearly said 'harp'. From then on they were able to develop a simple spoken as well as movement vocabulary. Nia was able to answer yes or no when asked specific questions.

She remained alert all through the group session and responded to other dialogues, usually with a smile or an angry sound, showing her interest, approval or disapproval. Over time she was also able to develop contact work with an object, like the ball and stretch rope. This work provoked a smile from her and a direct gaze with the therapist, as if intrigued by her sense of achievement. For someone who had been so isolated and who had not been able to relate at all in a social context, she had been able to become an important part of the group.

In addition to the specific effects on Nia, having a therapist willing to work with someone so disturbed and disabled had a positive and encouraging effect on the staff working there.

The effect of one person's grief on the group dynamic

Some of the group had started to dance to ballroom music and Nia began to shout and cry. Ruth got exasperated and shouted at her to 'shut up', muttering that they had enough to put up with themselves. The therapist then explained to the group that Nia had loved dancing so much, it had made her feel very sad because she was not able to stand up any more. The group suddenly fell silent, with a sigh of recognition from Ruth; a swift change from her previous self-centred expression of anger. There was a moment when the group recognised a feeling of universality (Yalom, 1995).

They had been working with this theme for some time, in their songs and rhythms, where they had recognised the feeling of being together 'in the same boat'. From that time on, there were visible signs of people turning towards each other, speaking and sharing moments. For group members who had not been able to speak, the therapist observed people giving a gentle touch against some-one's face, or a pat of the head. Harry was much more able to modify his movements, finding an acceptable balance between passive and over aggressive. He was able to regulate the fine motor movements, so that he did not have to go into a 'gripping' flexion. He was also able to regulate the loudness of his singing to soft and gentle.

Nia's reminder of infirmity had provoked the most extreme projections of anger and self-loathing in other members of the group. However the expression and acknowledgement of these feelings had also eventually been able to invoke the opposite experience of love and gentleness, when the group had enacted the drama of their grief through their empathy for her.

CONCLUSIONS

Change had taken place in the clients over this period of work, both in their individual means of expression and in their response to each other and to members of staff. In some, medication was reduced. Staff saw changes in behaviour and consequently in their relationship with their clients. This was noticed not only during the group but also carried over into daily life. There were indications that movement, gait and posture had become more co-ordinated and flexible; communication had improved and even speech had returned, either through the use of words or phrases unheard before, or sentences had become more ordered and relevant in the cases of dysphasia. Patients had gained confidence and had become more relaxed within the setting, as they felt that their deep anxieties and concerns had been seriously listened to and possibly understood.

Dance movement psychotherapy in group work is suited to the needs of clients with dementia, because of the nature of their physical and psycho-social needs. Regular, long-term, dance movement psychotherapy groups enable patients to access and express their creative skills. They also enjoy reminiscence and shared memories using this framework. This model pro-vides another method of communication when the usual verbal means of contact is very limited or misunderstood. With this technique dementia suf-ferers may be able to express very difficult and frightening feelings and in doing so, reconcile conflicts with other residents and staff.

Recent research has demonstrated that there is a subtle relationship between the influence of organic damage and environmental stress on changes in neuronal function (Kandel & Hawkins, 1992). The psychotherapeutic movement intervention described here was a considerable factor in mediating this process. This method of intervention needs to be long term. The therapist found that, in view of the co-morbidity and high care needs amongst the group members, there is an important need for trained care staff to act in a supporting role, assisting clients to attend the therapeutic group.

From the observations made using this method of working with procedural memory, it was also possible to define certain aspects of the structure, for use in a training scheme for care staff. This was effective in developing a wider understanding of the needs of dementia sufferers, and extending the possible range of communication techniques for them with their patients. The training encouraged person-centred care and wellbeing for residents in the home and also equipped staff to run social activity groups, using movement and singing, enabling a deeper level of social interaction and sense of relationship.

Staff working within this framework have been able to observe changes in their clients which have motivated and inspired their daily practice and instilled a sense of hope (Violets, 2001).

NOTE

'Education through music' (Richards, 1985) is a method of teaching using children's traditional song dance and movement games – the link being the essential nature of movement reinforcing memory. I studied this technique in the United States and Canada. A few of us were just beginning to adapt the uses for children with disabilities but I am the only person I know who has linked it with dance movement therapy and used it as an influence in dementia work.

MARION VIOLETS-GIBSON, 2004

ACKNOWLEDGEMENT

Lyrics from 'Never Is Too Late' by Joan Armatrading. © 1977, by kind permission of Rondor Music (London) Limited.

REFERENCES

Bowlby, J. (1988). *A Secure Base: Clinical applications of attachment theory*. London: Routledge.

Chaiklin, H. (1975). *Marian Chace: Her papers*. Columbia, MD: American Dance Association.

Damasio, A. (2000). *The Feeling of What Happens*. UK: Heinemann.

Erfer, T. (1995a). Treating children with autism in the public school system. In: F. Levy (ed) *Dance and Other Expressive Arts' Therapies*, pp. 191–211. London & New York: Routledge.

—— (1995b). Dance movement therapy with children with autism. In: F. Levy (ed) *Dance and Other Expressive Arts' Therapies*. London & New York: Routledge.

Hannaford, C. (1995). *Smart Moves: Why learning is not all in your head*. Virginia: Great Ocean Publishers.

Kandel, E., & Hawkins, R.D. (1992). The biological basis of learning and individuality. *Scientific American*, 267(3), 78–86.

Kaplan-Solms, K., & Solms, M. (2000). *Clinical Studies in Neuropsychoanalysis*. UK & USA: Karnac Books.

Kestenberg, J. (1967). *The Role of Movement Patterns in Development*, Vol. 2. New York: Dance Notation Bureau Press.

—— (1973). Comments on movement therapy as a psychotherapeutic tool. *Journal of the American Psychoanalytic Association*, 21(2), 347–350.

—— (1975). *Children and Parents: Psychoanalytic studies in development*. New York: Jason Aronson

Kitwood, T. (1997). *Dementia Reconsidered . . . The Person Comes First*. Buckingham, UK: Open University Press.

Laban, R. (1992). The Mastery of Movement. UK: Northcote House (reprint).

Leventhal, M. (1992). Knowing and beyond. In: P. Greenland and P. Hilton (eds) *Dance in a Changing World*. Leeds: Jabadao.

Levitt, S. (1995). *Treatment of Cerebral Palsy and Motor Delay*. Oxford, UK: Blackwell Science Ltd.

Mahler, M. et al. (1975). *The Psychological Birth of the Human Infant*. New York: Basic Books.

Malan, D. (1979). *Individual Psychotherapy and the Science of Psychodynamics*. USA: Butterworths.

Moore, C., & Yamamoto, K. (1998). *Beyond Words – Movement Observation and Analysis*. Amsterdam: Gordon Breach.

Opie, I., & Opie, P. (1969). *Children's Games in the Street and Playground*. UK: Clarendon Press.

—— (1985). *The Law and Language of School Children*. Oxford: Oxford University Press.

Richards, M.H. (1985). *Education Through Music*. California: Richard's Institute.

Sandal, S., & Johnson, D. (1983). Structure and process of the nascent group: Dance therapy with chronic patients. *Arts in Psychotherapy*, 10, 131–140.

—— (1987). *Waiting at the Gate. Creativity and hope in the nursing home*. New York: Harworth Press.

Schilder, P. (1950). *The Image and Appearance of the Human Body*. New York: International Universities Press (reprint 1978).

Sinason, V. (1992). *Mental Handicap and the Human Condition*. London: Free Association Books Ltd.

Spotnitz, H. (1971). Touch countertransference in group psychotherapy. Presented at Annual Conference of American Group Psychotherapy Association.

Squire, L. (1987). *Memory and Brain*. New York: Oxford University Press.

Stanton-Jones, K. (1992). *Introduction to Dance Movement Therapy in Psychiatry*. London: Tavistock & Routledge.

Stern, D.N. (1985). *The Interpersonal World of the Infant*. USA: Basic Books & Harper Collins.

Stockley, S. (1992). Older lives, older dances. In: H. Payne (ed) *Dance Movement Therapy: Theory and practice*. London & New York: Routledge.

Violets, M. (2000). We'll survive. In: D. Aldridge (ed) *Music Therapy in Dementia Care*. London: Jessica Kingsley.

——— (2001). *Movement and Communication*. Research project in Camden: Group Movement Therapy for People with Dementia.

Wadell, M. (2000). Only Connect: Developmental issues from early to late life. *Psychoanalytic Psychotherapy*, 14(3), 252.

Winnicott, D. (1953). Transitional objects and transitional phenomena. *International Journal of Psychoanalysis*, 'IV(2), 89–97.

——— (1971). *Playing and Reality*. London: Routledge.

Yalom, I.D. (1995). *The Theory and Practice of Group Psychotherapy*. New York: Basic Books.

Chapter 15

Dementia

Jane Garner

> I have forgotten the word I intended to say, and my
> thought unembodied returns to the realm of shadows
> (O. Mandelstam)

Old age and dementia are not synonymous. Seventy-five percent of people over 80 are not affected by the disease, but brain disintegration, possible at any age, is one of the fears associated with getting older. Within this is fear of the loss of the self. The existential terror which this may occasion has not been alleviated by the attitude of professionals over the years, although current talk of a 'person-centred' approach may help. Analysts and psychotherapists, reluctant to take on older people following Freud's suggestion of a narrow range of analysability, have done less for those with dementia. At the same time old age psychiatrists have concentrated on the biological and social aspects of their work and patients, and often have not recognised the potential for a psychodynamic approach.

Homes set up to 'care' for patients with dementia usually know very little about the personal history and circumstances of the people residing there. Society tends to warehouse its older citizens, bearing scant regard for them as individuals. Bell (1996) reminds us that in the current ruling market hegemony human need is seen as despicable dependence. The dislocation of long-stay care from other aspects of a comprehensive psychiatric service into the fragmented private sector may be making matters worse.

THE VALUE OF THE PERSONAL HISTORY

However, as Freud was constantly revising his theories so too have the heirs to his theoretical models, and some have started work in areas previously neglected. Sinason (1992) has worked with people with a mental handicap and has made us think about the word 'stupid' which in the *Oxford English*

Dictionary is defined as 'numbed or stunned with grief, stupified'. Not all the symptoms we see in dementia are organically determined. In Sinason's moving account of psychotherapy with an academic who had to retire early because he had developed Alzheimer's disease, she explains to him that some words his brain was losing all by itself, and he could do nothing about that, but some words he was losing himself for reasons they might ascertain. If we do not take the needs of dementia sufferers seriously because they have brain damage we are guilty of 'metaphorical decapitation' according to Miesen (1998), who has long been a proponent of the need for more life history information on patients so they can continue to be treated as individuals throughout their care.

THE CONTRIBUTION OF PSYCHOANALYTIC THINKING TO AGEING AND DEMENTIA

Psychoanalytic theory is a theory of development. Freud's focus was on reconstructing very early aspects of patients' lives. Later analysts have seen development continuing throughout life. Erik Erikson's model using Eight Ages of Man (see Chapter 6) is particularly useful in understanding the elderly condition. At each stage there is a particular polarity, a contention between opposites. At the same time there is as an interaction between current development and early experience. The developmental task in late life is to negotiate between the contrapositions of ego-integrity and ego-despair. Integrity here is the capacity to value one's life experience and one's self, 'to be – through having been'. This involves holding on to the worthwhile aspects of one's life, memories of having been loved and valued. In the task of negotiating between opposites, this is balanced against despair at facing not being and disgust at physical and mental degeneration. The epidemiology of dementia is such that it is at just this time that actual disintegration of the self is most likely to occur. The self here is not used in any specific psychoanalytic sense but generally to denote personhood and identity. Dementia is a global impairment of functioning affecting intellect, memory, language, skills, personality, affect, behaviour and sense of self. The process of dementia fosters feelings of uncertainty, lack of security and fear of abandonment as if all one's known 'givens' are changing, this uncharted persecutory world will not feel safe.

Old age and particularly dementia is associated with increasing dependency. The way in which early experiences of physical and emotional dependency are remembered greatly determines the capacity to face this time of life (Martindale, 1998). Being dependent either on family or staff brings the capacity for trust – the first task for the baby, once more to the fore; 'Will they hate me? Will they be disgusted by me?'. The younger staff need to be reliable and dependable, accepting the dependency of the person with dementia in a manner which acknowledges the struggle the patient may be having to trust and rely on another for everyday and intimate tasks.

Early in the disease the patient defends himself from acknowledging the losses occasioned by it. He withdraws from activities and from meeting people, becoming more egocentric. He may project unacceptable feelings onto others and so blame them for his difficulties. Character traits may be emphasised – the previously aggressive man may become more so, the obsessional one more inflexible. If these defences fail the patient may also become depressed or develop catastrophic reactions; these were first described in relation to wartime head injuries. The emotional reaction seems out of proportion to the stimulus. For Kohut (1972) it is a 'narcissistic rage' defending against the shame concerning a defect in the self. O'Connor (1993) describes how the increased energy required in the attempt to maintain some sense of a core self means there is less available for attending to the needs of others. The patient may become self-centred, insensitive and inconsiderate. He needs someone to fill this hole in the sense of self and to take on the organising and containing function he has lost. He may follow his wife incessantly around the house, not able to bear separateness, not allowing her out of his sight. We are all familiar with the feeling of loss; with one loss all feels lost and the world a terrible place. Although cognitively impaired the patient may still be contending with extreme emotional states.

Strong emotion can 'unlock' a flow of words and recollection. We recognise the almost mute patient with dementia who when furious will become temporarily coherent and comprehensible. Reaching someone emotionally with therapeutic understanding may also integrate recollection and experience for a few moments.

ASPECTS OF ATTACHMENT

The concept of attachment grew out of work with children and their mothers but the theory is of relevance across the life cycle (see Chapter 4) and in different settings. Attachment theory postulates that we are driven by a need to be in a relationship with others, and acknowledges the continuing need for dependency. Magai and Cohen (1998) have demonstrated that the attachment pattern and style of individuals contribute to the emotional and behavioural symptomatology developed in dementia. Ambivalent patients had more depression and anxiety; avoidant patients experienced more activity disturbance than the ambivalently attached and more paranoid symptoms than the securely attached. We are familiar with the patient with dementia who believes their parents are alive. Miesen (1992, 1993) has termed this 'parent fixation'. As patients become more impaired cognitively, they seem to exhibit less overt attachment behaviour and more parent fixation. This has traditionally been viewed as a dysmnesic problem. Miesen sees it as an equivalent of attachment behaviour, a response to the fear and feeling of loss evoked by the dementia.

For Bowlby (1969) attachment serves a biological function of protection. The proximity is sought of someone seen as more able to cope. With dementia and the re-experience of fears of abandonment the protective function of attachment behaviour feels apparent, as does the need for regular and dependable staff as attachment figures in wards and homes.

THE NEUROBIOLOGY/PSYCHOLOGY INTERFACE

Freud's training and early professional work was in neurology. His early theories had a biological basis. When he later departed from this theme it was with the thought that psychoanalysis, biochemistry and neurology would rejoin in time (Schore, 1997). A century later this conjunction is still awaited and patients with dementia are rarely offered a psychodynamic understanding. Damasio (1994) writes that the distinction between diseases of the brain and those of the mind, i.e. neurological or psychological, is 'an unfortunate cultural inheritance that permeates society and medicine. It reflects a basic ignorance of the relation between brain and mind'. Diseases of the brain are tragedies for which the sufferer is not to blame, diseases of the mind social inconveniences for which the sufferer has some culpability. Dementia has achieved the distinction of straddling this divide but perhaps because most sufferers are elderly, only to be ignored until recently by both sides. The advent of the human genome project, antidementia drugs and some forward-thinking psychologists has increased research and clinical interest of late, but still the two halves, psychological and biological, rarely communicate.

An increase in neurobiological research, however welcome, could be in danger of reducing phenomenological empathy and understanding. Solms (1995) observes that as 'the boundaries of the brain are being extended, the mind is getting progressively smaller'. However, Gabbard (2000) reports that advances in neuroscience research have led to a more sophisticated understanding of how psychotherapy may affect brain functioning. He cites the work of Finnish researchers who found psychotherapy to have a significant effect on serotonin metabolism (Viinamäki et al., 1998) and of Spiegel et al. (1989) who found an increased lifespan of eighteen months in patients with metastatic breast cancer who had group therapy in comparison to those with the same diagnosis and only conventional treatment.

This raises the question of whether there is a biological substrate for psychotherapy. The orbital pre-frontal cortex has been suggested (Schore, 1997) as the interface for biology and psychoanalysis. Mental phenomena, while arising from the brain, are altered by environmental factors; conversely subjective experience affects the brain. Kitwood (1990a) writes of the dialectical interplay between neurological and psychosocial factors in and around the dementia sufferer. The 'malignant social psychology' surrounding the patient, which diminishes their self-esteem and personhood, makes them function at a lower level than that determined by the organic aspects of their dementia alone.

Memory in a simplistic sense, being able to recall the Babcock sentence or the name of the monarch, is not necessary for psychological work. Freud (1914) emphasised that what the patient does not remember will be repeated in the transference relationship and that during treatment this compulsion to repeat is replaced by the ability to recount. Freud was referring to patients with repressed memories but the same seems to be true of people with cognitive impairment. Patients still communicate through the relationship. Representations of object relations are laid down in infants too young to later recall specific detail. Fonagy and Target (1997) and Fonagy (1999) have suggested that the therapeutic action of psychoanalysis is unrelated to the 'recovery' of early memories; although early experience is formative it is encoded, stored and retrieved separately from reiterated autobiography.

Cognitive psychologists distinguish between declarative/explicit memory involved with conscious retrieval of information and procedural/implicit memory which is retrieved without the subject having the experience of remembering. Those who have spent time with people suffering from dementia know that explicit memory is impaired from early in the disease process and the patient will do badly on tests of cognitive functioning involving direct questions requiring specific answers. However, implicit memory is retained much longer and the patient may spontaneously relate the answer to the question much later in the interview when not pressed to remember.

Organic brain disease may predispose to regression to earlier modes of thinking, earlier both in terms of personal and human history (Garner, 2000). The capacity to think symbolically is diminished. Dementia exemplifies the complex inter-relations and borderline between the many bio-psycho-social aspects of man's experience. Genetics, location and extent of brain damage, drives and instincts, personal history, previous personality and attachment style, experience of and reaction to loss, previous and current environment and affective atmosphere, combine and coalesce to influence the presentation of dementia in an individual. Despite the clearest evidence of so far irreversible organicity in the aetiology of dementia, nevertheless a psychodynamic understanding may illuminate and improve the experience for both patients and staff.

THERAPY SESSIONS

Basic psychological needs for respect, security and self-determination persist throughout life and diagnoses. The earlier in the dementing process therapy begins, the less complicated some of the logistics so that the therapist remembers the words used and stories told even when the patient later forgets. When spontaneous recall is lost, recognition persists. If the therapist is able to narrate the patient's tales he may be less repetitive. Sessions as always should be in a regular, quiet place, perhaps including the possibility of the patient making simple choices, e.g. deciding where to sit, so he has some mastery over his environment, to enhance self-esteem and confirm retained competence. The therapist should speak clearly, frequently referring to the patient by name and while leaving little silence should confine each interaction to a few words or brief sentences. The therapist will need to be more flexible and active, it is usually better to have three fifteen-minute sessions each week rather than a single fifty-minute meeting. The use of favourite objects or photographs may be helpful as may writing something down for the patient to read again before the next session. Questioning the patient will not be helpful as he cannot be expected to operate in a cognitive mode he has lost – to push for that creates frustration and despair on both sides.

From the beginning the therapist will recognise and acknowledge the fear and terror which threaten to engulf the patient. The sessions provide an emotional but containing outlet. The patient's affective memory remains as cognition decreases, probably with an increased sensitivity to affective tone. The ability to make a relationship is retained, a therapeutic attachment and alliance develops quickly with an empathic therapist. Intimacy is important throughout life and touch may be used occasionally in a way that would be inappropriate in other therapy settings. Life review techniques may be used while these are still possible, helping the patient to mourn what is lost while also acknowledging achievements.

The elderly often feel in a state of disintegration – the ego can feel too frail to be containing. Ambivalent feelings may be unbearable, particularly the dread of being abandoned in a state of helplessness while at the same time resenting assistance and hating those who help. The therapist needs to support the ego, functioning as an auxiliary ego (Unterbach, 1994). Sterba (1934) wrote of patients' capacity, which is therapeutic, to split the ego into an observing and an experiencing part, the analyst siding with the former. With dementia the 'observing ego' fails and the therapist has to take on more of its role. Eventually the disease will protect the self, before then at times denial may be a very good defence and it is not always appropriate to tackle it.

In any conversation, communication takes place on a number of levels – meaning is not only implied or inferred verbally but is imparted and received multidimensionally. An emotional life continues without language. It is up to the therapist to be open to the subtext even when linguistic logic is impaired or absent (Duffy, 1999) and non-verbal cues from the patient and internal feelings of the therapist are the only key to the patient's state. The patient will repeat in the relationship with the therapist ways of being with others which have been with them throughout life and to which they return in this time of crisis. Old insecurities resurface. The person who has negotiated the 'paranoid-schizoid position' (see Chapter 2) and for the most part can acknowledge others and their needs with 'depressive concern' may in some cases return to a persecutory state of mind with the dementing process. For Waddell (2000) the therapist needs to 'tolerate the disturbing projections and still go on thinking about the meaning of the experience'. This communication is likely not to be verbal but by a process of projective identification, the patient may give the therapist or care staff some notion of their experience which could then be recommunicated in a more manageable form.

Hausman (1992) points out some of the obstacles in this type of work, one of which may be the family, who may be resistant to the patient engaging in therapy and because they have the means may sabotage it by not reminding the patient or bringing them to the appointment. Splitting can be painful, particularly as at some point the therapist is likely to be idealised and the family or other staff denigrated.

Due to the particular countertransferential feelings evoked by this type of work, the therapist requires good support and supervision. The patient will almost inevitably be older, maybe much older, and may represent a close elderly relative or the therapist's imagined self in old age while at the same time expressing infantile needs and dependency on the therapist. Identifications may be painful, not only in terms of personal history but also personality and affective style. Working with someone with an irreversible illness may stimulate hostility, helplessness, frustration and therapeutic nihilism. The therapist and other staff need to suspend their need for gratification in the treatment setting, accept the wound to their 'medical narcissism' (Meerloo, 1955) and cope with the fact that whatever we do, however skilled we are, the patient will deteriorate cognitively and physically. We want our patients to get better, to be cured. Unconscious determinants of our chosen healthcare profession may not be satisfied by patients whose condition is chronic, even deteriorating. Main (1957) reminds us that in spite of professional ideals, ordinary human feelings are inevitable and we need to recognise and examine them. The patient who does not get better may provoke feelings of aggression and sadism accompanied by anxiety, guilt, depression and reparative wishes. All this despite our intellectual understanding that we are unable to 'cure' dementia is not dissimilar to the spouse who knows that his wife has an irreversible progressive brain condition but also 'knows' that she puts things in the wrong place deliberately. The undeveloped space between our cognition and our emotional understanding gives us more in common with our patients than we usually like to imagine. Outcomes for therapy need to be modified. Psychodynamic therapy may alleviate suffering, it may diminish the terror and feeling of uncontainment for the person with dementia by establishing an affective understanding and continuity so that the patient may end in some peace.

CARE AND THE TEAM

The countertransferential feelings described for the therapist may affect each member of the team; difficult feelings brought about by the age difference, the progressive nature of dementia and the potential for splitting, disturbing non-verbal projections and identification with the patient. In addition the clinical team can feel deskilled by dealing with a deteriorating condition. This is a deskilling brought about by a combination of helplessness and mindlessness. Sutton (2001) writes of the double jeopardy awaiting the sufferer from dementia. He is losing his mind and he is treated with mindlessness. The cause of that mindlessness and unthinking is complex and multilayered. The microcosm of the staff team reflects the wider society which is undoubtedly ageist. Clinicians bring into their work the conscious and unconscious negative images of old age which we all carry. If you are elderly you are stigmatised, if you are elderly and mentally ill you are doubly marked. This stigma is compounded by also being played out on the staff. Working with people with dementia has traditionally been seen as not particularly skilled, low-status work. Some are employed on very poor terms and conditions. These attitudes to staff can have a domino effect in the way they perceive their work and their patients.

Old age psychiatrists and their teams are often overworked, 'jacks-of-all-trades', running a comprehensive service for a larger than reasonable catchment area, negotiating the benefits and housing system, being experts in the legal and medical aspects of mental capacity, understanding ethical dilemmas at the end of life, knowing something about neuroimaging, the most effective treatment for constipation and the best floor covering for a long-stay ward. For the most part we rather like this manic overactivity. It is a good reason, perhaps excuse, for not thinking. It helps us maintain 'clinical detachment'. We create a physical and emotional distance from our patient (Duffy, 1988). We are pleasant but distant and say that it is necessary to keep perspective. It is a very small step from clinical detachment to mindless detachment. Terry (1998) links the infantilisation of older people and the difficulty in thinking with and about them. It emphasises the split between patients and staff; them and us. He sees both as connected to a dread of our own infantile feelings and in its most extreme a dread of death.

The capacity of the NHS to take on individuals with dementia for psychotherapy is extremely limited. When it does occur the experience is valuable not only for the patient but also for the therapist who comes to understandings which can be used to inform the service as a whole (Ardern et al., 1998). If the team understands that odd verbal communications and curious behaviour are not only attributable to brain damage and the disease process but may also have personal meaning, the staff can be more empathic in their approach to the patient who at some level will 'know' they have been understood. Kitwood (1990b) writes that good dementia care aims to support the patients' sense of themselves as people of worth and value and may therefore be inherently psychotherapeutic. Understanding the patient's behaviour may also involve focusing on what staff are doing or feeling, which may stimulate an increased dependence or aggression or other reaction in the patient.

The pattern of care for patients with dementia is necessarily different. For most conditions maximum input is at the beginning, perhaps an admission followed by a spell in the day hospital, then a CPN visiting and an occasional outpatient appointment leading to eventual discharge. A dementia service on the other hand may give minimal input at the beginning, but as the disease progresses domiciliary care, day care, respite and eventually admission until death. This is a major assault on our therapeutic narcissism. We will not witness the gradual recovery of a patient who will be grateful for our attentions. Despite recent licensing of three antidementia drugs, we are made to feel helpless by the disease, which may account for the overprescription of major tranquillisers to this patient population (McGrath & Jackson, 1996) – in some cases the prescription acts to temporarily tranquillise the doctor and nurse in the face of them feeling overwhelmed by the patient's difficulties.

The potential for abuse in this relationship of unequal power is enormous. Abuse ranges from gross physical illtreatment to adopting that faintly patronising attitude which is so easy to assume. The causes of abuse are complex and varied (Royal College of Psychiatrists, 2001). Research suggests that older people with mental or physical impairment are at greatest risk. Patients in long-stay settings are not always easy to care for – they may be aggressive or resistive, repetition of a phrase or action may be irritating or the patients may evoke a sense of physical distaste. In these circumstances thinking about what we are doing should be our highest priority, but it rarely is. A remedy for this unthinking is essential. It is about recruitment policies, management practices, training, clinical supervision – but above all it is about having time and space and permission to reflect and to say. Having a forum to discuss and understand work-related problems and feelings may prevent them being acted out. Staff need freedom to recognise negative as well as positive feelings and the freedom to say these things in order to remain able to use their personal and professional skills for their patients.

SEXUALITY

Desire for intimacy, tenderness and also sexuality continues throughout life (see Chapter 17). When memory is deteriorating, physical expressions of affection may open recognition and links with the past. Dementia may raise practical issues surrounding sexuality. Deteriorating habits and self-care may disgust a previously affectionate spouse. For some, however, this may provide hitherto unexplored opportunities for intimacy, for example taking a bath together. Sexual intimacy can be a source of comfort and coping for both.

Issues of competency may need to be considered, certainly for a new relationship but also in some marriages. Some spouse carers relinquish genital aspects of sexuality, feeling that the partner acquiesces passively or as an obedient child rather than agreeing to a sexual life with adult understanding (Garner, 1997). Sometimes patients with dementia may behave hypersexually or inappropriately. This is rare. When it happens it is often as a result of frontal lobe pathology although the nature of the behaviour may reflect previous impulses or fantasies. Although it is usually possible to manage inappropriate behaviour via distraction techniques it can be distressing for the partner or create a furore in a care home. Sometimes the behaviour or obscene language may be a reaction to feeling diminished or to shock others into a response.

Wright (1998) investigated longitudinal changes in affection and sexual intimacy in couples in which one partner had Alzheimer's disease, and compared them to a group of couples where neither partner had cognitive impairment. In the couples affected by Alzheimer's disease affection declined and fewer of the couples were sexually active. Frequency of activity was not related to the Mini Mental State Examination score of the patient but to the physical health and mood of the spouse. Patients within a sexually active couple were less likely to be admitted to a home. Davies et al. (1998) found more sexual dysfunction in males with Alzheimer's disease than in similarly aged men without the dementia.

Being pushed out of bed for being 'a dirty old man' or 'horrid old woman' seems even more painful to a loving spouse than misrecognition in other situations. The potential for misunderstandings and misrecognition can be greater in institutional care. A fellow patient may be seen as a spouse. Staff friendliness may be erroneously interpreted. Often unskilled relatively untrained staff are employed to look after patients who need the most intimate of care which needs to be cautiously approached, carefully boundaried, clearly and repeatedly explained or the patient may feel an intimate assault is being perpetrated against them.

Sexual abuse of vulnerable people does occur. Due to the nature and illegality of the acts it is impossible to quantify. The patient who is unable to subsequently relate their experiences may be subjected to sexual exploitation in part stimulated by their vulnerability and apparent childlike state. The overtly unequal power relationship between a fit younger person and an elderly patient suffering from dementia can induce unhelpful feelings of pity or of sadism which may be acted out in verbal communication, in instances of maltreatment in day-to-day interactions or sexually. Occasionally the patient may seem to invite or welcome sexual advances and collude in the activity. Whatever the attitude of the victim, staff behaving sexually towards patients is abuse. At the same time treating people with dementia as if they were sexless, not even gendered, may be dehumanising. One of the skills for staff lies in acknowledging the manhood or womanhood of the patient in ordinary human ways while realising that subtle, sophisticated comprehension is lost, so that flirtation may be overwhelmingly tantalising or conversely leave the patient feeling humiliated and denigrated.

The current cohort of people with dementia will have lived with traditional gender roles and expectations. It may be helpful, whatever the views of younger staff who will have had a different life experience, to continue activities in day care or institutions which the patients recognise as gender appropriate. One's gender even if one is no longer sexually active may be an enduring source of gratification and self-knowledge.

THE FAMILY

There is an increasing body of research and literature about the effects of having a family member with a dementing illness. Much of this work has used a stress/burden perspective where the stress of caring is measured as physical, psychological and social burden and interventions are aimed at burden reduction. This model may serve well but it is not always successful and some carers refuse or sabotage 'help'. Gilleard et al. (1984) using the General Health Questionnaire (GHQ) identified distress in family carers sufficient in the majority of cases to warrant a psychiatric diagnosis, but there was no association between GHQ score and reported levels of formal and informal support. However, the poorer the rated health of the carer, the more negative the view they had of the premorbid relationship. Anthony-Bergstone et al. (1988) found an increase in hostility and anxiety in female carers but an increase in depression only in wives. There is great variability between individuals and families, what they find stressful and how they deal with stress. To the concrete burden of caring is added the quality and nature of the premorbid relationships. Carer spouses who experienced lower levels of marital intimacy currently and before the onset of the dementia had higher levels of self-perceived strain and depression (Morris et al., 1988).

The carer has the dual burden of the conscious problems of coping with a close relative with dementia plus the unconscious conflicts evoked by being in this role (O'Connor, 1993; Garner, 1997). The woman who has to some degree solved her oedipal problems by marrying a man onto whom she transferred her feelings towards her father will have difficulty when he topples from paternal grandeur to needing care like a child. The passive-seeming daughter who has never questioned her dominant imperious mother for fear of emotional dismissal will not be able to tolerate the necessary role reversal and take the lead in initiating referral for care when mother develops dementia.

Denial, anxiety, sadness, depression, hypervigilance, fatigue, anger, resentment and guilt have all been reported as psychological responses to dementia in a close other, in someone in whom there is intense emotional investment.

Most suffer a deep sense of personal and psychological loss (Zarit et al., 1985) sufficient in some to prompt thoughts of suicide. This sense of loss experienced by an intimate other can happen early in the disease when only subtle changes are apparent; 'He's not the man I married, doctor.' In other terminal illnesses there may well be time and space for resolution of personal relationships but when a partner has dementia this is a solitary time. The patient will have a declining interest in the world, an increased egocentricity, a change in level of drive, activity and initiative, and will have a reduction in emotional warmth and failure of a sense of humour. There will be mis-identification, inability to recognise a familiar face and loss of shared memories. To be unrecognised and unremembered by one with whom one has had a lengthy and intimate relationship can cause great pain. One is losing a partner but also that part of the self which is invested in the other. The husband of a patient touched on this when he spoke of committing a 'double suicide'. He would be killing that part of him introduced into her, a part to which only his wife had access, only she knew, and also killing his identification with the introjection of his wife into himself. The shadow of the object had fallen on the ego (Freud, 1917). With loss of a confidant(e) and of intimacy, the mutu-ality of the relationship is lost. A number of psychiatric studies have impli-cated the lack of a confiding relationship in the aetiology of depression (e.g. Livingstone et al., 1996).

The disease is one which occasions progressive losses over a long period of time, much longer than the two years from diagnosis initially described by Roth (1955). Freud (1926) differentiates mourning and anxiety – mourning as a response to loss and anxiety for anticipated loss. The partner of the patient with dementia is struggling with both, and with internal conflicts stimulated by their situation which also include at times the wish that the patient were dead.

With progression of the disease the patient will inevitably put increasing physical, psychological and social demands on their partner whose own health may be deteriorating, and it becomes less and less likely that their own emotional needs will be met by the patient.

The illness trajectory of the patient is not solely determined by the neuro-physiology of dementia. High levels of interaction between spouse and patient predict not only who will be at home but who will still be alive after two years. Lower caregiver commitment predicted death during two years follow-up. These findings have been linked to early work on attachment and maternal deprivation (Wright, 1994; Wright et al., 1995). Magai and Cohen (1998) found that attachment style in the patient predicted caregiver burden; carers of securely attached individuals experienced less total burden than did caregivers of both ambivalently attached and avoidant patients.

THE FAMILY AND THE WARD

When the time comes that the person with dementia needs to move to residential or nursing care, some partners and families are able to cope with that despite sadness and grief and may continue to help with caring in ways that they can. For others the failure which the admission may represent with concomitant feelings of guilt may prompt the family to be hypercritical of and hostile to staff. 'No one can care for my husband as I did' is likely to be true but if oft thought and spoken may obstruct staff doing anything useful either for the patient or for the family.

Different members of the same family will react differently to the situation and to staff as a group and as individuals. There is potential for unhelpful, even destructive splits and alliances to be made. The situation may be an opportunity for pre-existing family difficulties to be acted out, e.g. who will be the best, most caring of the children may be played out as the one who makes the most complaints. Staff need to be alert to these possibilities. A cooperative relationship needs to be made with the family including an understanding of their spoken and unspoken conflicts and fears. At the same time staff need to speak with each other, sharing experiences and anxieties so that a coherent and containing plan of management can be formulated and implemented for the patient, his or her family and the staff team.

There are no easy ways of helping the spouse or family of the dementia sufferer whose actual burden of caring and coping will not be reflected in their own perceived stress. It is unlikely that in the NHS many family members will be offered psychotherapy, therefore the keyworker and other staff need to be multiskilled, giving direct psychoeducational advice about the condition and available services and at the same time offering a psychodynamic understanding, helping the grieving relative discern something of the meaning of their current situation, the meaning of the illness, its symptoms and myriad losses. Over time the grief and anger may be changed to acceptance and sadness.

CONCLUSION

Despite stereotyping and prejudice, patients with dementia are not so different from other groups that a psychodynamic perspective to their care is inappropriate. Such an approach introduces an understanding of the uniqueness of each patient and their experience. While maintaining objectivity and perspective clinical staff need to be able to make an empathic and phenomenological connection with the internal experiential world of the patient. At the same time staff need an understanding of the intense loss for the spouse and shifting family dynamics in coping with the simultaneous presence and absence of the patient. Staff need an understanding of their own and colleagues' feelings and the potential for abuse of patients in the absence of thoughtfulness.

Although caring for someone with dementia and meeting their family is traditionally not seen as skilled work, to do it well requires skill, patience, imagination and understanding. Continuing care for dementia can be at the forefront of biological and psychological research and development.

REFERENCES

Anthony-Bergstone, C.R., Zarit, S.H., & Gatz, M. (1988). Symptoms of psychological distress among caregivers of dementia patients. *Psychology and Ageing*, 3, 245–248.

Ardern, M., Garner, J., & Porter, R. (1998). Curious bedfellows: Psychoanalytic understanding and old age psychiatry. *Psychoanalytic Psychotherapy*, 12(1), 47–56.

Bell, D. (1996). Primitive mind of state. *Psychoanalytic Psychotherapy*, 10(1), 45–57.

Bowlby, J. (1969). *Attachment and Loss Volume 1: Attachment*. London: Hogarth Press.

Damasio, A.R. (1994). *Descartes' Error*. New York: G.P. Putnam's Sons.

Davies, H., Zeiss, A., Shea, E., & Tinklenberg, J. (1998). Sexuality and intimacy in Alzheimer's patients and their partners. *Sexuality and Disability*, 16(3), 193–203.

Duffy, M. (1988). Avoiding clinical detachment in working with elderly in nursing homes. *Clinical Gerontologist*, 7(3/4), 58–60.

—— (1999). Reaching the person behind the dementia: Treating comorbid affective disorders through subvocal and non-verbal strategies. In: M. Duffy (ed) *Handbook of Counselling and Psychotherapy with Older Adults*. Chichester, UK: John Wiley & Sons.

Fonagy, P. (1999). Memory and therapeutic action. *International Journal of Psychoanalysis*, 80, 215–223.

——, & Target, M. (1997). Perspectives on the recovered memories debate. In: J. Sandler & P. Fonagy (eds) *Recovered Memories of Abuse: True and false* (pp. 183–216). London: Karnac Books.

Freud, S. (1914). Remembering, repeating and working-through. (Further recommendations on the technique of psycho-analysis II.) In: J. Strachey (ed) *Standard Edition 12* (pp. 145–156). London: Hogarth Press.

—— (1917). Mourning and melancholia. *Standard Edition*. London: Hogarth Press.

—— (1926). Inhibitions: Symptoms and anxiety. *Standard Edition XXVIII* (pp. 83–86). London: Hogarth Press.

Gabbard, G.O. (2000). A neurobiologically informed perspective on psychotherapy. *British Journal of Psychiatry*, 177, 117–122.

Garner, J. (1997). Dementia: An intimate death. *British Journal of Medical Psychology*, 70, 177–184.

—— (2000). Reduplication phenomena: Body, mind and archetype. *British Journal of Medical Psychology*, 73, 339–353.

Gilleard, C.J., Belford, H., Gilleard, E., Whittick, J.E., & Gledhill, K. (1984). Emotional distress amongst the supporters of the elderly mentally infirm. *British Journal of Psychiatry*, 145, 172–177.

Hausman, C. (1992). Dynamic psychotherapy with elderly demented patients: Caregiving in dementia. In: M.M. Jones and B.M.L. Miesen (eds). London: Routledge.

Kitwood, T. (1990a). The dialectics of dementia: with particular reference to Alzheimer's disease. *Ageing and Society*, 10, 177–196.

—— (1990b). Psychotherapy and dementia. *Newsletter of the Psychotherapy Section of the British Psychological Society*, 8, 40–56.

Kohut, H. (1972). *Self psychology and humanities*. London: Penguin (1985).

Livingstone, G., Manuela, M., & Katona, C. (1996). Depression and other psychiatric morbidity in carers of elderly people living at home. *British Medical Journal*, 312, 153–156.

McGrath, A.M., & Jackson, G.A. (1996). Survey of neuroleptic prescribing in residents of nursing homes in Glasgow. *British Medical Journal*, 312, 611–612.

Magai, C., & Cohen, C.I. (1998). Attachment style and emotion regulation in dementia patients and their relation to caregiver burden. *Journal of Gerontology*, 533(3), 147–154.

Main, T. (1957). The ailment. *Medical Psychology*, 30, 129–145.

Martindale, B. (1998). On ageing, dying, death and eternal life. *Psychoanalytic Psychotherapy*, 12(3), 259–270.

Meerloo, J.A.M. (1955). Psychotherapy with elderly people. *Geriatrics*, 10, 583–587.

Miesen, B.M.L. (1992). Attachment theory and dementia: Caregiving in dementia. In: M.M. Jones and B.M.L. Miesen (eds). London: Routledge.

—— (1993). Alzheimer's disease, the phenomenon of parent fixation and Bowlby's attachment theory. *International Journal of Geriatric Psychiatry*, 8, 147–153.

—— (1998). *Dementia in Close-up*. London: Routledge.

Morris, L., Morris, R., & Britton, P. (1988). The relationship between marital intimacy, perceived strain and depression in sparse caregivers of dementia sufferers. *British Journal of Medical Psychology*, 61, 231–236.

O'Connor, D. (1993). The impact of dementia: A self psychological perspective. *Journal of Gerontological Social Work*, 20(3/4), 113–128.

Roth, M. (1955). The natural history of mental disorder in old age. *Journal of Mental Science*, 101, 281–301.

Royal College of Psychiatrists (2001). Institutional abuse of older people. *Council Report 84*. J. Garner and S. Evans. London: Royal College of Psychiatrists.

Schore, A.N. (1997). A century after Freud's project: Is a rapprochement between psychoanalysis and neurobiology at hand? *Journal of American Psychoanalytic Association*, 45, 807–840.

Sinason, V. (1992). *Mental Handicap and the Human Condition. New Approaches from the Tavistock*. London: Free Association Books.

Solms, M. (1995). Is the brain more real than the mind? *Psychoanalytic Psychotherapy* 9(2), 107–120.

Spiegel, D., Bloom, J., Kraemer, H.D. et al. (1989). Effect of psychosocial treatment on survival of patients with metastatic breast cancer. *Lancet*, ii, 888–891.

Sterba, R. (1934). The fate of the ego in analytic therapy. *International Journal of Psychoanalysis*, 15, 117–126.

Sutton, L. (2001). When late life brings a diagnosis of Alzheimer's disease and early life brought trauma. A cognitive-analytic understanding of loss of mind. Unpublished paper.

Terry, P. (1998). Who will care for older people? A case study of working with destructiveness and despair in long stay care. *Journal of Social Work Practice*, 12(2), 209–216.

Unterbach, D. (1994). An ego function analysis for working with dementia clients. *Journal of Gerontological Social Work*, 22(3/4), 83–94.

Viinamäki, H., Knikka, J., Tilhonen, J. et al. (1998). Change in monoamine transporter density related to clinical recovery: a case-control study. *Nordic Journal of Psychiatry*, 52, 39–44.

Waddell, M. (2000). Only connect: developmental issues from early to late life. *Psychoanalytic Psychotherapy*, 14(3), 239–252.

Wright, L.K. (1994). Alzheimer's disease afflicted spouses who remain at home: Can human dialectics explain the findings? *Social Science Medicine*, 38(8), 1037–1046.

—— (1998). Affection and sexuality in the presence of Alzheimer's disease. A longitudinal study. *Sexualtiy and Disability*, 16(3), 167–179.

——, Hickey, J.V., Buckwalter, K.C., & Clipp, E.C. (1995). Human development in the context of aging and chronic illness: the role of attachment in Alzheimer's disease and stroke. *International Journal of Aging and Human Development*, 41(2), 133–150.

Zarit, S.H., Orr, N.K., & Zarit, J.M. (1985). *The Hidden Victims of Alzheimer's Disease*. New York: New York University Press.

Chapter 16

Elderly couples and their families

Sandra Evans

> *Martha:* Truth and illusion George, you don't know the difference.
> *George:* Yes, but we must carry on as though we did.
> > (*Who's Afraid of Virginia Woolf?* Albee)

There are occasions when it is helpful to consider patients in the context of their interpersonal relationships, current as well as past. This can be in the presence of partners or families, and doing so may provide valuable clues to the factors which provoke or prolong symptoms of mental illness or distress (Bennun, 1994; Kivela et al., 1999; Rubenowitz et al., 2001). The most obvious time for this kind of evaluation is when the couple themselves view that they have a problem and wish to explore it, or attempt to resolve it with professional assistance. Marital therapy *per se*, is not commonly sought by older couples. We do not know the reason for this, but might surmise that generational differences in the value of life-long commitment, as well as differing expectations of marriage and financial arrangements between partners, give rise to alternative strategies in the face of domestic discord. In addition, age itself may be a factor in the view that people may take of disharmony within marriage; better a life with the devil you know.

There are a number of different theoretical models from which to view the interpersonal relating of patients and these should apply to older couples in similar ways to their basis in younger adult pairs. The differences occur in the clinical applications of these therapeutic models, and in the settings of the older relationships. It is a feature of the partnerships of elderly people that one is forced to think of death as separation; of the potential of illness in one or both individuals, and the clamour of opinion of one's grown-up children who may believe that they know best when it comes to their parent's needs. In older people, the family looms large once more, as it does in the lives of children and adolescents. Life-changing decisions such as divorce or the making of new relationships may meet with unexpected resistance from others with vested interests. Laurence Ratna and his co-author Davis (1984) demonstrated that 60% of patients referred to an old age psychiatry service were experiencing life changes or conflicts of a sort that often involved their family or partner.

Experience has shown that spouses of depressed or physically ill individuals become depressed and require support (Carnwath & Johnson, 1987). They may complain of feeling guilty and inadequate in the face of their partner's difficulties. An additional dynamic can sometimes be seen where the healthy partner relates more and more to their spouse as a patient; with the potential of a detrimental effect on their relationship. The healthier the relationship had been at the onset of illness, the better. However the effect of chronic illness on family and marital relations is well documented (Kivela, et al., 1999).

Taking a psychoanalytic approach, one can theorise that the healthy part of the patient is invested or 'projected' into the healthy partner. It seems equally reasonable to suppose that reinvesting the patient's healthy functioning selves into their total personality rather than adopting and living the role of a sufferer, might yet further improve their depressive symptoms. Alternatively a systemic approach (Minuchin, 1974) would proffer an explanation based on the shift in the usual equilibrium of the relationship, in which dependence becomes too weighted in one direction only, having equal and opposite effects on the other partner. Altering the dynamic or re-adjusting this imbalance might also have some ameliorating effect on a strained relationship, thereby improving the quality of life for the healthy spouse.

Significantly, we are aware of first psychiatric presentations coinciding with the loss of a spouse, demonstrating the importance of partnership bereavement in the onset of depression (Murray Parkes, 1972; Brown & Harris, 1978). We know that the more ambivalent the relationship, often the more difficult the bereavement can be to negotiate. (Bereavement is dealt with more fully in Chapter 19.)

Marital partners may also act as a buffer between an individual and the rest of the world. Those people with unresolved dependency or narcissistic issues will be coping with more than simple bereavement when their partner dies. There may be a sense of loss of a major part of the self or loss of 'selfobjects' (Kohut, 1971). People with pre-existing personality disorders or problematic personality configurations may experience a lapse into previous difficult behaviours without the ameliorating effects of an understanding partner; the so-called 'unmasking theory' (Hepple, 1998). The demands made on the surviving family may be overwhelming and unsustainable, hence the referral to psychiatric services.

Ambivalence, in the psychoanalytic sense, is about the co-existence of feelings of love and hate for the same person. To an extent it corresponds with the Kleinian view of the depressive position, which is the mature position of whole-object relating: the realisation that one hates and attacks the object of one's love and desire. 'Hate' may be the expression of healthy rivalry or a 'life-instinct' of an individual. Absence or denial of hate may cause a fusion with the partner, with subsequent loss of self. Too much hate, or love confused with dependency can infect a relationship with negativity and potentially have a toxic effect on both partners.

Case Illustration
Malcom and Brian have been together for many years. They cannot easily identify a time when things began to go wrong between them. Malcom is still unsure why Brian is so vitriolic, and is referred to a counselling psychologist because of tearfulness and general unhappiness. There exists a danger that he may become clinically depressed in the continuing hateful environment. Brian sees no reason to seek couple therapy as he has identified Malcom to be the sole culprit, having demonstrated disloyalty, by helping a friend's widow for a considerable time. Malcom can neither confront Brian nor leave.

WHEN OLDER COUPLES ARE IN TROUBLE

Therapeutic change for couples is most effective and efficient at times of crisis (Fisher, 1999). However, the modern day NHS caseload is still unlikely to reveal elderly partners who mutually agree on a marital problem, and see it as a source of stress for one or other as service user or partner. In the 1996 statistical returns of activity of Relate, formerly The Marriage Guidance Council, the service received less than 2% of referrals from couples where either partner was over 65. An NHS Couple and Sexual Health Clinic recently demonstrated similar findings. It received only one enquiry from an older couple during operations in the year 2000 (Medawar, 2000). This is almost certainly an aspect of cohort effect, in which couples now in their seventies and eighties would have married at a time when expectations of marriage would have been different from those of the present day; there may also be a lower referral rate from primary and secondary care providers, due to general ageism on all fronts (Murphy, 2000; Evans, in press).

In the arena of NHS provision of psychiatry and psychology to older adults, the most common difficulties for patients are depression, dementia and anxiety. Depression is a particularly common presenting complaint and despite a wider appreciation of the treatable nature of late life depression, there remains a significant proportion of people with chronic illness and intractable symptoms. Elucidating the meaning of the depression for one particular individual may be more helpful than identifying every biological symptom. For some, depression may be the expression of the multiple losses of ageing; for others it may be heralding the as yet unregistered cognitive decline; while for yet other individuals depression may be a place of retreat to escape the unacknowledged hatred or ambivalence for their spouse or partner, or the weapon with which to mount an attack (Freud, 1917).

The depressed individual may be at odds with his surroundings and may find little pleasure or meaning in life. It can be appreciated that partners will also be affected by these changes. A number of studies looking at stress in carers identify a significant proportion who succumb to mood disorder themselves. These partners may become service users themselves and be at risk of the same morbidity and mortality as others with late life depression (Murphy et al., 1988). The importance of this in terms of suffering and service use is undisputed and therefore new treatment approaches need to be developed and evaluated.

DOMESTIC VIOLENCE

Little is known about domestic violence between elderly couples and even less is talked or written about (Mezey et al., 2003). What is known is that abusive young men age into abusive older men and that they are unlikely to alter their behaviour until they become physically incapable (Bengston, 1995). The reasons why women stay with violent men are many, but often involve issues around children and finance (Mezey, 2001), both of which may resolve over time thereby providing the opportunity for freedom. It is the author's experience that older couples can be physically violent towards each other, and certainly may continue to be mutually abusive, contrary to popular stereotypes. Violence is often exacerbated by alcohol and drug consumption (Pillemer & Suitor, 1990). This is something that affects both sexes and may include the regular ingestion of benzodiazepines in night sedation.

Violence and abuse can also arise *de novo*. This is particularly the case if one or both partners develop a dementia. In these cases the dynamics of a relationship can be altered considerably, and even reversed so that a previously passive and submissive partner will return years of threats or aggression, when the abusive partner becomes progressively frail and loses their faculties. A cognitively impaired partner may become disenfranchised by being placed in a residential home, when others in a more stable marriage may continue to reside with their spouse. This is not to say that only partners who are not loved are placed in care. Devoted couples are often separated in this way by the shear force of the illness and the physical frailty of the unaffected partner. However it is also true that the quality of the relationship is one factor in the amount of behavioural changes that can be tolerated, which does tend to influence the timing of institutionalisation (Spruytte et al., 2001).

TREATMENT APPROACHES WITH COUPLES

The treatment approaches most commonly employed are based on psycho-analytic theory, and some derivations thereof. Psychodynamic counselling or therapy with a psychodynamically informed basis, can be helpful to the motivated couple who wish to examine their relationship and who are capable of a degree of self-reflection and sufficient ego strength to risk the loss of illusions that may be comfortable but phantasy based (Clulow, 2001).

Christopher Clulow uses Edward Albee's dramatic play, '*Who's Afraid of Viginia Woolf?*' to illustrate the way in which a couple weave a shared phantasy in order to cope with childhood trauma and continued adult disappointment. George and Martha cannot bear too much reality; they are also unable to comfort each other over their disappointment. Their insecurity in attachment terms is respectively avoidant and ambivalent.

Attachment theory

The theoretical basis of attachment theory, which is dealt with in much greater detail in Chapter 5, is a most useful framework with which to view couple relationships. As a psychodynamic model it is based on object relations, meaning the interpersonal relating of infants with their parental objects. The style of relating is thought to derive directly from the kind of containment, responses and rearing to which each infant has been subject. The predominant attachment styles are secure, insecure/anxious (fearful), insecure/avoidant (dismissing) and insecure/ambivalent (preoccupied) (Bartholomew & Horowitz, 1991). A fifth more sinister attachment pattern is seen in children who have been abused by their caregivers. They display a disorganised pattern of attachment where the normal seeking of reassurance in the face of threat, is replaced by bizarre behaviours explicable only by the knowledge that the caregiver is also the source of potential threat (Main & Hesse, 1990). Victims of domestic violence may continue to demonstrate this disorganised pattern of attachment to their abusive partners, remaining locked in a dangerous dance with the person who provides them with some measure of security or at least consistence of insecurity and abusiveness.

Individuals will tend to form romantic/partner attachments with others who are likely to demonstrate the kind of relating of their early objects. For example, the anxiously attached individual is likely to object-seek another who will recreate the tension of the insecure attachment, thus reconfirming his or her model of the universe; that it is an altogether frightening and lonely place. Moreover a potential partner who is offering consistent security and stability may not be a source of sufficient interest; they may even elicit derision and scorn. The anxiously attached person is likely to project their own insecurity into this other person. An attraction between two such individuals may have the more anxiously attached of the two identifying with the aggressor (Freud, 1939) and becoming elusive and emotionally unavailable.

Birtchnell (1993) devised an interpersonal theory that is derived to some extent from an attachment perspective. It regards the power dynamics of

Upperness and Lowerness, and the dimensions of Closeness and Distance to be the atomic particles of Attachment. Birtchnell's theory is useful as a research tool in couple therapy (Evans et al., 1997) and can be used to demonstrate change in interpersonal relating. Birtchnell (1991) himself has done significant work on the effect of depression on marriage and vice versa.

Clinical Illustration

George came from a small family where his younger brother died a cot death when he was two years old. His mother developed a clinical depression and could not cope with his needs. His father was at work and it was not considered reasonable for him to look after his son. George was sent away to distant relatives and experienced a sense of abandonment and emotional distance.

On his return home he was quiet, clingy and well-behaved. He could not risk the possibility of being sent away again. His own explanation was that something of his behaviour had caused his brother's death and his family's rejection of him. He had internalised a sense of someone who is likely to be rejected.

His marriage to Clara had been long, but strewn with petty jealousies, the worst of which occurred at the birth of their second child, a boy. His attachment style tended to be an ambivalent one.

Clara also had a tendency to depression. She had a family history of bipolar disorder and her father had committed suicide while she was still a young girl. Her internalisation of this event as abandonment by her most loved father gave her a sense of being unlovable. Whenever George withdrew from her out of his jealousy of his son, Clara experienced this as an abandonment. Her attachment style was more of the anxious type.

In later life, Clara's increasingly frequent bouts of mania and depression were experienced by George as his fault. (Similar to the experience of feeling that he had harmed his sibling.) At those times he would withdraw emotionally from Clara. She felt unsupported and that he blamed her for getting ill. George began to get increasingly depressed also. There seemed to be a rivalry between them in their illnesses and in the emotional support they would receive from the hospital staff, on whom they both began to develop emotional dependence.

Psychoanalytic theory

Within a psychoanalytic framework the understanding of the above scenario would be in terms of introjected parental objects. The internal objects that George and Clara both carried were of abandonment and inconsistency. Their attraction to one another may have been due to the recognition of similar needs. Their wish for order and containment however, was often outweighed by their inability to sustain a satisfactory parental object for each other. Thus they recreated a sense of being abandoned in the other partner whenever their own narcissistic needs were threatened.

Narcissism

The narcissistic personality structure is one that develops in the absence of or withdrawal of the emotionally available parent. Generally and in Freudian terms, narcissism describes a turning away from relating with others who are either threatening, or a denial of those parts of the self that recognise a need to relate to others. Classically, the narcissist prefers to relate to himself; a far safer and more dependable companion. The narcissistic individual may be unable to make significant relationships, if the damage is profound and early. Alternatively, the individual with narcissistic personality traits will be more likely to withdraw from potentially damaging relationships or conflicts with partners, rather that remain with the anxiety or the ambivalence. Kohutian narcissistic self (Chapter 3) applies to a different structure, with far more positive connotations and not relevant to this discussion of narcissism.

Narcissistic relating in a couple

As Fisher (1999) points out, T.S. Elliot provides us with a brilliantly illuminating example of narcissistic relating in a couple. All kinds of reasons, many to do with transference, cause an attraction between two people. However it is also the case that the very root of the attraction is also the root of the differences and difficulties. The man who was badly scarred by emotionally aloof parents feels incapable of love; autistic in the psychodynamic sense. His partner who was offered a love complicated by many conditions and then abandoned, feels unlovable. The two are unhappy in their relationship, certain it is the fault of the other.

In Elliot's play, the resolution appears to be impossible; as it is with many couples who choose to continue in an unhappy state and find solace in their belief that it is not they but the partner, who is the cause of the unhappiness. Moving away from this position, involves a requirement for each person to accept responsibility for their part in the miserable drama. This kind of self-reflection is painful and requires a reasonably healthy ego (ego-strength) to tolerate the taking back of projections of unwanted and unacknowledged parts of themselves.

This taking back of unwanted parts of the self requires that the individual mourns the loss of the perfect self, and acknowledges the cause of the damage without transferring responsibility to a previous generation. Some people cannot get further than recognising that there is a problem, even with support. When there is property in common that neither is willing to relinquish, some partners will prefer a dreadful war of attrition, and will court misery and depression, rather that give one inch of their position. No understanding is reached. Despite onlookers being able to identify the cause of the difficulties, and offering potential solutions, without the engagement of the couple in question, the situation will remain unchangeable. It is possible that these bitter wars cause or prolong mental illness; and professionals are often called upon to 'do something'. Family and friends may get drawn in; however, as long as the partners have 'capacity', meaning responsibility over their lives, and remain implacable and entrenched in their individual positions, no one else has the right to enforce an intervention, nor the power to change anything.

Clinical Illustration
Clifford, who used to hit his wife whenever she made him angry, has suffered a series of strokes which have left him physically weak and emotionally labile. He cries at the smallest thing. After years of neglect and psychological abuse, and the occasional physical abuse, Vera extracts her revenge by excluding her husband from her relationship with the children. She denigrates every thing he says and does and attacks his sense of himself as a man by gloating over his impotence. The couple argue constantly and the home environment is unpleasant and demoralising.

In the past Clifford's need for his wife's affections was always defended against by his attacks against her. In his enfeebled state, he must acknowledge that he desires her love and care.

Working in the transference

Working with elderly couples and their families using psychodynamic models involves working with transference issues; or at least being aware of them and their potential for getting in the way of treatment as well as the positive benefits they might bring. Other chapters deal in detail with these transference phenomena and how they pertain to the individual and group settings. With couples, transferences may be particularly intense. Patients may hope for an understanding with the therapist, which may set up a triangulation, particularly if it is in any way reciprocated by the therapist. The intensity of feelings is a two-way process, hence countertransference responses need to be carefully checked, supervised, and ideally protected against by the presence of a co-therapist if possible.

It is common to find oneself relating better to one of a couple. A co-therapist may take the opposite view and the conflicts can be enacted in the therapeutic couple. This may occur irrespective of the genders of the players, and requires good communication between therapists. In older couples, the complication of generational issues comes into play, and for some therapists it may feel as though some taboo areas have been broached.

For example involving oneself in one's parents' relationship; or discussing the details of one's grandparents' sexual life.

FAMILIES

Systems theory

Although other theoretical models exist for the treatment of patients in the context of their families, systemic thinking is probably best suited to working with older adult patients (Pearce, 1999; Roper-Hall 1992, 1994). This seems to be because of the particular problems which contribute to the development of mental illness in later life, particularly chronic illness, mental or physical, and dependency. The systemic family therapists may assist sufferers to re-frame the way they see their situation and cause a shift in the system. Alternatively systemic therapy may assist a family to cope with a situation that will not improve; such as the dementia of a pivotal family member.

Another kind of family therapy has been described for use with older couples who become angry due to illness and ensuing stress. This involves the other family members in their various subsystems. The therapist is required to ascertain the family's unconscious strategic allegiances which compensate for threats to the integrity of the system. These are described as *positive wedging* (one or more family members encouraging others to increase their support of the index patient, when they have previously directed their alliances elsewhere), and *disentanglement failure* (meaning conceding to emotional blackmail or threats; this constitutes a severe threat to the stability of a partnership as it may escalate, becoming untenable).

Defensive paralleling is another couple-mounted defence strategy in couples who remain together despite having any real remaining attachment to each other. The partnership is a virtual one and each member pursues their separate and parallel lives. The stress on this modus vivendum comes when one or other becomes ill; and there may be an implicit expectation for the other to help and support the sick partner. Systemic therapy is then mounted to try to alter these dynamics or to encourage explicit separation (Montalvo et al., 1998). The therapist's task is to identify family actions, 'mobilisations' that improve or reduce healthy functioning in the couple; such as actions that particularly challenge or dismantle existing boundaries and established patterns of misdirected behaviour. This is very like group couple therapy, where the 'group' is the patient's own family.

RATIONALE FOR A COUPLES GROUP APPROACH

The theory behind doing couple therapy in groups, by contrast, is aimed at providing support, partly by offering a peer group which allows couples to see that they are not alone with their suffering. In addition, because they are all confronted with their own behaviours and responses to stress, they are given the opportunity to change.

Literature review

Elderly couples have been offered group work in the past. Richman (1979) described one such group. Skynner (1980) detailed the analytic and process elements of couples work in groups but described work with younger patients. Le Wall (1981) gave an account of work with older couples in a psychiatric context and in a more traditional mode of therapy with older people; that of conjoint therapy. In this situation, each member of a couple is also in receipt of individual treatment, therapists communicating separately about their various positions.

Mainly the kind of work with older adults in this format has been approaching the whole family utilising a systemic approach (Benbow & Marriott, 1997) or in a case work style, as with conjoint therapy which specifically reinforces the carer/patient dynamic. Evans and colleagues (1997) ran a time-limited couples group for older people in a psychiatric day hospital setting. There was strict adherence to group analytic principles and some attempt was made to examine outcome. Significant change was apparent. Group analytic work (Foulkes, 1964) purports to be effective in changing entrenched behaviours through a process of mirroring. Seeing one's own behaviour enacted by another person or couple, gives an opportunity to reflect on the behaviour and its effects on others.

Male and female co-therapists enable us to model certain desirable behaviours, such as mutual respect, listening to one another and enjoying a healthy disagreement. They can also act as objects for the counter-transference projections which can be useful. The exploration of these issues can be diagnostic, particularly in exposing dynamics of which the couple themselves are unaware.

> *Clinical Illustration*
> *Mary, whose mother attempted suicide when Mary's father left home, becomes overtly depressed, and anxious on behalf of the female therapist when the male co-therapist misses a group. Other couples joke about his 'other woman', and the female therapist is sensitive to having lost some social status within the group on that occasion.*
>
> *Upon the return of the male co-therapist Mary comments on how much better the female co-therapist appears. Mary perceives her to be less*

'depressed'. The group explores the recreation of a constellation of factors which gave rise to Mary's anxiety and the threat of the loss of both therapists, and of course, in the transference her main care-taking objects. She is also better able to bear another perspective to her own, which is that of herself as the depressed partner who defuses her husband's anger by threatening her own suicide.

DEATH IN A COUPLES GROUP

Death may happen to any group but is statistically more likely to occur in groups of people who are over 65. In a couples group, the widowed partner has rather lost their reason for remaining in the group, but should be offered some leaving time to work through their loss and to make sense of their place within the group. The process of re-adjustment of how one is seen and more importantly how one sees oneself can be begun in microcosm in a small group, and the experience may be valuable. Therapists have to work particularly hard to prevent scapegoating and alienation from occurring, as the presence of a widow may be too much of a painful reminder of members' own mortality, to face full on. Bloch et al. (1981) and Yalom (1976) describe the therapeutic factors, in a group. The existential factors, including the mortality of group members and the therapist, are more pronounced yet often underplayed in a group of elderly people.

Clinical Illustration
When Morris died suddenly of a heart attack at home in his wife's arms, the group was relieved to hear that he didn't suffer and that they had had time for some tender words.

Later there is the expression of some envy that his widow is now free to pursue many of her heretofore frustrated dreams; but the other members seem to be willing for her to remain in the group. She nonetheless decides to leave as the atmosphere is a little awkward and people don't seem to know what to say to her.

Groups provide the possibility of different permutations of sub-groups. These can reinforce or counteract stereotypes, and can alter the power dynamics within couples and between groups. For example, members who identify as the 'index patient' may defend another 'patient' from the 'healthy partner'. Sub-grouping is an interesting phenomenon in group dynamics, and not always easy or obviously therapeutic. However, in this particular instance, a number of different sub-groups developed; therapist couples and non-therapist couples. Men and women, patients and 'carers', young people and older people. Here, the presence of sub-groups acts quickly against the normally tenacious assumptions made by individuals in their usual roles.

Roles that the author believes would ordinarily take considerable time and effort to unravel.

> *Clinical Illustration*
> *During a group, Frank was told by his wife Doris that he couldn't go out by himself, because of his anxiety. She continued by referring to all the potential dangers on the street to a frail elderly man, citing examples of muggings she had read about in the papers. Frank remained quiet. The atmosphere in the group altered and one by one, the other 'patients', men and women, suggested to Doris that she wasn't exactly inspiring confidence in Frank who had not been out for some time. It was also tentatively mooted that it might be comfortable for Doris to know that Frank was safely at home whenever she herself was out braving the streets. If he remained indoors, he could not meet anyone else who might threaten their relationship and her position in their marriage.*

Comment

In this example, a sub-group of patients had identified themselves and had found strength in their unity. They were able to challenge the views of the carer partners, which they would have found more difficult alone. Moreover they were able to recognise the potential for strength and independence in a man whose chronic anxieties had incapacitated him for years. What may have started out for his wife Doris as a way of continuing to 'help' her husband, may have become an uncomfortable experience in which her own anxieties were being exposed. Both parties would need considerable support to maintain that new position and not retreat (i.e. leave therapy) to a familiar if unsatisfactory way of life.

CONCLUSION

Despite the clear theoretical optimism for this kind of work, little evidence-based research is published about working with older couples and families. Interventions with younger adult populations, however, are promising in terms of family and couple approaches to treatment of depression, alcoholism and deliberate self-harm (Leff et al., 2000; Asen, 2002); and some work exists on family interventions with suicidal older people (Richman, 1999).

This chapter gives qualitative descriptions of patients in the ordinary clinical setting of an NHS hospital. One can see how people who are stuck in a depressive frame of mind can be inched out of it by working with their partners, their families or their peer group. Twenty years after the publication of Richman's paper, we may now be at the threshold of a recognised discipline of family and couple therapy as a useful adjunct to the treatment of old people with major depression and other types of mental illness. Family and couple therapy also provide useful models with which to help and support families and carers; something that is an essential part of modern old age psychiatry services and required by the National Service Framework for Older Adults.

ACKNOWLEDGEMENT

Extract from *Who's Afraid of Virginia Woolf?* by Edward Albee, published by Jonathan Cape, used by permission of The Random House Group Limited.

REFERENCES

Asen, E. (2002). Outcome research in family therapy. *Advances in Psychiatric Treatment*, 8, 230–238.

Bartholomew, K., & Horowitz, L.M. (1991). Attachment styles among young adults: A test of a four category model. *Journal of Personality and Social Psychology*, 61, 226–244.

Benbow, S.M., & Marriott, A. (1997). Family therapy with the elderly. *Advances in Psychiatic Treatment*, 3, 138–145.

—— Marriott, A., Morley, M., & Walsh, S. (1993). Family therapy and dementia: Review and clinical experience. *International Journal of Geriatric Psychiatry*, 8, 717–725.

Bengston, V., Rosenthal, C., & Burton,. L. (1995). Paradoxes of families and aging. In: R. Binstock & L. George (eds) *Handbook of Aging and the Social Sciences* (pp. 253–282). New York: Academic Press.

Bennun, I. (1986). Group marital therapy: A review. *Journal of Sexual and Marital Therapy*, 1(1), 61–74.

—— (1994). Recent advances in couple therapy. *Current Opinion in Psychiatry*, 7, 216–221.

Birtchnell, J. (1991). Negative modes of relating, marital quality and depression. *British Journal of Psychiatry*, 158, 648–657.

—— (1993). *How Humans Relate: A new interpersonal theory*. London: Routledge.

Bloch, S., Crouch, E., & Reibstein, J. (1981). Therapeutic factors in group psychotherapy. *Archives of General Psychiatry*, 38.

Brown, G., & Harris, T.O. (1978). *The Social Origins of Depression*. London: Tavistock.

Carnwath, T.C., & Johnson, D.A. (1987). Psychiatric morbidity among spouses of patients with stroke. *British Medical Journal*, 294, 409–411.

Clulow, C. (ed) (2001). *Adult Attachment and Couple Psychotherapy: The 'secure base' in practice and research*. London: Brunner-Routledge.

Elliot, T.S. (1950). The cocktail party. In: *Collected Works 1909–1962*. London: Book Club Associates.

Evans, S. (in press). Who does what for whom? A survey of psychotherapy services to older adults in the NHS. *Psychiatric Bulletin*.

—— Goodwin, M., Winnett, A., & Birtchnell, J. (1997). Group psychotherapy for elderly couples. Qualitative, and quantitative results from a 30-week group. Abstracts, *International Psychiatric Association*, Israel.

Fisher, J.V. (1999). *The Uninvited Guest: Emerging from Narcissism Towards Marriage*. London: Karnac.

Foulkes, F. (1964). *Therapeutic Group Analysis*. London: Unwin.

Freud, A. (1939). Identification with the aggressor. In: *The Ego and the Mechanisms of Defense*. London: Hogarth Press, 1979.

Freud, S. (1917). Mourning and melancholia. Standard Edition 14. London: Hogarth Press.

Hepple, J. (1998). *Unmasking theory*. Personal communication.

Kivela, S.L., Luukinen, H., Sulkava, R., Viramo, P., & Koski, K. (1999). Married and family relations and depression in married elderly Finns. *Journal Affective Discord*, 54(1–2), 177–182.

Kohut, H. (1971). *The Analysis of the Self*. London: Hogarth Press.

Leff, J., Vearnals, S., Wolff, G. et al. (2000). The London Depression Intervention Trial. Randomised controlled trial of antidepressants versus couple therapy in the treatment and maintenance of people with depression living with a partner: Clinical outcomes and costs. *British Journal of Psychiatry*, 177, 95–100.

Le Wall, J. (1981). Conjoint therapy of psychiatric problems in the elderly. *Journal of the American Geriatrics Society*, 29.

Main, M., & Hesse, E. (1990). Parents' unresolved traumatic experiences are related to infant disorganised attachment status: Is frightened and/or frightening parental behaviour linking the mechanism? In: M. Greenberg, D. Cicchetti, & M. Cummings (eds) *Attachment in the Pre-school Years: Theory research and intervention*. Chicago, IL: University of Chicago Press.

Marriott, A. (2000). *Family Therapy with Older Adults and their Families*. Oxon: Winslow.

Medawar, C. (2000). *Referrals to the Barbican Psychosexual Clinic*. Personal communication.

Mezey, G. (2001). *Economic and Social Research Council. An exploration of the Prevalence, Nature and Effects of Domestic Violence in Pregnancy*. London: ESRC.

——, Evans, S., Gopfert, M., & Hall, A. (2003). Domestic violence. *Council Report 102*. London: Royal College of Psychiatrists.

Minuchin, S. (1974). *Families and Family Therapy*. London: Tavistock

Montalvo, B., Harmon, D., & Elliott, M. (1998). Family mobilizations: Work with angry elderly couples in declining health. *Contemporary Family Therapy*, 20(2), 163–179.

Murphy, E., Smith, R., Lindesay, J., & Slattery, Z. (1988). Increased mortality rates in late-life depression. *British Journal of Psychiatry*, 152, 347–353.

Murphy, S. (2000). Provision of psychotherapy services to older people. *Psychiatric Bulletin*, 24(5), 181–184.

Murray Parkes, C. (1972). *Bereavement: Studies of grief in adult life*. London: Tavistock

Pearce, M.-J. (1999). Systemic therapy in old age psychiatry. *CPD Bulletin Old Age Psychiatry*, 1(2), 40–41.

Pillemer, K., & Suitor, J.J. (1990) Prevention of elder abuse. In: R. Ammerman & M. Herson (eds) *Treatment of Family Violence: A sourcebook* (pp. 406–422). New York: John Wiley & Sons.

Ratna, L., & Davis, J. (1984). Family therapy with the elderly mentally ill. Some strategies and techniques. *British Journal of Psychiatry*, 145, 311–315.

Richman, J. (1979). A couples group on a geriatric service. *Journal of Geriatric Psychiatry*, 12, 203.

—— (1999). Psychotherapy with the suicidal elderly: A family-orientated approach. In: M. Duffy (ed) *Handbook of Counselling and Psychotherapy with Older Adults*. New York: John Wiley & Sons.

Roper-Hall, A. (1992). Better late than never? Family therapy with older adults. *Clinical Psychology Forum*, October, 14–17.

—— (1994). Developing family therapy services with older adults. In: J. Carpenter & A. Treacher (eds) *Using Family Therapy in the 90s*. Oxford: Blackwell.

Rubenowitz, E., Waern, M., Wilhelmson, K., & Allebeck, P. (2001). Life events and psychological factors in elderly suicides – a case-control study. *Psychological Medicine*, 31, 1193–1202.

Skynner, A. (1980). Recent developments in marital therapy. *Journal of Family Therapy*, 2, 271.

Spruytte, N., Van Audenhove, C., & Lammertyn, F. (2001). Predictors of institutionalisation of cognitively impaired elderly cared for by their relatives. *International Journal of Geriatric Psychiatry*, 16(12), 1119–1128.

Yalom, I.D. (1976). *Group Psychotherapy*. New York: Universal.

Chapter 17

Sexuality

Jane Garner and Lorenzo Bacelle

> You think it horrible that lust and rage
> Should dance attention upon my old age
> ('The Spur', W. B. Yeats)

Scant attention is paid to the needs of older adults and even less to questions of their sexuality, either by clinicians or society generally. This is in stark comparison to the information available about and interest shown in the sexuality of younger people. For Zoja (1983) this could be attributed to ongoing gerontophobia and the Freudian Zeitgeist of the twentieth century which centres psychic life on and around sexuality that is linked biologically and archetypally with youth (see Chapter 1). Rather than a phobia with implications of individual pathology, the reluctance to approach the topic of sexuality in old age may be viewed as a centuries-old historical attitude, a taboo. Taboo is an anthropological term for the setting apart of something forbidden, maybe sacred, a space which cannot be entered without a violation of the culture's system of thought. Ham was cursed for looking at his drunken father's penis, whereas Noah's other sons had looked away. The taboo is greater regarding older women than older men and greatest in consideration of an old couple; two old people together. This has something to do with the parents' closed bedroom door but also perhaps with the lessening of gender difference with age, a homosexual suggestion might add to the avoidance. The taboo has been elaborated into a myth that old people are asexual and undesirable. Gerontophilia is no longer classified as a paraphilia, but the word and image is still in people's minds accompanied by derisory smiles.

Negative stereotypes are common in old age. The potential for this is increased considerably for the homosexual. The 'old queen' is pitied or despised. Although the same can be true for lesbians they are more likely to be 'triply invisible' (Kehoe, 1986) by reason of age, gender and sexual orientation.

RECENT LITERATURE

There has been some recent literature on the topic; however, most has presented a rather narrow view of sexuality, emphasising physical aspects and frequency, the quantitative rather than qualitative aspects of sexuality. There is little correlation between quantity and quality. Intercourse may paradoxically be a way of avoiding intimacy. Most of the studies involve volunteers who are partnered heterosexuals. Volunteer samples are usually unrepresentative, particularly when questioned on sexual matters.

Kinsey et al. (1948, 1953) from their survey found a peak of male sexuality in the 20s and for women in the late 30s, both with a decline thereafter so that 27% of 70-year-old men and 75% of over 80s have permanent erectile impotence. However, fewer than 200 of Kinsey's 11,000 respondents were over 60 and only 4 over 80. Masters and Johnson (1966) included 6 men and 3 women over 70; they were able to conclude that if sexual activity continues into old age then it may continue further. Their work prompted the idea of disuse atrophy ('use it, don't lose it'). Starr and Weiner (1981) questioned 800 subjects aged 60 to 91 years old; 99% expressed a desire for a sexual relationship; 80% reported they were still sexually active.

Reported behaviour may not be directly correlated with interest and desire; the complex nature of sexuality may increase with age, physical bodies will change but in parallel with learning, experience and psychosocial development. Individual variability obvious from birth continues into old age with probably greater differences.

Cultural expectations anticipate a loss of sexual functioning in old age. Schiavi (1990) presents some evidence of loss, although it is difficult to separate the effects of old age *per se* from effects of disease. However, this widespread expectation of loss is not necessarily believed at a personal level; young people imagine they will be sexually active well into old age; but when they consider the older people they know, such a thing is unimaginable. The Internet, which offers a plethora of sexuality resources, rarely touches the topic of sexuality for an ageing population (Harris et al., 1999).

QUESTIONS

Professionals reflect socio-cultural attitudes to sexuality in old age and contribute to its invisibility not only in terms of research but also in the clinical setting. Doctors who do not always feel easy treating old people feel more uncomfortable discussing sexual matters and the patient is trapped into this 'Hammerlock of Myths' (Hodson & Skeen, 1994). Bouman and Arcelus (2001) found that psychiatrists (general and old age) are less likely to take a sexual history from an 83-year-old than from a 40-year-old with a similar presentation of low mood. In managing sexual dysfunction the 40-year-old would be sent to a specialist clinic and the 83-year-old to a community psychiatric nurse (CPN) (sexual therapy is not a usual part of CPN training). If the doctor does not ask, there is a tacit assumption by some patients who would like to discuss a problem that sexuality is not important. As in all similar interactions the questioner needs to be open and non-judgemental. If physicians routinely ask about sexual matters rather than waiting for the patient spontaneously to complain, they discover twice as many problems (Burnap & Golden, 1967); doctors who were uncomfortable with the questions elicited only one-fifth of the patient concerns compared with those who felt easier.

Direct questioning is a way of gathering information, either by clinicians or by researchers, and can to some extent dispel the myth of an asexual old age and aid individuals with specific difficulties. There may be something missing from this approach. If one crashes into the 'forbidden sacred space' the quantitative parameters of the space may be measured but the essence has shifted and remains hidden and elusive, and there is a risk of hypersexualising old age in a way that has happened to younger ages. To really have a better understanding of the quality of sexuality in old age the subject needs to be approached laterally; collectively via cultural representations in art, literature, religion and myths; individually, when in a clinical setting, through transference and countertransference. In addition the topic has the part of an old person as a subject, what excites and pleases them; and the part of an old person as an object, what representations they have as an object of desire. What is the goal or purpose of sex in old age, is it the same as when young, is it orgasm? Is the experience of orgasm and its linkage with death '*la petite mort*' different when one is nearer to death? Old couples who no longer attempt a genital sexual contact preserve in their minds a partnership-long sexual knowledge of each other evidenced by memories, photographs, children, relatives, friends. They still have a sublimated sexual relationship based on the day-to-day sharing of intimate behaviours; eating the same food, drinking from the same glass, washing his underpants, watching while she gets dressed, helping him clean the urinary mess caused by his enlarged prostate or taking her false teeth for repair if she does not want to be seen without them. Some couples may find questions about their 'sexual life' redundant or intrusive – they are 'man and wife', they are a couple with sexual intimacy between them even if not by the interviewer's standards. For other couples questions may be relevant and it will be helpful to explore directly all aspects of intimacy with them.

Disclosure of homosexuality occurs even less than other aspects of sexuality in old age. 'Coming out' and gay liberation are fairly recent phenomena (the Stonewall riots were in June 1969) and may be seen as appropriate for the young or for activists only. In this country (UK) homosexual acts even between consenting adults were a criminal offence until 1967 (they are still illegal in many parts of the world). Some still prefer to conceal their sexual orientation either for self-defence or to protect friends and family, although for the majority, fears of the consequences of discovery will be exaggerated.

Little has been written about old age sexuality from a psychodynamic stance. Berezin (1976) regrets that missing from much of the literature is any sense that sexual relations in old age are in the service of an object relationship in which tenderness and affection are significant.

Gussaroff (1998) ascribes the reluctance of the psychoanalyst to work dynamically with older patients in part to be due to denial by the analyst of elderly sexuality, which contributes to negative transferences and resistances in this work. Stereotypes can be incorporated into the countertransference. Non-productive sexuality has a negative image, e.g. for post menopausal women or homosexuals of either gender. However, sex can be creative if not literally productive.

LITERATURE AND ART

Non-clinical literature and arts present a mixed picture of passions spent or passions continuing. Colette in her 70s is said to have been asked by her niece, 'When do the fires of love die down?' She replied, 'It's no use asking *me*, my dear.' Another view is reported in Plato's *Republic* by Cephalus: 'How well I remember the aged poet Sophocles when in answer to my question, How does love suit with age, Sophocles – are you the same man you were? Peace, he replied; most gladly have I escaped the thing of which you speak; I feel as if I had escaped from a mad and furious master.' The painter Bartolomeo Manfredi depicted an 'Allegory of the Four Seasons' (circa 1610): male, virile, fertile Autumn with produce of luscious sweet fruits is kissing Spring and embracing Summer, both beautiful women. Winter, as an old man, is shivering excluded outside the group. Giuseppe Verdi, at the age of 79, composed an opera with Falstaff, a lusty, foolish old man, in the title role.

Relationships across age groupings have been criticised although they have existed throughout time. Helen of Troy was the most beautiful woman who ever lived. The first and best description of her beauty is given in the *Iliad* by Homer (traditionally represented as a blind old man, he is the first significant author in western culture). He speaks through the eyes of Troy's elderly men after ten years of war, murmuring together as they catch sight of Helen cloaked in shimmering white veils with a tear in her eyes. 'Ah, no wonder the men of Troy and Argives under arms have suffered years of agony all for her, for such a woman. Beauty, terrible beauty!'

Susannah of biblical time was beautiful too, a popular subject for renaissance painters – she a young naked woman bathing while two elderly men secretly watch her with coveting eyes. In some paintings she seems to know of and enjoy their unconditional desire, lacking as it does the element of competition which may be present between younger men and women. The cultural legend is that it is older people, particularly men, who desire a relationship with someone younger. However, the Earl of Rochester (1647–1680) has written a powerful and moving poem, 'Song of a Young Lady to her Ancient Lover':

> Yet still I love thee without Art
> Ancient Person of my Heart.

There is an extensive literature on the tale of Little Red Riding Hood. It comments from an historical, artistic, socio-cultural and psychodynamic perspective (see Zipes, 1993) but none discusses that the same fate that befalls Little Red Riding Hood has also occurred to her grandmother. Both young and old are devoured (a clearly sexual metaphor) by the wolf but all thought and sympathy is with the girl who lay in the grandmother's bed with the wolf, rather than the old woman who had previously suffered a similar deceit and the same end. The collective expectation is that it is young girls who are vulnerable to sexual attack and murder. Young and old are vulnerable in similar ways to the predatory rapist: the girl in the woods, the old woman in her home.

PHYSICAL ASPECTS

In many cases it may not be helpful to have a hard dividing line between that which is considered organic and that which is thought of as psychogenic. Doctors dealing with medical problems need to be alert to psychological antecedents and consequences of disease. Psychotherapists need to understand the physical reality of people's lives and health. Later years undoubtedly bring with them an increased risk and rate of physical ill-health. Heart disease, stroke, longstanding diabetes, malignancy, medication can all affect sexual functioning, not always via a direct physical route. Patients worry that following a myocardial infarction sexual activity is dangerous and may lead to death. There is little information about this except that such a cause of death is extremely rare. Ueno (1963) documents that a myocardial infarction is rather more common in the bed of a lover outside marriage than of a spouse; couples are anxious and deprived unnecessarily without adequate information. Surgery may have disrupted pelvic nerves or blood supply but more often has its impact on self-image. The worry of a woman following mastectomy of being rejected by her partner can be alleviated by the couple sharing intimate anxieties and hopes in anticipation of the operation.

The autonomic neuropathy that affects patients with diabetes and with Parkinsonism can cause erectile failure. A prostatectomy may produce retrograde ejaculation into the bladder. Over-the-counter and prescribed medication, including most psychotropics, can affect functioning: thiazide diuretics are a major cause of erectile failure; L-dopa may actually increase libido. Alcohol and tobacco cause many problems in this area at any age. Disease may limit enjoyment due to pain, malaise, nausea or disfigurement: the person is likely to feel traumatised and withdraw into themselves at the expense of intimacy. It has been estimated (Morley & Kaiser, 1992) that vascular problems are the main source of erectile failure with age, but decrease in male sexual activity may be due to a fear of failure as well as to the physical effects of ageing. Ageless sexual anxieties may continue throughout life. Sexual behaviour within heterosexual couples still tends to be driven by the male in terms of types of activity and frequency. His fear of failure will greatly determine the sexual life of the couple. Worrying about impotence is a self-fulfilling anxiety with spectatoring of performance making matters worse and intimacy less.

Physiological problems may account for some dysfunction but will rarely be the sole cause. Sexuality is not only biologically driven, it also has socio-cultural and psychological determinants. In addition to an individual perspective, couples co-construct attitudes and behaviour in their relationship.

Health problems are seen as the main constraints to sexuality. Fooken (1994) challenges this assumption and suggests an alternative view that sexuality promotes health in later life. Palmore (1982) found frequency of sexual intercourse to be a significant predictor of longevity in men; past enjoyment of intercourse of longevity in women.

With increased age the sexual response retains its four phases: excitement, plateau, orgasm and resolution with some changes first detailed by Masters and Johnson (1966). Essentially the cycle of stages will take longer, with men more dependent on physical stimulation to achieve and maintain an erection (some women may not be comfortable with a more active role). The ability to delay ejaculation increases, ejaculatory inevitability is lost and premature ejaculation is rarely an issue for this age group; resolution is quicker and the refractory period extends much longer. For women arousal may take longer with delayed clitoral tumescence without direct stimulation; thinning of the vaginal walls and less lubrication can make intercourse uncomfortable; orgasm may be shorter and less intense. Gender response differences, often a problem for the young, may be better synchronised in old age, particularly the requirement for longer foreplay and the delay in male orgasm.

If a physical treatment is recommended, e.g. sildenafil or penile implant for erectile failure, it is important not to ignore the psychological aspects of this for both individuals and for the couple whatever the age. If there has been abstinence for a long period the wife needs time to adjust both physiologically and psychologically to this further shift in the sexual balance.

PSYCHOLOGICAL ASPECTS

In addition to chronological age, when considering populations the effect of the cohort from which the sample comes needs to be taken into account. Kinsey's sample would have been brought up in Victorian times. The cohort influences upbringing and culture and perhaps has more impact on the lives of women. Young women of today when they reach old age will have had a more extensive and varied, though not necessarily satisfying, sexual history than current elders. Older people are also recipients of expectations from their middle-aged children who may be disapproving and from the staff with whom they come into contact.

For most homosexuals, homophobia, experienced at a cultural as well as at a personal level, is one of the greatest problems with which they must cope (McDougall, 1993). Society's negative attitudes may be internalised by the homosexual person, generating, often unconsciously, self-hatred as well as hatred for homosexuality and for other homosexuals. Self-hatred may be expressed in the use of derogatory slang or pronouns of a different gender when referring to self or to others, or in more frankly self-destructive behaviour (conversely these terms can be 'reclaimed', neutralised and used in defiance against a 'straight' world). In the homosexual community with its stress on youth, a young man may find it more difficult than his heterosexual counterpart to find an identification model in an old man and an old man may find it more difficult to leave his legacy to a young one.

There is a need for intimate connectedness whatever the age or the sexual orientation. The benefits of a stable long-term relationship may accumulate over the years, with the couple able to treat and acknowledge each other in ways that are not available to the single person trying to make a contact. However, for some long-term couples unresolved emotional issues of hostility or resentment will impact on or destroy intimacy. Hostility may provoke sadism or lack of interest.

In discussing the problems associated with old age, one risk is of ignoring the capacities associated with ageing and the strengths individuals bring into the senium. Sex is an activity thought of first and foremost as one in which participants must get excited. Perhaps the first requirement is to get relaxed – in this, age itself should not be a barrier. Despite resistances, sexuality is always present in psychodynamic/analytic work whatever the age of the patient or therapist. There is an element of timelessness to the unconscious and to impulses and wishes.

The Freudian view of sexuality as a drive is perhaps too mechanistic to explain the complexities of sexuality in later life. Jung (1931) observed older men moving towards femininity and women towards masculinity. This is seen in some somatic characteristics – greater adiposity in men, increased hirsutism in women – but is also a psychological phenomenon with men becoming more 'effeminate' in their attitude and women more incisive, paying less attention to feelings and heart. Later authors (Gutmann, 1977; Hildebrand, 1982) have elaborated this theme: men in later years relinquish some of their stance of active mastery and agency and become more diffusely sensual, more affiliative and communal; women become more autonomous, aggressive and managerial, turning away from community. These transformations may be disastrous for a marriage, with the husband discovering his tender side and the wife her sharpness of mind. It may also be disturbing for the individuals; men may be alarmed by the emergence of a feminine side and women now troubled by competitive aggressive aspects of the self. For others, however, redressing the gender and power balance in a 'traditional marriage' may resolve unspoken tensions.

Subjective body image and unrealistic expectations for physical perfection are consuming preoccupations for some women. In old age, with echoes of adolescence, Pines (1993) writes 'the body resumes its important role in a woman's life'. Good health can no longer be taken for granted, 'physical ageing thus undermines omnipotence'. Outpatient clinics often have a number of female patients for whom pleasurable investment in the body image in younger life has turned to hypochondriacal preoccupation in later years. Perhaps a continuing overt sexual life could be healing to the narcissistic wounds of old age. Pines (1993) describes a patient who, when catching a reflection of herself in a shop window, felt that she who was youthful and attractive had been invaded by a strange older woman. How one reacts to looking more and more like one's mother depends again on early relationships and identifications.

Changes in body image affect not only women. Men may mourn the loss of strength, stamina and self-perceived attractiveness. The erect phallus is part of the iconography of most civilisations, often with cultural expectations of loss of functioning with age. The older man can feel diminished comparing himself unfavourably to the all-powerful male symbol or, if he is more secure, he can feel that competition and performance are no longer necessary. The fantasy of achieving wisdom with age may include the sexual life. In some cases the fantasy may come to be. It is true that with the decline of physical robustness, sexual behaviour can become more sensual, with couples not clinging on to traditional sexual roles but becoming more sophisticated with a focus on pleasure from intimacy rather than on performance. To assume that energetic intercourse is the only component of a sexual life is to oversimplify.

Berezin (1969) succinctly reminds us of social pressures on older men: 'what is virility at 25 becomes lechery at 65'. Older people as a cultural reflection may also adopt a negative view of their own sexual desires, feelings and fantasies so that the myth of a sexless old age may become a self-fulfilling prophecy. Premature loss of sexual functioning can contribute physically and emotionally to deterioration in later years and add to feelings of helplessness which may accompany some in later life. For some old age is a painful and terrible time without pleasure.

What, then, is life if love the golden is gone? What is pleasure?
Better to die when the thought of these is lost from my heart:
The flattery of surrender, the secret embrace in the darkness . . .
. . . Hateful to boys a man goes then, unfavoured of women.
Such is the thing of sorrow God has made of old age.

(Mimnermus, 7th century BC)

Some older patients may be suicidal for these same reasons. The lovely young self has been internalised like a lost object for the bereaved. Attacks on the lost object are attacks on the self. Depression and sexuality have a complex relationship. Libido may be diminished in a depressive illness or manically acted out. Sexual problems may be an aetiological factor in depression. In 'Mourning and Melancholia', Freud (1917) wrote of erotic sadism; melancholics disappointed in their partners withdraw love, however, unable to recognise hate, they become depressed, deriving pleasure from self-torment, due to sadistic attacks against the ego, which has been identified with the internalised disappointing object as well as from the torment caused to their partner through their illness. In a more open relationship, with room for expressing hostility, if 'the secret embrace in the darkness' should go, solutions other than depression could more easily be pursued.

Some authors such as Balint (1957) and Bibring (1966) have emphasised the regressive re-emergence of pregenital, infantile sexuality in later life with eroticisation of vegetative functions, increased importance given to food and rigidity of habits. There is a tendency for post reproductive sexuality to be labelled as a regression with implications of pathology. In describing and explaining similar phenomena, Jung from 1912 onwards repeatedly pointed out a healthy as well as a pathological aspect of regression, viewing it in some cases as a potential 'period of regeneration, or retrenchment prior to subsequent advance' (Samuels et al., 1986). Similarly Abraham et al. (1980) consider it a healthy state that in some elderly people 'genitality and pregenitality merge' to produce 'a dialectic exchange far richer than in the young person'.

The bedroom has been a potent and dramatic venue for acting out battles for some couples. Changes associated with age may prompt further wars in bed. The passive-aggressive woman can make sure by attitude and comments that her partner will fail to obtain or maintain an erection. The hostile husband will not be supportive to the woman feeling vulnerable and insecure with age or may punish her by not having an erection. Sexual anxieties, latent when the physiological response was vigorous, now come to the fore. For some men the lack of spontaneous erections induces great anxiety. Some use age as a convenient alibi for disengaging from a sexual life with all its complications and potential difficulties. Kaplan (1990) describes some of the conflicts couples experience with the ageing process: the male's increased sexual dependency on direct stimulation by his wife may give rise to conflict, particularly in a male with unresolved oedipal problems or dependency on his mother; the insecure or narcissistic woman losing her youthful appeal may feel too threatened by her own changes to support her ageing husband and may paradoxically make increased sexual demands with consequent failures, disappointments and recriminations. Some women may attribute their husband's diminished erectile responsiveness and perhaps increased use of fantasy or erotica as a personal rejection; 'he needs something more/other than me'. Same sex couples may experience some or all of the above.

Homosexual men are not a homogeneous group (Friend, 1991). Many are well-adjusted and content with their lifestyle and sexuality. There are a group of older men, fearful throughout life that sexual orientation would be discovered, who have experienced little sexual intimacy and in internalising negative ideas about themselves have increased their isolation. Some bisexual men have content marriages and lives. There is another group of homosexual men who, from social pressure and having thought it was the only option for them, have married, and still in later life have not disclosed to their spouse; they may continue to have brief genital encounters with strangers and develop a rather fragmented sense of self.

It is still more acceptable for women to live together. Older widows with a previously totally heterosexual life may seek support, companionship and also a sexual life from other women in similar situations.

The death of a same sex partner may bring particular difficulties. A grieving widow or widower has an acknowledged cultural place but there is no social role in response to the loss of a same sex partner.

There are two schools of thought about how homosexual people adjust to later life. One is that there is greater difficulty with age because of a focus on youth and body image in gay culture, so old age brings eccentricity, isolation and depression. The other is that the homosexual person from previous experience is able to manage stigma and crisis, and so is better able to survive with self-esteem in the face of societal pressure about age. Probably no generalisation is helpful, 'homosexuals and heterosexuals are more similar than different' (Lee, 1987). The main issues for old age are health and the quality of relationships.

Relationships characterised by non-communication and poverty of sexual interaction may continue with neither person complaining until a life event, illness, retirement, etc. intervenes and edifices, strong enough up to that point, collapse. Even then the couple may deny that the main issue is the relationship, preferring to concentrate on the life event. Non-communication can cause premature cessation of an active sexual life for the couple when open discussion could have led to different ways of intimacy and pleasure. Any therapeutic work with older couples presenting with sexual difficulties must begin, as in all sexual therapy, in ensuring that each of the couple is able to express themself, their feelings and wishes to the other with some anticipation of being heard and understood (see Chapter 16). An ongoing satisfying and satisfactory sexual life for a couple is a function of closeness in the relationship. Affective tone and communication between the two is more important than who does what to whom and how often. Close and empathic couples, able either to speak directly about sexual changes and needs or to intuitively understand and sense vulnerabilities and wishes, are able to successfully negotiate and adapt to changing situations and desires.

Clinical Illustration

Mr B was 69 when he first sought psychotherapeutic help, following his wife's death a year earlier. His wife, who was his own age, had been ill with cancer for several years and had undergone chemotherapy and a double mastectomy. Since his retirement at the age of 65 he had dedicated himself to looking after her. He washed her, changed her clothes and combed her hair when it started to grow again, experiencing a sense of satisfaction from making her comfortable. From the beginning of their marriage they had an active sexual relationship, which continued throughout her illness. He remembers making love to her for the last time two weeks before she died, only two days before she was taken to a hospice. They did not have any children, the reasons for which were never medically investigated. A week after her death and two days before her funeral he had a one-off sexual encounter with a neighbour, which was totally uncharacteristic of him as he had been faithful to his wife. The encounter occurred when the neighbour paid a visit to offer practical help. It happened in a daze and was accompanied by aching sensations reminiscent of flu. He could not have an erection and eventually she left. The episode was never mentioned and did not re-occur. He coped with funeral arrangements, immediately afterwards he spent a week in Spain. In his perception problems started after his return.

Initially he could not stop crying, not so much for missing his wife, but for reasons he felt involved the whole of his life. He was angry with everyone, but no one in particular. He felt his wife's soul was still in the house, watching him. One morning he got up at 4 a.m. feeling agitated and it seemed natural to him to wrap his body with a blanket. He then unexpectedly noticed a decrease in his agitation and sat on the sofa feeling happy. He felt like masturbating, but on that occasion he did not. He walked around the house enjoying the sensation of being cloaked in the blanket. Familiar memories rushed through his head, secret fantasies of being dressed as a woman, wearing a frock or a shawl. Such images had frequently been in his mind when he made love, but they had receded when his wife was ill. Now they came back with full force, and being on his own in the house he felt exhilarated at the thought that he could act them out unseen by anyone – apart from his wife's continuing and disapproving 'presence'. Having confined these fantasies to a secret space in his mind, now he felt he was finally free to be 'himself'. In a short space of time cross-gender practices became established and escalated. They were often accompanied by masturbation, reinforced by sexual pleasure and by relief from psychological pain. He bought a quantity of women's clothes which he wore indoors. One evening he felt compelled to go out still wearing a dress, driving his car to a different part of town then walking in a park in the dark. It was after this episode that he sought therapy, fearing that he might lose control over his cross-dressing behaviour and that he might go mad.

Internally he suffered violent attacks of self-blame and self-recrimination, viewing himself as a disgusting monster who deserved to be killed for causing grief and indignity to his wife, whose watchful eyes he could not stop.

In the initial stage of the therapy, the therapist (a man) attempted to explore the patient's quasi-delusional belief that his wife was still alive. The patient was reluctant to engage in this exploration; one day he responded with a sudden scream, the effect of which was to frighten the therapist as well as the receptionist who knocked on the door to see if help was needed. The therapist felt threatened and also recognised a prickly sensation in his own eyes, a potential for tears. In this countertransference response he found some clue to the patient's internal state. The patient, unable to communicate with an appropriate use of language, 'transferred' his internal state, through projective identification, into the therapist, partly to get rid of it and partly to make the therapist understand it. By inducing tears in the therapist, he was putting his own tears in the therapist's eyes, whilst his eyes remained dry to the pain of his wife's final loss. By threatening the therapist, he was showing the threat he had experienced from the therapist, when he felt pushed to leave the security of his fantasy cocoon and think about reality. It emerged that a propensity for not thinking and for retreating to a world of fantasy had featured throughout the patient's life. He panicked at the prospect of being helped by the therapist the way he had panicked at the prospect of being helped by the neighbour after his wife's death. Both times, he associated panic with sex.

He had worked as a lawyer, with an image of himself as a helper of other people. Although he chose to have psychotherapy, part of him had never really thought of himself as a person who might need to be helped by another. This same part made him suspicious of the therapist's unspoken intentions, which he thought might be of a sexual nature. When he was young he had had some homosexual experiences, these stopped when he got married because of the guilt involved. Now the therapist became, in projection, the repository of the patient's homosexual traits, which diverted his attention from the need to think about the reality of his wife's death and about his own problematic sexuality. He admitted that when he went for a walk in the park dressed as a woman, he hoped to meet a man, although he met no one. Slowly he began to think about his ambivalence in the relationship with his wife. Although she never knew about his secret world, he resented her way of controlling him, preventing him from acting out his fantasies. He had hoped to have a daughter who, as an extension of himself, he imagined might have freed him from the internal image of himself as a woman, by incarnating that image externally to his body. For the first time he felt angry with his wife for not giving him that opportunity, and angry with himself for not seeking medical help at the appropriate time. He felt troubled by the physical changes of her illness. After the mastectomy and the chemotherapy, a barrier had dispersed between them. Without her breasts and with her hair short, he thought of her as a wounded boy and her body seemed a continuation of his own body, so that making love to her seemed like making love to himself, viewed as partly man and partly woman. He also felt a sense of phallic power, probably of a sadistic nature, as she appeared so fragile in comparison to him. These fantasies however prevented him from recognising the horror and the disgust he felt at seeing and touching her mutilated body. It was a body he had also loved and the pain of thinking about its damage was hard to bear. How could he cheat on her with the neighbour, when her body was still in the crematorium? Guilt about cheating turned into anger about being cheated. How could she die on him, after all he had done for her?

The experience of cheating had longstanding roots in his personality. As a child he felt his masculinity was cheated by his mother, who played with him, together with his aunt, by dressing him with her clothes and teasing him about his little penis. Mother's mindless behaviour was mirrored by his mindless response, which split anger off and only left him aware of being involved in a pleasant erotic game. The cross-dressing fantasies and behaviour reversed that position, by giving him an illusion of control which he previously did not have: this time he was the one who directed the plot, by dressing himself up as a woman, secretly hiding what he imagined was a huge erect penis underneath the clothes. In fantasy this was not a penis that could be teased; the sudden revelation of its potency was meant to startle and to frighten a hypothetical observer (once his mother and his aunt). The attachment formed with the therapist triggered fears of abandonment. What if the therapist died, like his wife and his parents did? What if the therapist disregarded the patient's reality, as mindlessly as his mother and aunt did, or as ineffectively as his father?

The next line of exploration concerned his retirement. When he retired he lost contact with his colleagues and became the helper of his wife instead of his clients. Keeping busy, avoiding what he called 'disposable time', had contributed to minimise and contain his cross-dressing fantasies. After his wife died he felt, for the first time in his life, alone with nothing to do and limitless time to fill. How could a 69-year-old man re-invent himself, form new interests, maybe seek a new partner? Was it too late?

It took Mr B approximately three years of once a week psychotherapy to find in himself an answer to the latter question, that after all maybe it was 'not too late'. Determinedly unhurried despite pressure of waiting lists and the patient's age, the therapist did not crash into the sacred space of the patient's sexual states of mind. Few direct questions were asked, meanings unfolded and Mr B over time acknowledged that he had needs which could be attended by another person.

INSTITUTIONAL CARE

The failure of health and social service professionals to acknowledge and understand sexuality in old age is most marked in long-stay institutions, where older people, more dependent because of mental or physical deterioration in their health, may spend their final years. Attitudes and behaviour of staff will directly affect the expression of sexuality by the residents (Eddy, 1986) who are quick to pick up both consciously and unconsciously the expectations of the 'carers'. At the same time the residents themselves hold similar ideas about the unacceptability of their sexual expression, in some surveys expressing more negative attitudes even than the staff (Walker et al., 1998). The design of buildings and management of the day allow little space or privacy for residents who wish to continue a relationship with a spouse, make new contacts within the home or to masturbate in private.

Training programmes for staff can address questions of knowledge and to some extent negative attitudes but more in-depth psychological work may be necessary to assist the staff in understanding their prejudices and distaste about sexuality in the elderly. Group work with the residents sharing thoughts and feelings in this area may promote a more positive reflection of their sexuality and the possibility of devising practical approaches to the issue in an institutional setting. White and Catania (1982) showed that an education programme for elderly persons, their family and nursing home staff resulted in an increased rate of sexual intercourse for the residents by 400%.

CONCLUSION

Sexuality, however it is expressed, is relevant throughout life. It is underestimated as an issue for older people, with young and old in a tacit collaboration. For some, 'elderly sexuality' is an oxymoron. A continuing sexual life in whatever way suits the individual can be healing and comforting, perhaps more important as one gets older, to compensate for losses inherent in ageing. It remains potentially an enduring source of gratification. Future cohorts will bring different experiences into old age but will have the same human requirements for intimacy and connectedness and sexual expression.

Sexuality in old age is characterised only by individuality and diversity. Elderly people form the most heterogeneous of populations. Their relationships too are multiform. Age is but one variant and determinant of sexual life which is multidimensional. Activity is dependent on physical and mental health, previous adjustment and behaviour, self-esteem and feelings of desirability as well as availability of a partner and a private space. There is a tendency for sensuality to become a more important aspect of sexuality and there is an increased use of fantasy and need for direct stimulation.

Clinicians working with older patients need to actively facilitate communication about sexual matters in history taking and as part of life review. Complaints about sexual problems should not be dismissed as an inevitable part of ageing. Management may be medical, practical, behavioural and psychotherapeutic, informed by the needs of the individual.

ACKNOWLEDGEMENT

Extract from 'The Spur' by W. B. Yeats, reprinted with permission from A. P. Watt Ltd. on behalf of Michael B. Yeats (from *W. B. Yeats Selected Poetry*, Penguin Books, 1991).

REFERENCES

Abraham, G., Kocher, P., & Goda, G. (1980). Psychoanalysis and ageing. *International Review Psycho-analysis*, 7, 147–155.

Balint, M. (1957). The psychological problems of growing old. In: *Problems of Human Pleasure and Behaviour*. London: Hogarth Press.

Berezin, M.A. (1969). Sex and old age: A review of the literature. *Journal of Geriatric Psychiatry*, 3, 131–149.

—— (1976). Normal psychology of the aging process revisited. Sex and old age: A further review of the literature. *Journal of Geriatric Psychiatry*, 9, 189–209.

Bibring, G. (1966). Old age: Its liabilities and its assets. A psychobiological discourse. In: R.M. Loewenstein et al. (eds) *Psychoanalysis – A general psychology*. New York: International University Press.

Bouman, W.P., & Arcelus, J. (2001). Are psychiatrists guilty of 'ageism' when it comes to taking a sexual history? *International Journal of Geriatric Psychiatry*, 16, 27–31.

Burnap, D.W., & Golden, J.S. (1967). Sexual problems in medical practice. *Journal of Medical Education*, 42, 673–680.

Eddy, D.M. (1986). Before and after attitudes towards aging in a BSN program. *Journal of Gerontological Nursing*, 12, 30–34.

Fooken, I. (1994). Sexuality in the later years – the impact of health and body image in a sample of older women. *Patient Education and Counselling*, 23, 227–233.

Freud, S. (1917). Mourning and melancholia. Standard Edition 4, pp. 152–170.

Friend, R.A. (1991). Older lesbian and gay people: A theory of successful ageing. *Journal of Homosexuality*, 20, 99–118.

Gussaroff, E. (1998). Denial of death and sexuality in the treatment of elderly patients. *Psychoanalysis and Psychotherapy*, 15(1), 77–91.

Gutmann, D. (1977). The cross-cultural perspective: Notes towards a comparative psychology of ageing. In: J.E. Birren & W. Schaie (eds) *Handbook of the Psychology of Aging*. New York: Van Nostrand.

Harris, S.M., Dersch, C.A., Kimball, T.G., Marshall, J.P., Negretti M.A. (1999). Adults with sexual concerns. *Journal of Sex Education and Therapy*, 24(3), 183–188.

Hildebrand, P. (1982). Psychotherapy with older patients. *British Journal of Medical Psychology*, 55, 19–28.

Hodson, D.S., & Skeen, P. (1994). Sexuality and aging: The hammerlock of myths. *Journal of Applied Gerontology*, 13(3), 219–235.

Homer (7th century BC). *The Iliad* translated by Robert Eagles (1990). Penguin Books, 1991.

Jung, C.G. (1931). The Stages of Life. *C. W. 8*.

Kaplan, H.S. (1990). Sex, intimacy and the aging process. *Journal of the American Academy of Psychoanalysis*, 18(2), 185–205.

Kehoe, M. (1986). Lesbians over 65: A triply invisible minority. *Journal of Homosexuality*, 12(3/4), 139–152.

Kinsey, A.C., Pomeroy, W.B., & Martin, C.E. (1948). *Sexual Behaviour in the Human Male*. Philadelphia, PA: W.B. Saunders.

——, Pomeroy, W.B., Martin, C.E., & Gebhard, P.H. (1953). *Sexual Behaviour in the Human Female*. Philadelphia, PA: W.B. Saunders.

Lee, J.A. (1987). What can homosexual aging studies contribute to theories of aging? *Journal of Homosexuality*, 13(4), 43–71.

McDougall, G.J. (1993). Therapeutic issues with gay and lesbian elders. *Clinical Gerontologist*, 14(1), 45–57.

Masters, W.E., & Johnson, J.E. (1966). *Human Sexual Response*. Boston, MA: Little Brown.

Mimnermus (7th century BC). In: *Greek Lyrics* (2nd edn) translated Richard Lattimore (1960). Chicago, IL: University of Chicago Press.

Morley, J.E., & Kaiser, F.E. (1992). Aging and Sexuality. In: B. Vellas & J. Albarede (eds) *Facts and Research in Gerontology* (pp. 157–165). New York: Springer Publishing.

Palmore, E.B. (1982). Predictors of the longevity difference: A 25-year follow up. *Gerontologist*, 22(6), 513–518.

Pines, D. (1993). *A Woman's Unconscious Use of Her Body. A Psychoanalytical Perspective*. London: Virago.

Plato (3rd century BC). *The Republic*. Translated B. Jowett (1894). [Dover Thrift Edn (2000). New York: Dover Publications Inc.]

Samuels, A., Shorter, B., & Plant, F. (1986). *A Critical Dictionary of Jungian Analysis*. London & New York: Routledge & Kegan Paul.

Schiavi, R.C. (1990). Sexuality and aging in men. *Annual Review of Sex Research*, 1, 227–249.

Starr, B.D., & Weiner, M.B. (1981). *Sex and Sexuality in the Mature Years*. New York: Stein and Day.

Ueno, M. (1963). The so-called coition death. *Japanese Journal of Legal Medicine*, 17, 333–340.

Walker, B.L., Osgood, N.J., Richardson, J.P., & Ephross, P.H. (1998). Staff and elderly knowledge and attitudes towards elderly sexuality. *Educational Gerontology*, 24, 471–489.

White, C.B., & Catania, J.A. (1982). Psychoeducational intervention for sexuality with the aged, family members of the aged and people who work with the aged. *International Journal of Aging and Human Development*, 15(2), 121–138.

Zipes, J. (1993). *The Trials and Tribulations of Little Red Riding Hood.* New York & London: Routledge.

Zoja, L. (1983). Working against Dorian Gray: Analysis and the old. *Journal of Analytical Psychology*, 28, 51–64.

Chapter 18

Bereavement

Rosamund Oliver and Erdinch Suleiman

No one ever told me that grief felt so much like fear.

(C.S. Lewis, *A Grief Observed*, 1961)

This chapter is written in two parts: the first part is a study of group bereavement counselling within an NHS setting, and the second presents some illustrated cases in a description of a community bereavement counselling service, one of many around the country. These services run on a shoestring budget on charitable money. They offer individual bereavement counselling, often in the person's own home and often for as long as the client wants it.

Grief is a natural process; a proper reaction to loss and death. The word bereavement derives from an old English word *reave* meaning to commit robbery; which emphasises the strong feelings of outrage that can be felt after the death of someone. This is especially the case in acute, close bereavements, such as the sudden death of a partner, parent or child. If a bereaved individual is able to contact their grief, and follow their own natural process of mourning, either alone or with the support of others, a resolution can often take place. Loss happens to everyone, including those of us who are well and those who are already frail, having sustained things that life puts in our way.

The basic process of grief work are outlined in the writings of Worden, Kubler-Ross, Murray-Parkes, and Scrutton; and may be adapted to personal circumstances meaningful for both counsellors and client group. Death itself a natural process, is often treated as something abnormal. Elizabeth Kubler-Ross (1975), with her work on the cultural taboos on death and dying, emphasises: 'We are mandated to make certain that this last period of life be as anxiety free as possible.' However, a tension exists between this ideal and the need for a realistic preparation for, and acceptance of, death. Only a minority of people today die in the familiar surroundings of their home. The terminally ill are often removed to the sterile atmosphere of a hospital, and the dying person is estranged from family and familiarity at the point of greatest emotional trauma.

In Colin Murray-Parkes' (1972) work on stigma and deprivation he states:

By stigma I mean the change in attitude that takes place in society when a person dies. Every widow discovers that people who were previously friendly and approachable become embarrassed and strained in her presence. Expressions of sympathy have a hollow ring and offers of help are not followed up. It often happens that only those who share the grief or have themselves suffered a major loss remain at hand.

In our twenty-first century society we have less fear of the newly bereaved, but we still find it difficult to accept their need to mourn, and when forced to meet them we find ourselves at a loss. Geoffrey Gorer (1965), in his study of grief and mourning in contemporary Britain says: 'Mourning is treated as if it were a weakness, a self-indulgence, a reprehensible habit instead of a psychological necessity; we do not burn our widows, we pity and avoid them.'

Steve Scrutton (1989), in his work on the medicalisation of old age, comments:

Fears and worries can be tranquilized, but they are rarely discussed. In this way, medication can be used to hide the underlying problems, and in doing so, it can help us to avoid the time-consuming process of looking deeper into the causation of many 'elderly conditions'.

Scrutton continues on this theme suggesting that while in younger people medicine boasts the ability to prolong life, in older (suggesting less productive and therefore less valuable lives) people decline is inevitable, therefore nothing is to be gained from intervention. Bereavement counselling could be seen as a prime example of medical ageism, where older people are recognised to be the group most commonly affected by bereavement, yet seem to have the least access to counselling services.

An example of adapting key theories through the filter of local experience would be in William Worden's 'tasks of mourning' (1991). These are: 'to accept the reality of the loss; to work through the pain of grief; to adjust to an environment in which the deceased is missing; to emotionally relocate the deceased and move on with life.'

These can be interpreted by experienced counsellors less as tasks to be performed (which seem to imply a steady methodical progress) and more as phases (which implies that people tend to move forth and back in their grief throughout their time and work with bereavement counsellors). The theoretical insights are useful in recognising where people may be in the grieving process, but can only provide an overall map. The detail, intensity and rhythm of each individual's grief process is the core of grief work. If there is denial, even though some people find their loss too overwhelming, traumatic and unbearable, there is a need to accept the reality of the loss. If there are feelings of anger, guilt or sadness they need to be experienced and worked through. Reconstructing an everyday life and sense of purpose requires reflection, creativity, support and a feeling of being valued. This may be particularly difficult for older people to find. Some bereavement counsellors work with older people who are not only bereaved, but may also be losing their physical abilities, or perhaps experiencing relationship breakdown. They may be suicide survivors or refugees arriving in unfamiliar landscapes. Eventually, after a period of mourning, they can resume their life again. Allowing the process of mourning to unfold helps not only with the immediate loss, but may also heal an older unresolved grief, leading to a renewal of life's pleasures. (Murray-Parkes, 1972; Leick & Davidsen-Nielsen, 1991).

Acute grief may be accompanied by physical pain and other somatic distress. There may also be anxiety, confusion, guilt, fear and anger, and other strong emotions. The bereaved person may suffer psychic disturbances such as visual and auditory hallucinations, nightmares or upsetting memories, or they may need to regress. They may take on the behaviour of the lost person. They may need time off from normal life.

Because grief is such a powerful and disruptive response to loss, it may be denied or partially denied (Murray-Parkes, 1975; Pincus, 1974: 122). 'Complicated grief', which is avoided rather than experienced, occurs when a person becomes stuck in the grief process, and is unable to mourn. This arrest can occur an any stage but tends to happen in the early phases, when the loss is still raw and overwhelming. It occurs most commonly when feelings of unacceptable anger and guilt predominate (Lendrum & Syme, 1992: 134). Responses to a recent loss may also be complicated as earlier unresolved losses surface. If the inability to allow mourning persists, mental and physical illnesses can ensue, and may even result in psychiatric admission. Grief can manifest symptomatically through phobias, severe depression (some depression is a normal part of the grieving process, see Chapter 4), panic attacks, psychosomatic illness or psychosis. It may lead to suicide attempts. Our cultural denial of death and bereavement further reinforces this inability to mourn.

Elderly people who survive will, with advancing age, outlive their generation and sustain the cumulative losses of friends, family and sometimes even children. The debilitating effect of this is intensified by the increasing tendency for the elderly to live in more isolated circumstances as communities break down and families become more dispersed. This presents health services and local charities with a growing necessity to address the difficulty, in as creative and comprehensive a manner as is possible, often with few resources. The support of a bereavement group can provide a lifeline to those struggling with bereavement alongside increasing mental and physical disability, often alone or with little support. Offered as part of psychiatric care, it is not only an important part of treatment, but can help to prevent readmission.

SETTING UP THE GROUP

In recognition of the importance of this facility, a bereavement group was set up in the Old Age Unit, at a psychiatric day hospital in East London. The group ran for three years until the day hospital closed down. It was an ongoing, slow-open group of eight clients with two facilitators. This hour-long, psychotherapeutic group ran weekly. As clients were discharged and left the group, their places were taken by new members.

In all about two dozen clients attended the group during its lifetime. Patients known to be suffering from bereavement who might benefit were referred to the group by the consultant psychiatrists and other members of the hospital multidisciplinary team. Before joining, clients were assessed by the facilitators as to whether they might benefit from such a therapeutic group and were asked to make an initial commitment of eight weeks. The group facilitators had weekly group supervision with other members of the multidisciplinary team.

THE GROUP MEMBERS

There were some important and particular factors about the people who comprised this group. Despite being elderly there was a considerable age span amongst its members. All the group members were over 65 and some in their late 80s. They not only suffered from the psychological and emotional effects of bereavement but all had mental health problems severe enough to be in psychiatric care, such as behavioural difficulties, depression and high levels of anxiety. Some came from a nearby inpatient psychiatric ward and could not function at home. In addition, some had physical illnesses, for example Paget's disease, Parkinson's disease, respiratory illnesses, arthritis, diabetes and cancer, while others had physical disabilities caused by strokes or injury and could not walk unaided. Some members suffered from organic causes of mild cognitive impairment, such as early dementia, as distinct from psycho-logical causes of illness. Most were on medication as part of their psychiatric treatment or for other medical conditions.

The different cultural backgrounds of the group members reflected the diversity of the multi-ethnic and multi-cultural London borough in which the hospital was based. This was one of the poorest and most deprived in the country, with high crime levels and poor social support, having many of the disadvantages of inner city life. Several group members had been victims of crime, mugging and theft, and this had affected their confidence and ability to go out.

Another major factor with this age group was that many carried severe trauma from Second World War experiences. Most had been very affected by the war; losses and traumatic events going back to that time were often mentioned. Some had suffered family losses or had been bombed in the Blitz and some had lost comrades in the army. Members included a man who had been a Japanese prisoner of war camp survivor, a woman who had been involved in the French Resistance and a man who had been in the French Foreign Legion. The fiftieth anniversary of the ending of this war, during the running of the group, greatly reactivated memories.

None of the factors mentioned above impaired the members' ability to make constructive and good therapeutic use of the group. Because grief is a natural process, not a state, it lends itself to being worked within a group. The members of this group were brought together by the basic human experience of loss and in this there was a community. The losses that brought people into this group were often acute, sometimes as a result of violence or sudden accident. Another prominent factor was multiplicity of losses. The losses experienced by people did not only involve death.

Other losses such as divorce or those associated with getting older such as physical disability, loss of sight, memory or mobility, were often very difficult to withstand. In addition, the loss of a job or of being an active member of a family affected some very deeply.

METHOD OF WORKING

The group was facilitated by the author as psychotherapist, and a psychiatric nurse. The group ran along integrative psychotherapeutic lines, emphasising empathy and resonance, and combining these with a psychodynamic awareness of transference, the developmental age of the group and of group process elements.

In addition to incorporating the understanding of Colin Murray-Parkes (Murray-Parkes, 1975) and others of grief as a natural process, two other models were drawn on for this work; the existential model of Irvin Yalom (1995) used in running psychotherapeutic groups, and the tasks of mourning Worden (1991). The work of J. William Worden has been adapted by Nini Leick and Marianne Davidsen-Nielsen in Denmark in the running of bereavement groups (Leick & Davidsen-Nielsen, 1991).

Existential issues, which arise due to the changing circumstances of life, provide a useful focus for work with older clients. For example, older people many need to look at personal issues around their own fear of dying, and this may have been rendered intolerable by earlier, unresolved bereavements. Yalom outlines four existential 'givens'; impermanence, meaninglessness, isolation and freedom. These existential factors can give rise to conflicts as follows. The struggle with impermanence manifests through complicated grief or fear of death. Meaninglessness can accentuate or become a debilitating lack of purpose in life. Isolation may be expressed through withdrawal or intolerable loneliness, or fear of loneliness. Freedom is conflicted through a fear of choice, or an inability to make use of choices.

In accompanying grief, therapists naturally access their own existential and even spiritual sources of meaning, and through awareness of these, therapists may be able to follow clients into places where they are struggling for survival. Meaning is an aspect of life or continuation, while impermanence is an aspect of death or change. As Laura, an 84-year-old woman in the group said: 'We no longer have much of our life ahead of us, so our thoughts are not about the future but about the past.'

Members of the bereavement group looked for meaning in the life they had lived. Some found it in their children, others through religion or through reminiscence. It was important for most to find a sense of purpose somewhere in their life and a continuing sense of being of value in old age. A central part of the therapeutic work with grief in a group is each person simply listening to others and being heard, and through this, clients can share their experience and hear that of others, enabling them to distil out their own meaning around death and loss. When a person was not able to find this, perhaps because of estrangement from their family or a sense of failure in life, their despair at the losses they suffered could be intensified in the group, an example of the amplification effect of group dynamics (see Chapter 6). Through listening to others, people could begin to look into how they might have contributed to their unhappiness and consider changes.

Clinical Illustration
Henry, an 82-year-old man, cut off emotionally after the death of his wife, to whom he was married for over 50 years – a strategy that he felt had served him well throughout his life, to the extent that he denied any feelings of the loss. The group was able to question him on his lack of feeling in contrast to the love he had expressed for his wife, and after some weeks, he admitted that he had been very distressed by her long and painful final illness. The group reflected back to him how caring he had been as a husband, spending many hours visiting her hospital. Shortly after this, he informed the group that he would take up the offer of accommodation from his sister-in-law and move outside London to live with her, an offer of which he had previously been very dismissive.

This demonstrates the possibility that the deeper contemplation of bereavement through a therapeutic group may free its members from their previous psychological limitations and enhance their ability to live a fuller life.

In bereavement work, many practitioners draw on Worden's 'Four Tasks of Mourning'. In the bereavement group, these interwove throughout the work. The tasks were not necessarily followed sequentially, but as newer members came into the group, older members would provide an important modelling of an ability to work through grief that was a resource for the newcomer, often implicitly giving them hope. This would also bolster the confidence of the 'older' members, who would have reflected back to them the progress that they were making in working through their own process of mourning.

WORKING THROUGH LOSS

Naturally, impermanence and the experience of loss and change regularly recurred as a theme in the group. The experience of the loss was often initially difficult to express.

Clinical Illustration
Jack, a 74-year-old man, spoke of the murder of his daughter. Initially, he needed to express his anger and despair at her death, as well as his shock and disbelief. As he continued to share his sense of outrage, and tell his story of loss, he began to be able to disclose that he had never been able to visit her grave, and since his divorce, he no longer had access to photos of her. He had not been able to talk about this with anyone, including his much-loved second wife. Gradually encouraged by the per-mission to express himself in the group and drawing on the group as witness to his intention, he set himself the goal of going to the cemetery. Each week he reported back how he was gradually getting nearer and nearer to doing this. How he was taking buses past the cemetery gates but not getting off. Then one day, crying as he talked, he told the group that he had visited the grave and put flowers on it. A few weeks later he discovered hidden away in the bottom of an old wardrobe an envelope of photos of his daughter, which he brought to the group like lost treasure. This process developed, step by step, over several months with Jack using the group as a resource to give him courage to complete this essential part of his mourning and to rediscover his emotional connection with his daughter.

The group had worked actively with the continual process of death. Several people had family members facing terminal illnesses. This enabled members to work with anticipatory grief. On a few occasions, members of the group died between one week and the next; a consequence of working with this age group with all their physical fragility.

Clinical Illustration
At 67, Sybille was one of the younger more lively members of the group, with an outgoing social life. Her unexpected death deeply shocked the group. Later, in reflecting what she had brought to the group, it was remembered how she had been able to find the energy to complete many

things left over from the death of her husband. She had scattered his ashes abroad and sorted out some long standing bequests with her children. She had also, two weeks before she died, written her will, although seeming in perfect health. The group's holding of this process had been an important factor in supporting her to sort out this unfinished business.

THE PAIN OF LONELINESS

Isolation was the most intractable issue explored in the group and there was a great reluctance to stay with the painful feelings that discussion of this brought up. Coming into hospital care did relieve some of this and, although not a long-term care facility, was an important antidote to loneliness. The sociability, care and friendship people found there was mentioned many times, but several still spent long periods on their own at home, especially those with agoraphobic difficulties. The hospital staff, aware of this issue but unable to take people on beyond their need for psychiatric treatment, would gradually help a client move towards attending day centres while dovetailing their treatment at hospital. This could be then built in as part of their social life after discharge, helping the patient to make that transition.

Clinical Illustration
The experience of loneliness was an extremely painful reality for some members of the group. One long-term member Ed, a man in his early sixties, was immobile having led a previously active life. He would cry often as he spoke of his loneliness, especially if shown any sympathy. He spent hours alone with only the television for company, friends and family rarely visited. He had multiple losses, both family members and his physical ones, which had lost him his job and independence. New group members would initially project their fears of ageing and incapacity onto him. Some new people would describe feeling embarrassment or pity for Ed when they first met him. They would ignore him or talk down to him. Men particularly would find it difficult to witness his tearfulness. Gradually, as they came to know his story including his busy and exciting life prior to getting ill, they developed more tolerance for his emotional expressions. They witnessed the care and respect afforded him by other group members, freeing them to explore their own experience of grief; their projected disgust and horror of their own sadness having been contained and processed by the group's hold-ing of and refusal to shun Ed. In this way one group member can hold and mirror back uncomfortable, repressed emotions in individuals and enable them to find a voice for them.

The mirror can also be supportive. The experience of grief may be difficult to share, and people hurt by grief may feel misunderstood. One person described this as though they were speaking from another world. The sharing of their stories of grief reminded the members of the group that they were not alone. Even the most difficult loss could be described and emotions expressed.

THE GROUP PROCESS

The facilitators would encourage the exploration of emotions at the expression of the losses when they were brought into the group. The therapists used their awareness of the tasks of mourning in order to support the process for each individual, and for the group as a whole. Group members were not dissuaded from talking about other issues that they needed to bring to the group, as these were generally related to the life now being lived in the aftermath of the loss. Attention was also given to the deeper relevance of psychotherapeutic work, so that small talk was gently discouraged, but responding to each other was encouraged. Established group members would help orientate newcomers who would be invited to tell their story. A culture of mutual support developed, where each person would be given time to speak and reflect. Silence was respected, but when it was felt by the group that some members were avoiding entering the group, they were effectively challenged.

Clinical Illustration
When Irene began to forget her hearing aid, her excuses were tolerated only for a few weeks before others wanted to know why she persisted in 'forgetting'. They expressed the view that although she clearly felt supported by the warmth of the group, there existed a reluctance to hear what was going on.

The group was held in a bright sunny room overlooking a courtyard garden. In its forty-second week, seven members attended. Jack was voted in because he had been 'cut off' by the ending of the previous week's group. He began by thanking Nancy for talking about her husband's death in a way that had made him reflect on it during the intervening week, and how it had made him less angry about his own lost daughter. It had also made him focus on his wife's current ill health. Nancy followed by repeating how much she still missed her husband and recounted the manner of his death. In response to Jack's request for more detail of the circumstances she repeated that she really did not think his death had been her fault. However, she felt that she had been held responsible by her family. Laura suggested that Nancy had been fortunate not to be killed alongside her husband, an idea that was supported by the group. Jack spoke of his recent visit to his daughter's grave when he had been able to talk to her in his mind. He was sad that her headstone did not bear his name, only her own and that of her mother. Nancy empathised as her husband's grave did not have her name on it either.

Bill, now approaching ninety, spoke of an army photograph he had looked at during the week, and reflected rather sadly that he was now the sole survivor of thirty soldiers pictured there. Six of the men had been his closest pals with whom he had gone drinking en masse several times a week. They had all died in the previous seven years, as well as several members of his large family. He stated that he had wanted to cry when he had been admitted to hospital, but had been unable to. Jack and Bill said it was alright for men to cry; in fact they needed to. Nancy spoke again of missing her husband, particularly when she returned home to see his empty chair. She knew he was in Heaven but this was not a comfort.

Some were quiet that week. Ed was prompted to report what he had done since the previous group, but he remembered only that he had been lonely and had made a visit which had not been a success. He expressed sadness at the lack of contact with his remaining family. Irene was also quiet, but did feed back that she was getting her hearing aid fixed. Laura was reticent, but reported profound dysphoria during the week about her daughter's death, and emotions that she could not revisit today. Mary spoke last. She had been 'seeing' (hallucinating) her deceased husband in the room. Apparently he was 'still around' but she denied being distressed. Nancy wondered if he was there to protect her, but Mary shrugged the idea off.

Discussion

This account of one session in the life of the group gives some insight into the group cohesion of members in their similar plight. Only during the previous week had Nancy begun to talk of the difficult circumstances around her husband's death, and in this session she had brought painful feelings of guilt which had been hampering her mourning. Jack continued with work started in previous sessions, and Bill, who rarely spoke, was able to name his multiple losses for the first time; possibly inspired by the openness of others. Laura, who was silent in this group, opened up in sessions that followed.

CONCLUSIONS

The author maintains that this group could not have run so effectively, if at all, without the support and holding environment of the day hospital, and the context of care provided by its staff. A day hospital can contain this work in bereaved people who have pre-existing or who have developed a mental illness such as depression, because of the ability to assess and consider needs closely and respond accordingly. Patients attended the bereavement group as part of a programme of therapy and psychiatric care over one or two days per week, while they would continue to live at home the rest of the time. The hospital provided patient-centred care, offering people dignity and respect. Their understanding and agreement was sought at all levels of treatment, which was aimed at symptom relief, palliation and cure, depending on the degree of disability and distress. Age was no barrier to type of therapy offered. The patients were offered respect, particularly when they were in difficult, regressed or dissociated states, which was seen as empowering and important. Patients would attend only one 'therapeutic' activity at a time, but would be offered other kinds of supportive activities such as relaxation classes or cooking groups. In this way some men who had lost female partners had learnt to cook late in life, which would both enable them to cope independently, but also to re-introject something of the lost loved one, and retrieve a sense of unity.

The group members came from a comparatively older age group than might usually be worked with in psychotherapeutic groups. The combination of therapeutic work with bereavement and the whole person support offered by the day hospital manifestly benefits older people, enabling them to greatly improve the quality of their lives.

A COMMUNITY-BASED BEREAVEMENT COUNSELLING SERVICE: INDIVIDUAL WORK

Counselling work sometimes meets at the point where private pain and public events overlap. For example, the marking of the 60th anniversary of the start of the Second World War generated a large number of cases for the local bereavement project, where clients felt they had private and public permission to look at their losses and the disruption that the war had on their childhood lives (loss of home, family, friends, familiar environment, community). Clients whose relatives died on the same day as Princess Diana experienced the anxiety of measuring their own losses against history-making, media saturated loss: 'I know my bereavement is only small compared to . . .'. Clients whose relatives died during the millennium parties took private grief in the face of public celebration.

Discovering a bereavement through the mass media, e.g. friends and relatives of the Waco tragedy, the Soho bombing, and the New York World Trade Center disaster, with third-party interpretations and reminders, can make an individual client's focus on their own grief that much more complicated.

Many of our clients had little cultural reference to counselling and counselling processes, yet fell compelled to enter a therapeutic relationship and try to put words and feelings to their stories. One of the most common expressions from our clients is their won sense of what they found helpful or unhelpful at the point of being bereaved. They identify unhelpful comments and behaviours as: 'people giving me advice'; 'people ignoring me or not speaking about the loss'; 'being told to cheer up'; 'being offered a drink and told to forget about it'; 'being told not to cry or upset myself' (probably meaning 'don't cry and upset me'); 'I know how you feel'; 'Time will heal'; 'It's a blessing. They won't suffer anymore'. Many of these comments might be said with good intentions, but they usually make the person speaking them feel more comfortable, and the comments are addressed to close down their feelings. These kinds of statements deny the reality of the loss and the feelings surrounding the loss. Every loss is unique and needs to be mourned.

Helpful attributes identified by our clients include: 'People sent me letters and cards'; 'People being there for me'; 'I was allowed to be left alone when I needed to be alone'; 'I was allowed to feel the way I did'; 'I was listened to'; 'A friend let me talk as often and as long as I needed to'; '. . . and kept phoning, even after I'd been angry with them'; 'Remembering together'; 'People were patient with me'; 'Just sitting together, holding hands'. Many of the supports which clients describe as helpful seem to have little to do with 'giving advice' or 'managing' someone else's grief. They seem to have more to do with being listened to, held and acknowledged. In counselling terms 'being with' rather than 'doing to'. In many ways the skills the bereavement counsellors use are those to do with 'refraining', 'doing' less and 'being' more. The ability to be present with someone in intense distress or pain, without judgement or interpretation, is seen as being both healing and therapeutic by many of our clients.

CLINICAL ILLUSTRATIONS

Complicated grief reaction

A Muslim woman in her mid 50s who had settled in London for the last 30 years, had married, worked in shops and offices, raised a family and made a life in London. Her husband of 20 years unexpectedly died in his sleep. The client relived the sense of isolation and abandonment that she had first felt on arriving in the UK. She could not stop crying and found it difficult to maintain any routines in her eating and sleeping. Distressed family members took her to see the local mullah at the mosque who advised her that 'your husband is watching you from the clouds in heaven and can't be at ease until you stop crying'. This temporarily forced the client to maintain a façade of coping and 'getting on with her life'. However, after a few weeks she started to go out on to the fourth floor balcony (where she lived) in the early mornings and to howl inconsolably at the loss of her dead husband. At this point both the police and the Social Services became involved and referred this client on to a bereavement counselling service.

How we worked with this client

Sessions 1–8: These were used to establish a warm, supportive rapport with the client; building trust and a safe space for the client to reflect, cry and remember.

Sessions 9–20: The links and feelings between the client's other key losses were examined. This included her coping strategies when she felt her world was disappearing, both when she first arrived in London and with her bereavement, looking at how she coped then and how she was coping at this point in her life. The bringing of photographs, diaries and clothes to the counselling sessions was encouraged.

Sessions 21–30: Working with the client's shakiness. Would the act of remembering always keep the client in pain? Time was spent reassuring the client that grief and tears are a natural response to bereavement.

Sessions 31–36: Talking through memories and feelings. The client began making statements about how she might continue, reconnect to a wider world. She talked of finding local work and starting new activities.

Sessions 37–45: Working on strategies with client as she takes her place in the working world. How would she see herself through a 'bad' day? What support network and self-resources could she call on?

Sessions 46–48: Modelling a mutually good ending with the client. These final sessions were clear, structured, known and named.

Sudden loss

A man, in his mid 60s, had recently retired with his brother. They lived together in a small block of flats. They both made detailed plans about their post retirement lives. Neither had partners or children and both had been working in their trade since leaving school. Part of the promise they had made to each other was how they would 'mind each other'. There was a promise of holidays, travel, living well and having each other's company. One brother committed suicide two weeks after their retirement date. The older brother was in a complete state of shock, barely able to leave his flat, with relatives and friends bringing food for him, washing and cleaning him, and becoming increasingly concerned about him.

How we worked with this client

Sessions 1–10: Encouraging the client to articulate his sense of shock at the suicide of his brother. We endeavoured to create a warm, safe, uninterrupted environment for the client to work in, negotiating confidentiality with the client's friends and relatives (the counselling took place at the client's home).

Sessions 11–12: Despite warm invitations to say more about the relationship with his brother, their plans, their sense of each other, living together, the client was mostly quiet.

Sessions 13–40: The client repeatedly told us of the last day his brother was alive; the minutiae of what they ate, what was in the fridge, on the table, showing on television, the clothes they had on, their last conversation.

Sessions 41–45: He talked about his own lack of anticipation, of not foreseeing what was about to happen, and gave his first strong expressions of hurt and anger and deep sadness at what had happened in his life.

Sessions 46–50: The client was beginning to cry more openly during the sessions, whilst widening his vocabulary to describe his interior world: 'I feel a different kind of sad today . . .'. The counsellor responded: 'Do some days feel easier than others?' This offered scale to the client's overwhelming sense of pain and dislocation. He became able to remember and offer up humorous stories about his relationship with his brother and put back the photograph of his brother on the living room mantelpiece.

Sessions 51–60: He stated that eating and sleeping had become mostly routine again and felt that the medication offered by the GP was 'not necessary now'.

Extended sessions 61–62: Ending counselling relationship with agreed closing sessions – checking client's support network and sense of journey over the preceding 18 months.

Grieving at a distance

A Nigerian refugee (a political opponent of the Nigerian Government) had to leave his home country, as his own life had been threatened due to his political opposition to Government policies. Whilst trying to settle in his new environment in East London he was informed of several deaths of immediate family members. Both his son and his brother died in mysterious circumstances in prison, and his wife and his parents disappeared from the village where they had all lived. He was offered six counselling sessions at his local GP's surgery. Still feeling vulnerable and devastated, he contacted the Hackney Bereavement Service.

How we worked with this client

General: A contract was made with the client, committing him to keep himself safe whilst we worked with him over the year.

Sessions 1–12: The client was mostly sitting silently, comfortable with another person in the room, but finding it unbearable to voice what he was thinking and feeling. Weekly appointments were confirmed with him for reference, consistency and support.

Sessions 13–16: He was talking in short bursts about 'walking in front of the buses', 'leaving my unlit gas oven on . . .' The safety contract was consolidated with the client, encouraging him to stay with the raw feelings. He was reassured that we would be ready to listen when he was ready to talk.

Sessions 17–45: The client started tearfully to tell his story, looking at and talking through his family relationships, his politics, his losses, his bereavements. He opened up more and more to his own history; what he felt responsible for, what he could change, what he could not change, how he will honour memories, what he has to live with.

Sessions 46–50: These were spent with the client on how his life could continue in his new environment in East London. What did he need to sustain himself?

Sessions 51–52: We looked at other support services in the local community for him to move on to. He made contact with other exiles and refugee groups in the community. He explicitly stated that self-harm was not an issue for him any more.

Clients' comments

The effectiveness and importance of the work we carry out is confirmed to some extent by the outcome forms we use at the end of each counselling relationship. These are filled in and returned to the Project by the clients we have worked with.

'I didn't know what to expect.'
'I can say things here that I can't say to anyone else.'
'Exploring, deep, painful, feelings . . . uncomfortable to start with but as time went by I felt so much lighter.'
'I managed to release a lot of feelings about things I have never spoken about before . . .'
'Good to be able to talk to someone when I was feeling my life was pointless.'
'Your support and warmth helped me to come through the saddest time of my life.'
'Now I feel able to face my loss, I feel able to face the world again.'

REFERENCES

Gorer, G. (1965). *Grief and Mourning in Contemporary Britain*. London: Cresset Press.
Kubler-Ross, E. (1975). *Death: The final stage of growth*. Hemel Hempstead: Simon & Schuster.

Leick, N., & Davidsen-Nielsen, M. (1991). *Healing Pain. Attachment loss and grief therapy*. London: Routledge & Kegan Paul.

Lendrum, S., & Syme, G. (1992). *The Gift of Tears*. London: Routledge & Kegan Paul.

Murray-Parkes, C. (1972). *Bereavement, Studies of Grief in Adult Life*. London: Tavistock Publications.

Pincus, L. (1974). *Death and the Family: The importance of mourning*. London: Faber.

Scrutton, S. (1989). *Counselling Older People*. London: Edward Arnold.

Storr, A. (1989). *Solitude*. London: Flamingo.

Worden, J.W. (1991). *Grief Counselling and Grief Therapy*. London: Routledge & Kegan Paul.

Yalom, I.D. (1995). *The Theory and Practice of Group Psychotherapy*. New York: Basic Books.

Index